Stinson Jarvis

Letters from East Longitudes

Sketches of travel in Egypt, the Holy land, Greece, and cities of the Levant

Stinson Jarvis

Letters from East Longitudes
Sketches of travel in Egypt, the Holy land, Greece, and cities of the Levant

ISBN/EAN: 9783337244477

Printed in Europe, USA, Canada, Australia, Japan

Cover: Foto ©ninafisch / pixelio.de

More available books at **www.hansebooks.com**

LETTERS

FROM

EAST LONGITUDES;

SKETCHES OF TRAVEL

IN

EGYPT, THE HOLY LAND, GREECE, **AND CITIES**
OF THE LEVANT.

BY

THOMAS STINSON JARVIS,

STUDENT AT LAW.

> " Yet not the more
> Cease I to wander, where the muses haunt
> Clear spring, or shady grove, or sunny hill,
> * * * but chief
> Thee, Sion, and the flowery brooks beneath,
> That wash thy hallowed feet, and warbling flow."
> PARADISE LOST. **Book III.**

Toronto:
JAMES CAMPBELL AND SON.
1875.

HUNTER, ROSE AND CO., PRINTERS,
TORONTO.

Dedicated

BY PERMISSION

TO

HIS EXCELLENCY **THE EARL OF DUFFERIN**,

GOVERNOR GENERAL OF CANADA,

&c., &c., &c.,

IN HUMBLE APPRECIATION

OF HIS DISTINGUISHED ABILITIES

AS A

STATESMAN A SCHOLAR, AND A YACHTSMAN.

Preface.

EVERY person who has been bold enough to publish what is ominously termed a Book, which is to be scanned and criticised by that very awful drill sergeant, Public Opinion, has experienced, I suppose, the same doubts and hopes as I feel myself.

It is very pleasant to spend the long winter evenings refreshing one's memory and re-writing about places visited; but having now published the work, I dread its being actually read by others, and I feel like leaving for a lengthened trip into the country to escape "chaff."

It must, however, be considered as merely a compiling and arrangement of the long letters sent home at every possible opportunity, and as they were often written by **the** flickering light of the tent, on up-turned **trunks, in Arab mud huts,** or by the fading light of **Eastern** sunsets, and generally under most adverse circumstances, any " jerkiness " of composition must be attributed to my continually unsettled situations.

The pleasure of spending my spare hours **in this way has, for** the last few months, almost equalled the enjoyment **of the trip itself, and if** any others can pass a **pleasant hour or two in** reading the **result, I** shall feel that, **after all, the** greatest **pleasure of travel** is experienced **after it** is over. I feel, too, that my friends will excuse some of the defects on account of my youth, and **for the same reason** I hope that even the general **public will give** some *latitude* to my " East Longitudes."

> " There is a **land of** every **land** the pride,
> Beloved by **Heaven** o'er **all the** world beside,
> * * * * *
> Where shall that land, that spot **of earth be found :**
> Art thou a man ?—a patriot ?—**look around.**
> O thou shalt find, howe'er thy **footsteps** roam,
> That land thy country, **and** that **spot thy** home."
> Montgomery.

Bertie Cottage,
 Toronto, April, 1875.

CONTENTS.

CHAPTER PAGE

I. Begins the book, which is its chief merit, and takes me with seven-league boots through France and Italy to my starting point at Venice 1-6

II. Contains the only verbatim letter, on which the title is based—Venice—Trieste — Miramar — The Adriatic—Raræ aves, and other passengers introduced—Ionian Islands—An early glimpse of Egypt 7-14

III. Street scenes in Alexandria—Pompey's Pillar and Cleopatra's Needle—Mehemet Ali's Canal—The Seraglio—Egyptian landscapes—Heartless Jimmy—The run to Cairo—Caireen bazaars—Bargaining with Persians—Service on Sundays—The old geography eclipsed......... 15-24

IV. Day at the Pyramids—Nile Valley—Grand Mosque—"Egypt is the gift of the Nile"—Joseph's Well and other sights—Historical and Biblical associations—Departure from Cairo.. 25-33

V. Steamboat dodges—Suez Canal—Storm—Aggravations—On Holy ground at last—The tents—Jaffa and its sights—The pilgrimage commenced—Plain of Sharon—Lydda—The first encampment at Ramleh—Kirjath Jearim—Nice Sunday-school story—Approach to Jerusalem... 34-51

VI. First entrance to Holy City—The lepers—Ruins and rubbish—The Sepulchre, and the side shows for pilgrims—Hebron—Solomon's Pools............................ 52-66

VII. A glance at the history of Jerusalem—The modern City—A midnight adventure—Jews' Wailing Place—Nocturnal excursion to the tombs of the Kings and Solomon's Quarries—Sunday—Service on Mount Zion—Olivet.... 67-76

VIII. Surroundings of the camp—The monuments, tombs and fountains of the Bible—The view of the world—Mount of Olives—Bethany—Garden of Gethsemane—Storms and Hardships in the tents—Via Dolorosa—Mosque of Omar and *wonders* connected—Mahomet *vs.* Messiah—Stables of Solomon—(Solomon and Michel Angelo built the world) 77-90

IX. Pilgrims at the Sepulchre—To Bethlehem—Rachel's Tomb—Church of the Nativity—The Manger—St. Jerome and his abode—A new way of watching sheep—Boaz's field—Convent of Mar Saba, its appearance and occupants—A frightful ride by night—Jerusalem in snow... 91-108

X. Departure from the city—Who wouldn't be a flower?—Our guards Arab shepherds—Dead Sea—The Jordan—Plain of Jericho ....

CONTENTS.

CHAPTER.	PAGE
XI. Waking thoughts—Jericho—Bedawin dance—Music in the East — Bethel — Letters! hooray!—Shiloh, and the ideas suggested by it—Lunch in a Skeikh's house—In trouble—Pitiless weather—The mules—Jacob's Well—Arrival at Nablous	124–138
XII. The ancient Shecem and its curiosities—Gates of eastern cities—Similarity of the ancients and moderns—The Samaritans — Beauties of Nablous—Miseries of the people—Broad views—Samaria—Solemn thoughts—A dismal ride by night—Wrecked luggage—Jenin—Plain of Esdrælon—Jezreel—Shunem—Mount Tabor	139–160
XIII. Nazareth—The grotto business—Wanderings and ideas about Nazareth—Cana of Galilee—Mount of Beatitudes—Galilee!	161–170
XIV. Approach to the Sea—Hot baths—Sunday evening on the holy lake—The town of Tiberias, its Jewish population—The shores and sea—Magdala—Capernaum—Bethsaida—Chorazin—The ascent to Safed	171–184
XV. The mountain of the great Temptation and its view—Daybreak over the Holy Land—A few words about travel—Experience—A touching incident—The Arabs' ailments—Tibnin—Mount Hermon	185–194
XVI. From Tibnin to Tyre—Tomb of Hiram—General appearance of the Holy Land—Ras-el-Ain—Tyre and its prophecies, its past and present—Horse racing—Sarepta—Sidon—Lady Hester Stanhope and Jonah—The last day in the saddle	195–208
XVII. Beyrout—Our last sunset in the Lebanons—Cyprus—Rhodes—Cos—The voyage—Scio—Views framed by portholes—Smyrna—Run down to Ephesus—The old Ephesian theatre—As Ephesus now appears—Knocking about Smyrna—Naval review for the Pacha—Troy and Tenedos—Regatta up the Dardanelles	209–226
XVIII. Constantinople—Our ladies—Newspapers?—The Argonauts' course—A scare—Dancing Dervishes—Turkish baths—Mosque of St. Sophia and other sights referred to—Magic lantern views—Eastern ladies—The Bosphorus—Howling Dervishes—Honoured graves at Scutari—Death's Orchards—Golden Horn—The Sultan going to his Mosque	227–246
XIX. The Ægean Sea and Syra—"'These waters blue that round you lave"—Quiet life at Athens—Temple of Jupiter Olympus — The "Maid of Athens"—Eleusis — Two thousand years ago—The poetical old Grecian beliefs—Philosophers and Art—Acropolis—The Parthenon—Environs—Mars' Hill—Paulus ad Athenienes	247–262
XX. A hurried wind-up—Seven-league boots again—Northern Italy—Italian lakes—Over the Alps by the Simplon—Buzz-buzz, whiz-whiz, multum in parvo—Fast fiddling—Red fire—Faust bows and retires to change the *tenor* of his ways	263–267

LETTERS

FROM

EAST LONGITUDES.

CHAPTER I.

IT is not my intention to enlarge upon travelling in Europe. There are so many spots around which I would linger fondly, so many scenes to describe, that a volume would be filled before arriving at my desired starting point. Let me meet my gentle (or otherwise) reader at Venice, and while waiting for the steamer to take us to Trieste, and as we glide along the Grand Canal, let me shortly narrate how I came here, where I am going, and what I am going for. To begin *ab initio*, I would skip the parting from home, for I have a recollection of a strange gulping feeling that is uncomfortable, even to think about. All goes happily you know, till at the last moment when the trunks are being carried out of the house, and then, with its full force, the thought flashes through the mind that perhaps the last embrace from loving arms is now being received. On such an occasion, which may happen but once in a lifetime, it requires a strong will and firm jaw to stifle the inarticulate noise that sounds very like a sob; but once in the cab, the great difficulty is overcome;

the sense of self-responsibility comes to the rescue, and the mere necessity of having to check the baggage for the first time, collects the thoughts still hovering regretfully around the old home. I joined my friend at Hamilton, and after a few days we were gliding out of New York harbour, in company with several steamers similarly outward bound—among these fine vessels that were exchanging salutes with us was the *Ville du Havre*. Many of her passengers were taking their last view of land, and had bidden the last good-bye to friends on shore whom they were fated never to meet again. We were in sight of each other the next day, so that our vessel was perhaps the last one seen by those on the French steamer until the disaster which happened about a week afterwards, when they were awakened one night to meet a watery grave. Everyone who has undertaken the voyage across, knows how, when the people are overcoming their sea-sickness, every subject under the sun is discussed until there does not seem to be a topic left unbroached; few, however, even then enjoy pacing the decks on a wild night, when the spray is flying, the wind howling, and the good ship, straining under steam and canvas, ploughs her bows under the fleeing wave and throws it back over her decks, like an elephant in his bath. On such nights the wild spirit seemed rampant within me; there was a pleasure even in helping the sailors to set or take in the sails, and I often felt strongly inclined to follow them aloft.

London was dull, cold, and out of season, so we stayed but a few days there, and then flew south to Paris. Paris was also foggy and cold, so that we soon left it, marked with "to be continued" in the spring. Ho! to the South! was the cry that sounded uppermost in our breasts; and south we sped, till one morning we found ourselves passing between hedges of roses and orange trees, and before long the Mediterranean lay bright and sparkling before us.

Around the picturesque harbour of Marseilles we found ample sources of enjoyment in sailing the lateen-rigged boats out to the old Castle d'If, and in walking along the quays. Marseilles was the first Mediterranean seaport I had seen, and everything about it **had,** for me, the charm of novelty. Trading vessels from every country and of every size and rig were jammed up together, their cargoes of grain and other imports emptied out on the quay as if such a thing as a rain shower was never expected. Here could be seen Arabs, Lascars, Turks, Greeks, Russians, Italians, and Yankees, each walking about in his own national garb, each jabbering **in** his own tongue, **and trying to** " drive **a** hard bargain." Nice and Cannes **had that** deliciously calm yet picturesque scenery, and balmy, **sweet-scented atmosphere that** have always invited the **invalid or** the worn-out brain to take rest and find renewed **health** among their trailing **arbours,** and eye-gladdening groves of orange and lemon.

The luggage was sent on by **rail** to Genoa, while **my** friend and I, shouldering our knapsacks, left Nice for **a** walking tour on the Cornici Road. There **was a** halo of romance about this undertaking which the wondrous beauties of the everchanging views served to intensify. After passing Monaco, escaping scathless from the gambling there, and passing through Mentone and other towns well known to many of my readers, we **soon** found **we** had crossed the Italian frontier. Here, now, we were puzzled how **to** act, for the people at the inns where we stopped, **could speak** no French, though living so **near** France, and we could not manage a word of Italian, having forgotten to bring **a** dictionary of that language,—moreover our feet were rather used up with walking up and down the hills, so we were constrained to take the railway to Genoa. A week **was passed in** hunting about " La Superba" for the baggage which **had been** lost about the miserable Italian *doganas* **or** custom houses. What pantomimes, explanations, anxieties, telegraphing, and squabbles were gone through in that little week, **words cannot tell ;** let it suffice to say that before **the** luggage was found, hidden away in an obscure loft, I had become completely cured of all *worrying* and was fully competent to issue the moral to be observed in **all** Italian travel, " Never worry, and stick **to your** luggage."

Genoa never looked more superb than when we left it by steamer in the moonlight on our way to Leghorn, where we stopped long enough to enable us to run up to Pisa: and after making another landing at Civita Vecchia, a few hours more brought us before Naples, where, on tumbling up the hatchway in the morning, I found myself in the centre of a picture I had known all my life, floating on the azure Bay, with Vesuvius on one side and Naples on the other.

I would like to say something about Naples and its excursions—Vesuvius, Pompeii, Sorrento, Capri, and others, have all engraven their names upon my memory. We passed our Christmas there, and at that season, when families are always gathered together at home, I felt more than before the desire to get my first letters, directed to be sent to Rome. I yearned too, for the Eternal City, and went there intending to settle down for a month or so. My friend and I here parted; he returning to England, and I remaining to indulge my fancies for the quiet enjoyment of seeing the ruins of Rome and studying their histories. And yet it seems to me I was as much interested in them on account of the people I knew who had visited them, as I was in their antiquity; for does not the greatest pleasure derived from travel consist in the ability to recur to it with friends in after days? Five weeks spent there was continual happiness; though alone, I made warm friends at the Hotel d'Angleterre, and had the pleasure of meeting a Toronto lady and her daughter, in whose company the Catacombs seemed brighter, and the interminable galleries of the Vatican, less damp and cheerless.

The riding parties to Albano, Frascati, and Tivoli, drives beyond the gates, the afternoon strolls in the villas and through the galleries of art, were not the least among the attractions offered by modern Rome. To be sure, we had no gladiators, who, for our benefit, would spring into the Flavian arena shouting "Morituri te salutant;" but it was not hard to picture to oneself, whilst gazing down from the highest tier of seats in the bright moonlight, the sea of eager cruel faces, the hand to hand combat, the death and rapturous applause ensuing. Every visit to St. Peter's made me comprehend its size more and more: I tried to compare some of its measurements with objects well known to myself; for instance, the *baldachino* which **looks** like a mere monument set in the body of the Church, **is** higher than the elevators that run out into the Toronto Bay. This is only one object in the edifice partly explained; **the dome** was ever a conundrum to me, a view from the top being as deceptive as looking upwards from the floor. **Rome** was left with unfeigned regret, and although I **did not** drop the coin in the Fountain of Trevi, I was summoned back in a few days from Florence to meet some friends from Canada. But the gloss was off the picture—Rome did not seem the same place—when running down in this everyday sort of way to meet people. I would not even look at the old places I had bid farewell **to**. The Carnival was then at its height—one day of it being very good fun—but I would remember Rome as I found it at first, rather than as a city of confetti-throwing masqueraders; so after seeing my friends on board the steamer at Civita Vecchia I returned to Florence. In the excursions about the environs, at the table d'hôte, and in the parlours, what pleasant friendships spring up almost imperceptibly! It was here I first **met** the Americans I afterwards travelled with in the East, and although I had then no intention of taking such a trip, **we** often conversed on its feasibility. To appreciate Florence, less than three weeks will hardly suffice. Among books, letters, friends, and operas **I** would have dreamed there longer, if not awakened by what might almost be called a sense of duty to move **on** and see other places of interest. By this time my stock of Italian was considerably augmented; my plan for study being to take a little *vettura*, and with a dictionary to go for a drive into the country; making up sentences and thus extracting answers from the grinning Jehu.

Two days sufficed for Bologna. It was too cold to enjoy anything except a good fire, so I hastened on to Venice, which I found, as did the Irishman who said " I found it damp, sur, very damp." It rained a good deal. I was lonely, not quite well, and dreaded the cold journey further northward. At this point I suddenly stumbled upon my American friends who were going to the East. They discovered me shivering through one of the wretchedly chilly Venetian palaces, and said "Why don't you come to Egypt with us and get warm ?" " All right, DONE," I answered, as it suddenly struck me that that, at least, would take me out of Venice. They were quite startled with the abruptness of the reply, but Jimmy said " Wal now, that's what I call decision, give us your fin on it, old man." (Jimmy lives out West.)

I bought a light portmanteau, and taking my old knapsack stuffed them full of old clothes, wisely leaving my trunk and in it everything that would spoil at the Hotel Royal Danielli till my return.

And now I am ready to go on board the steamer, my short sketch being rather more long-winded than I intended to make it. I have answered the first question, How I came here; as to the second, I would say truthfully I don't know where I am going; and as to the third, I say that I am going to get warm.

CHAPTER II.

AS to the trip **down the Adriatic**, touching at Trieste, I might **as well** insert my letter written during the passage, verbatim, and if any body is averse to reading a letter **headed**, "My Dear Mother," he can **skip** this chapter.

"**S. S. ESPERO,**
"*on the Adriatic.*

"MY DEAR MOTHER,—As **we** plunge through these foaming waters towards that ancient land, whose monuments **of** antiquity are ever shrouded in mystery and gloom, as every mile is one more to increase the distance between **you and me, there** comes that pleasant **desire to** communicate **with** you, and keep **you by my** side, though **far** away. As the ship groans and strains till **the** varnish cracks, **as** the powerful screw keeps the huge vessel **in** continual tremor, as the groups around me in the handsome cabin are studying their books on the Holy Land, I get out the portfolio to inform you of my doings. **Two** stalwart gondoliers whisked me off from my hotel, **into the** harbour, in **front** of the thousands of lights which **line** the watery streets and quays of Venice, in the inky blackness of the night, lighting up the marble palaces with **a** sombre shade, suggestive of its might, wealth, mystery, **and** dread of former days.

"On the ruffled surface of the water came the innumerable reflections of those diamond lights, twisting and twirling like the hair of a beauty, or rather like the snakes of the Gorgon. Yes! I would call Venice the beautiful horror! Because to see her weird beauty in the damp raw air of winter was for me literally to become as stone—to chill into solidity, and petrify in my curiosity to view her strangeness.

"A few more sweeps of the oars brought me alongside of the Steamer *Milano*, that was to take us to Trieste, and from the deck I was hailed by one of the Pilgrims, who testified his faith in me by saying 'he reckoned I'd be on time.'

"If it had not been for the work of the day in getting ready, I should have had a hard night of it, there being certain *realities* on board little Italian steamers which are not calculated to superinduce sleep. The berths are piled close together, and there is no room to undress, much less to hang up anything; the air is foul to suffocation, the bedclothes cover about half the body, and are nearly a foot and a half wide, so that to get them anywhere near one's chin is to leave the extremities bare from the knee down, and to double up the body is to hang part of it outside the berth, which is inconvenient. I managed tolerably well under the circumstances by getting the clothes off some other bunks, laying them together in layers like the shingles on a roof; then slipping in, like a paper knife, with all my clothes on, I slept while others suffered. It blew hard all night and came on a 'snifter' in the morning, making us several hours past due.

"From a white speck, or a divided molecule, Trieste, on approach, grew into houses, churches, and streets, which could be seen through the forest of masts in the harbour. The ships had all their long lines out, every anchor and chain being required to withstand the gale; and threading our way into the dock I soon enjoyed a brisk walk on Austrian soil, and was much surprised to find Trieste the clean, handsome, well-built city it is. After breakfast at the hotel, we drove round the coast to Miramar, the palace of the unfortunate Maximilian. Situated on a promontory, this delightful abode overlooked shore, surf and sea for miles. The town, the harbour **and** the frowning mountains were backed by heavy **storm** clouds which, in their fleeting wrath, looked like other mountains driving through the air; and the **sea,** lashed into spray by **the** whirlwinds from the snowy peaks, dashed up to the base **of the castle** to meet with a **rude** rebuff **from its** solid foundations. Passing through an armoury, up a proud staircase, whose polished walls were hung with trophies of the **chase and** battle-fields, we **came to** a suite of delightfully cosy rooms, all inlaid with **various kinds** of woods, in the latest **patterns** and workmanship, and filled with beautiful cabinets, clocks, mosaic tables, and rare vases—even the books keeping their places as when left there by their royal owner.

"Wandering through these **rooms,** where riches and comfort, greatness and happiness, seem, for once, to have been combined, among paintings of distinguished looking members of the family, we are arrested by a picture of a lovely dark-looking woman. No need to tell us who that is! The drawn look on that wondrous face reveals to us her story. Though still the look of sanity is there, it seems the face of one with whose love might depart her reason. Another picture of the Mexican gentlemen presenting the Petition to Maximilian requesting him to govern the country; and he appears in the representation of **the** scene, standing handsome and noble before them. Why, I wonder, did he accept their offer? Why did he leave this Arcadia to meet a sudden and awful death? And why does the beautiful maniac Carlotta, whose picture we have seen, yet wander listlessly about? It is **one** of the saddest stories on record, and the beautiful abode, left thus desolate, intensifies the compassion for the royal sufferers. Just look at that miniature harbour approached by broad marble steps, and the breakwater of cut stone checking the waves that else would wash up into the garden! What a delightful place to keep a yacht! and close by, what lovely nooks invite repose! What rambling paths hedged with roses, and, as the guide says 'che belle pergole son qui!' Sad spot! Thy pictures and thy beauty recall most touching memories that teach again the oft-taught lesson of the evanescence of human happiness!

"Ho hum! the people have all gone to their berths, and I, as usual, am left to myself with the roar of waters and machinery. This is often the pleasantest part of the day to me; were it not for a sleepy garçon who shuffles through the saloon every instant to interrupt and induce me to retire for the night, I might scribble on till morning. We left Trieste last midnight in this large and comfortable steamer, and have ever since been wallowing in the trough of the sea. The Pilgrims have been as lambs to-day; with bowed heads and bended knees they have offered their sacrifices to Neptune at the lee-rail with becoming humility. Why did Byron neglect to put in his 'Ocean' something about the glorious uncertainty of the health of travellers over its ruffled surface? Thankful am I to be always free from sickness, and rejoice with the Pharisee, that 'I am not as other men are.' But now, to bed, and let this garçon sleep, or he will go mad.

"Sunday evening. It was very comfortable as I lay in bed this morning watching the mountains on the coast of Dalmatia and nothing but thoughts of a cold breakfast aroused me, which apprehension proved but too true on my entering the saloon. At twelve we had a prayer and a few appropriate remarks from Mr. T——, and a hymn sung in the weakest manner by the pilgrims. The wind having shifted to aft, gave us a nice little pitch and roll combined, but on the sun coming out and lighting up the waves which rolled bottle green, the old maids, who comprise our female community, aired themselves; and the males timidly partook of half a smoke to assure themselves of their recovery. Among smokers there is no more certain gauge of inward qualms than the pipe. One's salubrity can be estimated most correctly by the length of cigar smoked. The lady friends with us now, have, in common with their sex, their peculiar idiosyncracies, and are intensely pious. There is one very fat old maid who bullies everybody and sketches everything. She has painted the whole north coast of the Adriatic, and wonderful are the colourings; 'just for a little remembrance' as she says, when throwing paint at a wavy line which means mountains. She shows everybody her productions, all of which having **a** strong family likeness, the only thing one can say is 'How strikingly similar to that other one you showed me!' I made what **I and** some others considered **rather a** good picture; **but she said** 'You should blend your colours more,' and with a sweep of her brush suddenly enhanced its beauty to the level of her own.

"**Two** very thin, unmarried and aged sisters also adorn the decks. They wear long brown cloaks to their ankles, of which too much are generally seen; they have such a bird-like appearance that I am doubtful from what ornithological museum they have escaped. Rather a hard look out for the boys, is it not?

" It is always delightful to lean over the taffrail, watching the foaming of the water round the screw, and to view the boundless expanse of toppling glistening whitecaps; but it is more enchanting to have the mountains on one side towering from the water's edge, straight up into the clouds; or, where they lower in the foreground, showing others towering behind, grand, rugged and sublime, till they lose themselves in mist. Passing these islands and mainlands of Albania, uninhabited by human beings, and almost too rugged for the wild goats to scale, the scenery in the distance consisting of a soft, many coloured beauty, and, on approach, of an awe-inspiring grandeur—speaks to the heart in a way different from anything I have yet seen. When far out at sea the distant mountains lie **in** many shades of blue, in shape as endless and varied as the clouds that tip their peaks. The sea near us is a deep blue, changing to an emerald green before it reaches the bases of those indigo cliffs; and the line 'twixt earth and ocean is marked by a white dashing line of surf; while capping all, a rainbow, broad and brilliant, arches over the scene, setting the landscape in a natural frame which alone would be in keeping with the beauty of the picture. It is impossible to cease from feasting the eye on this banquet of beauty.

"The sun goes down as we still pace the decks. Now, with all sail set, and every spar and rope shining spectrally in the moonlight, we rush past a precipice which seems scarcely a stone's throw distant, the sides towering to an appalling height where clouds enwreath the summit. We are all now finishing letters to be posted at Corfu. My next will be from Alexandria, where, in the sunny clime of Egypt, I hope no shivers will run down my backbone, and in the softness of the atmosphere, I may be able to extract any ideas lying dormant or yet unsung.

"With much love, &c."

We lay off Corfu, at midnight, the lights on shore and partial moonlight giving us a queer idea of the mountain-bound harbour. Small boats keeping their distance till we stopped, boarded us like ants; orange-sellers, game-sellers, and Greeks in hairy, whitish cloaks came skulking on board without a sound, passing under the hatchways till they were lost to sight. The whole thing seemed very like a conspiracy to take the ship, and the extreme quiet of our entrance to the harbour, the absence of steam blowing, hallooing, and commanding usual on such occcasions, aided the imagination in the idea. Presently a boat with two ladies and two gentlemen came alongside, and we had at last the supreme satisfaction of seeing a fair face among us; so we went to bed feeling that some life might now be instilled into our party with this reinforcement. Corfu oranges were the best I had yet eaten, in fact everything received from that island proved satisfactory. One of the new comers played the guitar and had a very good voice, and as he seemed to know every song, he led the choruses which we often sang in the day time, and always in the night. In this passage, through the Ionian Islands, between Cephalonia and Ithaca—passing Zante, and, in the evening, Cerigo, not the slightest chill was perceptible in the air; umbrellas were even used in the daytime, and groups were

AN EARLY GLIMPSE.

scattered over the deck, too softened by the sensuous influence of the balmy atmosphere to do anything but listlessly enjoy it. Next morning we managed to make ourselves known to the new young lady, who, we found, rejoiced in the euphonious name of Day ; and certainly never was light hailed with such satisfaction **as was this Day** upon our ship.

"Many-fountained Ida" soon reared its snowy crest above the clouds at our left on the Island of Candia, then we passed Fair Havens and close to the solitary Isles of Clauda, which were certainly uninteresting except for their Biblical mention. But after again reading the twenty-seventh chapter of Acts, I took a more lively interest in the old mud bank before me, feeling a thrill of pleasure, as I saw that this was the place mentioned. Another day passed in the same lazy way. **On** approaching Egypt the sun becoming more genial **and the nights** still more balmy, all were separated at **even into** picturesque groups on **the** deck, and Cynthia's **rays** shone vertically upon us, so, no shadow being cast in any way around our little party, all thought of gloom was forgotton. Next morning we were anchored **off** Alexandria, waiting for daylight and the Pilot to take us in. Several of us were up before sunrise **to** get our first glimpse of Africa, and in the twilight **we** could see the low bank of land, and the huge Pharos or lighthouse revolving and flashing at intervals. A beautiful tint flushed the Eastern sky, faintly lighting **up** the **sea**, and bringing to view the graceful sails of **the** fishing boats skimming along the horizon, and as daylight came on we asked each other if we could realize that this was Egypt. It was hard to do so, but when the sun rose over the City and burnished the mosq**ues,** minarets, and domes, when the boat came alongside, **and** the Egyptian pilot walked the bridge in full, flowing Oriental costume, we then began to realize that we were nearing a strange land. A few minutes, and our steamer, threading its way through the mazes of shipping, dropped anchor amid vessels of all nations.

Moving bundles of rags were now to be seen swarming

everywhere, on the decks of the surrounding ships, which looked very odd until we saw the bronze faces of Arabs peering out from under their swaddling tatters, and, in sliding down the sides of the ships by ropes, they strikingly resembled the masses of old rags let down our chimneys at home by the sweeps. The disembarking was accomplished with great quiet and order, considering all things; and soon luggage, passengers, old maids and all, were bobbing towards the shore where we landed at the Custom House. As usual, having no passport, I entered the city as somebody's son, in fact I had been obliged to pass under so many names for entrance to different sights and cities, that I almost doubted my identity. My luggage was not looked at, owing to a judicious use of a little "back sheesh," and in carriages we were soon dashing to our first hotel in Egypt.

CHAPTER III.

ON landing at **Alexandria, one** feels how utterly unlike is **every inhabitant, every** building, and every street **scene to** anything one sees in Europe. With **the appearance** of the French, the Germans and the **Italians, the eye** becomes quite familiarized after a short sojourn **in their** respective countries; but with the different races seen in Egypt who, **in** their garb, figures and physiognomies, seem almost to **be** a different order of beings from ourselves, it takes **a** much longer time to accustom **one's self** to their peculiarities. **At the** Hotel **we assemble on** the balcony, and, for a while, amuse ourselves by watching the masquerade of passing natives. A large round fountain lies in front of us, in the Grand Square, where numbers of the rag-bundles previously spoken of are washing their extremities, beginning with their feet, as it is only right that in great undertakings people should begin low and work up. Camels carrying heavy loads string through the streets, each tied to the one in front, their forelegs practising the "goose-step" proudly, while the hind legs seem loath to follow, but get dragged along, after reaching about ten feet **behind.** And the donkeys! Those donkeys are too **much for** my gravity. Small donkeys, lean donkeys, **sore,** sleepy, blind, lame, stubborn, or lively donkeys—everybody has a donkey, which he rides on its tail, and if he is well-to-do has a runner behind to shove and beat his animal. Those who don't have a runner pick out a sore place and beat him there. The largest men have the smallest donkeys, and when they stir him up with continual kicks one feels that the hind leg may be kicked off at any moment. In no foreign country do the natives speak so much English. Each donkey boy brings his animal right across the path and declares that Africa has but one of these perfections, which is at the gentleman's pleasure. As to the money used, I think every coin in the world passes current—a handful of change generally being a collection from all countries. Rupees and piastres form the native coin, but Japanese pieces, with the square hole in the middle, which have strayed here up the Suez Canal may often rub in the same pocket against an old Yankee quarter-dollar; and the first thing to be done, after changing some money, is to adorn ourselves, while strolling through the bazaars, with the fezes and puggeries which we wore continually afterwards while in the East.

If the Moralist or the Philanthropist cannot find enough in London or New York to attract his attention or excite his pity, he should come to Egypt to dwell on the little interesting views of queer humanity, and on the strange collections of poverty, squalor, and misery here seen. Some great man once said that any one who could make an original remark should have a monument for it, he ought to have added, " and have the remark engraved thereon." The speech occurs to me often in the endeavour to make letters readable when written about a country so well known as Egypt. One by one the pictures in the old geography are viewed in reality; one by one the dreams of childhood have the gloss of imagination taken from them, and each sight dispels part of the pleasant early delusion that somewhere on earth there is a likeness to Paradise. It takes many years to get over the childish ideas conjured up whilst idling over Morse's Geography; for instance, that old column called Pompey's Pillar, standing on a small eminence outside of Alexandria, does not look half as big as it did on the margin of the old map.

But there it has been waiting and standing erect, like an old soldier guarding the spot, century after century, while the world kept passing by twos and fours to gaze at it. We all think of the stories of sailors ascending it, and the anecdote of Voltigeur who went up it by a rope with a donkey on his shoulders, leaving the beast up there all night. We try to think it is ninety-eight feet high, and wonder what polished its immense cylinder. Was it sandstorms, or the eyes of fair ones gazing hard? We would like to think that this Arab beggar has a real piece of the pillar to sell, but they have sold pieces for hundreds of years, and the Pillar is almost intact, so we would rather give him a piastre than take the stone. Near by, and overturned, lies an immense sitting figure of a god, lying supinely, while the multitude, walking over his face, wear his nose off—worthy subject for a Christian's reverie! For how changed since kings and rulers bowed before it is its position now!

Over the fields, now green and fertile, the eye rests with pleasure, and through the groves of palms which wave their plumes in the breeze, the white square-topped houses are seen, and many an Eastern scene we greet as a friend long looked for. But here in the yard of a peasant, and guarded by a snarling mongrel, rests the obelisk called Cleopatra's Needle, sunk in the ground, and in its lowly position still retaining its seventy feet intact. Three of its sides are rough and unpolished, with the hieroglyphics almost obliterated, while it still (like many men) turns its bright side to the sea, looking down over the sparkling water, seeing, at last, Alexandria the key of Europe, and Africa an island; but what changes in the histories of the world have taken place since it saw the Phœnicians glide past on their trading expeditions to the shores of the then barbarous Britain! Who could have foreseen that that far off isle, shrouded in Cimmerian darkness would in a few centuries be the mistress of the seas, and that about this same monument should reverberate the thunders of her fleet, doing battle for the liberties of Europe? This obelisk once stood at Heliopolis,

B

the City of the Sun, the On mentioned in Genesis (41-45), where Joseph received in marriage Asenath the daughter of Potiphera, the priest of On, "the Oxford of ancient Egypt," built three hundred years before Memphis or Thebes, where Plato and Herodotus enunciated the principles that rival Solomon in wisdom, and, even though springing from heathenism seem divinely inspired. More cutting and more erasing have been its experiences on the other sides, for since first erected, when Thotmes the Third and Rameses the Great flourished—whose names are yet legible upon it—the sandstorms have cut into its surface like dropping water; and it has seen nothing but disease and misery in an oppressed people, who for degradation vie with the animals. No wonder its bright side faces the sea!

An agreeable drive lies along a canal leading to the Nile, where the *dahabeahs*, with towering lateen sails, catch the wind over the trees on the bank, while men partly haul them by ropes from the shore. Many a scene for an artist is here, taking perhaps a group of mud huts in one corner and through the trees the tapering sails and winding river, with the palms and blue-coloured palaces of the grandees in the background, a picture could be made to rival Claude. This canal is forty-eight miles long, and in the magnitude of the undertaking and in the cruelty accompanying its accomplishment may compete with the gigantic labours of the Pharaohs. When Mehemet Ali desired a canal from Alexandria to the Nile 250,000 people were pressed from the adjacent villages and made to work at the excavations. Provisions had been supplied for a month only; then famine set in. The scourge kept them at work while their starving wives and children lay dying on the banks by thousands; the men dug into the ground with the last effort of desperation; children are said to have carried away the earth in little handfuls, while nursing mothers laid their dying infants on the banks to assist in the operations; and, at the cost of 25,000 lives and untold misery the waters of the Nile were in six weeks led into Alexandria.

BARBARIC MUSIC.

With steps to the water's edge and **its** base washed **by the** salt water, the Palace of the Viceroy rises with more than Venetian grandeur. The seraglio, where the beauties of the East bask in the partial sunlight of their capricious master, is a place worth seeing, if only to **form** ideas of its internal magnificence. The style of the palace is somewhat Italian, but the luxurious divans and worked tapestry of the interior give it a very Eastern look, the inlaid ebony floors, and beautiful glass candelabra, fifteen feet high, fully carrying out the idea of Oriental splendour.

In some **of our drives in the** country, through tracts of waving sugar-cane, **we** were attracted by the band playing in the Viceroy's gardens. These gardens, commanding **a** fine view towards Ramle, **are** well laid out and rich **in** tropical plants; but **like most** eastern gardens, have **few** flowers, and a greater **wealth** of foliage than our western ones. The bands tuned their instruments for a long time all together before commencing **to play;** and here Jimmy and I thought it **our duty to impress** upon **the** credulous old maids the peculiar **harmonies** of this barbaric music. Jimmy loved his joke, and we so deluded them as to make them think it was the correct thing to appreciate and praise it. When the band really did begin to play, (very well too,) James and I "made ourselves scarce," to escape the vengeance of injured innocence.

On the run down to Cairo, we passed through miles of low green land, where the wild fowl watched us fearlessly by thousands, and the sacred ibis stalked rather nearer to than away from us. How I longed for a punt and a couple of double barrels! All through the swamps were seen the wretched mud villages looking more like the habitation of the beaver than that of man; **and** how they lived in these cone-shaped huts I could not **then** imagine; it having been through after experience **only,** that I realised the delights of such abodes.

Africa never seemed so real, that **is,** never so like the old geography, as when viewing these scenes. A camel and a cow appear to be the favourite team for ploughing, or perhaps the only beasts they have; and the ploughs are the same as those the Children of Israel worked with, a long tongue or pole attached to a sharp-pointed crosspiece, which sticks into the ground. Buffaloes are also much used in the irrigation of the soil, and are supplied by the Government to the poorer farmers to turn the the water wheels; for which they pay a heavy tax. There was a strange scene at the half-way station where we Franks all turned out for an airing. Pretty English and American girls ran about bargaining for oranges and bananas with the Arabs. The Englishmen and Germans had a whiff from their pipes as they regarded complacently the scene; the Italians had a cigarette ready for the opportunity, and the Yankees said something "cute," as is usual on such occasions. The hubbub was increased by the loud cries for "backsheesh;" the first thing heard and the last thing we are reminded of is "backsheesh."

Shepheard's Hotel at Cairo, has long been the haven of rest to the worn out invalid, homeward bound from India, as well as to dusty Nile travellers: we were soon ensconced in its comfortable quarters, and ready to mount the donkeys assembled in front of the hotel for hire. It had rained hard the night previous to our advent and the mud was deep in some of the narrow streets; nevertheless, mud is preferable to the dust of Cairo. Once in the bazaars, every step of the way is full of interest to the observer. There were some scavengers cleaning the streets, picking up the mud in handfuls. Hands were made before shovels, and too much invention seems odious in Egypt, but the way the overseers thrash the poor workmen aroused both my ire and interest. If a carter does not look about him well, one of the men with canes flies at him and administers a tremendous thrashing, which the victim bears without murmuring, or, apparently, feeling. The bazaars form a perfect labyrinth, which one might walk through for hours without finding his way out. The houses with their little shops on the ground floor are generally lofty; from the upper windows lattice casements project; and matting in most places is hung across the narrow space between the roofs to shade the street below. Artificers and workmen of each different **trade**, have, from time out **of** mind, worked together in the same localities; so that **the** visitor finds himself walking for half a mile perhaps through the districts of the makers of donkey-saddles; then passing through a din raised by copper-kettle makers, he finds himself among the manufacturers of the long flexible pipe tubes **for the** *narghili*. Each nationality is represented **in their** different localities, the Turks, the Arabs, the **Persians,** the Copts, and many **others,** have each **a** portion **of** the town allotted to **them**, where they are seen, disposing of their countries' products, dressed in the garb peculiar **to their** native land.

The streets, in some places, reminded me a little of the Ghetto at Rome; each shop raised a foot or more from the ground, a good-sized one being **about seven** feet square. The turbaned occupants sit smoking their narghilis or tchibooks in all attitudes of repose, with their weighing scales before them, and the wares heaped up inside the shop. Now my donkey rushes into the cool dimly-lighted arcades, where the shops seem smaller, and their **owners**, more ghastly white than outside. Were it not for an occasional motion **of** the lustrous eye, one could easily mistake the motionless Persians **for** clothed statues. The voluminous garments are snowy white, their beards are silvery white, their faces are floury white, but once the sleepy eye rests with interest upon you, the latent fire in that sitting statue is immediately felt. The venerable gray-beard does not solicit custom, yet he will ask exorbitant prices; perhaps your suggestion of half the **price** asked will cause him **to** resume his pipe and become suddenly forgetful of your presence, till an offer **of** three-fourths of what he has asked awakes him. Now, become friendly, sit down on his mat, roll **a** cigarette, or accept the offer of his amber-mouthed tchibouk, and become as silently courteous as Eastern merchants and other gregarious animals generally are. If he understands any Italian, a good word about his wares will go a long way towards working down his price, and here is a good chance to air the Arab expressions picked up from the donkey boys; after a while, again suggest what you will give. He is looking the other way, and deep in thought. Presently one shoulder goes up into a long shrug of sacrifice, and he places the slippers, or whatever the object is, in your hands. He has probably charged you twice the price a native could buy them for, but the Koran does not forbid extortion with a "dog of a Christian." Having now finished all your bargains, the donkey-boy carries the purchases till the hotel is reached; but to get out of the endless ramifications of the arcades is not easy. It is often necessary to crouch in a corner, or get into a shop, as a camel, laden with firewood or clover, comes striding along, scraping each side of the alley with his burden. It is quite useless trying to guide the donkey, for he knows better then you how to get through the throng; the gadfly of a boy, who whacks him, continually uttering the cry "oowah" (get out of the way), or "alameenak," or "alishmahl," when he wants the pedestrians to take the right or left; and many are the scowls one receives from those who suffer hard knocks. In New Cairo the streets are wide and handsome, but not yet paved. The Khedive is going to make the city another Paris, and the stone is being brought all the way from Italy. As Augustus found Rome in bricks and left it in marble, so the Khedive intends to metamorphose Cairo. Does not this resemble in magnitude of idea the operations of the ancients, who, without modern machinery, built the Pyramids?

Service was held on Sunday in the ball-room or dining-room of the New Hotel, the accustomed hour of eleven seeing us wending our way to church in Cairo. When seated on chairs arranged into aisles, our memories were at once carried back to the small churches we were familiar with at home. My last service had been at Rome, in the hot-bed of Romanism; and this, my next, was in the stronghold of Mahometanism. "Dearly-beloved brethren, the Scripture moveth us in sundry places," had, perhaps, more of music to my ears than the words ever bore before, and I sung the old psalms to the end with real pleasure. The clergyman, who, I think, was "high church," had the good sense to descend a little, in consideration of the various sects he had in his congregation. He thought, no doubt, that the exhortation to Phæton, "Tutissimus ibis in medio," would be applicable to himself. In the prayer for the Royalty, was added, "and his Royal Highness the Khedive, by whose permission we are permitted here to worship:" but for this reminder, and the fact of dropping an Egyptian coin into the plate, I might have been in St. John's Church, at Toronto.

The water carriers of Cairo form an interesting study on account of the peculiar appearance of the receptacles in which they carry the water. They are generally the skins of large black pigs or sheep, which have been taken off with the least possible cutting, the holes made by taking off the hoofs being tied up, so that when they are filled, the legs stick out from the bloated dripping bodies, as if the animals had been drowned for about two weeks. They fill them at the fountains with the neck of the skins around the spout, then quickly twisting a thong around the apertures, they stagger off under their wobbling disgusting, looking burdens, about the most unhandsome sight ever seen. Of course the water is very good, and not affected in any way by the skin, but if all our people had known they were drinking the water carried in this way, more wine would probably have been consumed.

The Shoobra Road leads for miles out of the city, and the acacias "high o'er arched, embower" the whole road, which is the principal drive for the élite. After galloping helter skelter for a mile or so while the donkey boys untiringly keep up the pace, let us rest the animals and watch the passing panorama of strange sights. Three figures, draped gracefully in flowing white muslin, come bounding down the road, with every limb moving in perfect unison and ease, to clear the way for the carriages of their masters following; they carry long upraised wands in their hands, and woe to the donkey boy who delays making way when they utter "oowah, oowah." While looking at them the mind recalls the words, "Prepare ye the way of the Lord, make his paths straight;" and no doubt the cry and the custom date from the most remote antiquity. Then come a couple of guards mounted on fine Arabs, and after them, a carriage, generally containing some of the Khedive's wives, surrounded by more horsemen. The glimpse at the eyes, and face partly concealed yet enhanced in beauty by the light muslin *Yashmak*, is very good while it lasts. Nothing conveys a greater idea of *style* to my mind than the sight of these bounding, graceful, white-robed figures, wearing embroidered vests of different hues; with the leg and foot bare, heads thrown back and arms well up, they run for miles with more ease than the horses they precede.

Some grandees prance past on thorough-bred Arabs, which walk as if on springs, gaily caparisoned with embroidered saddle-cloths, their glossy coats that shine in the sun, their fine noses and clean cut limbs, the nostrils distended, and the eye with a well-bred flash about it—all tell their pedigree as if they had it printed on the saddle. We are not so well mounted, but join in the rush and ruck for another mile, where we ascend a slight eminence. What interest lay in that view over the Nile! There, cradled on the bosom of that River of Wonder, lay many a dahabeah with lofty sails impatient for the breeze; and fertile banks, rich in verdancy and perfume, stretched away in ever varying colour under the palms and Arab tents, till the Sahara abruptly marked the line 'twixt life and death of vegetation; and on the rising desert lay the Eternals of Earth, those of Ghizeh nearest, and farther, those of Cheops, dwindling in the distance till the vanishing point of the perspective was almost lost in the bluish light of Egypt.

I think the old geography was eclipsed here.

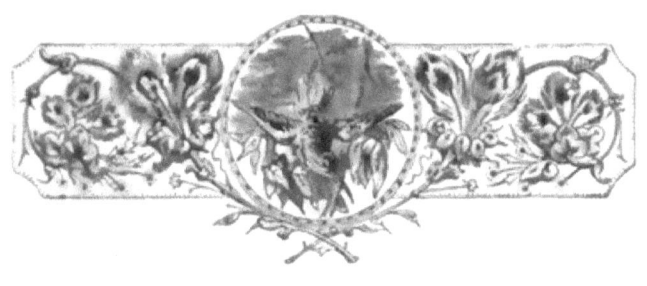

CHAPTER IV.

DURING our stay at Cairo there were additions made to our **party, which** now had several good-looking young **ladies,** several jolly ones, and the aged spinsters aforesaid, who hoped to die, if possible, at Jerusalem; besides, Jimmy and I by this time knew the other young fellows thoroughly, **and** better companions were **never** met with—so we **took** heart. A fine morning **saw us** starting for the Pyramids, each carriage filled with a party of four particular friends. The precious pretty ones kindly distributing themselves among the different carriages to brighten **up** the despondent; so the caravan had to be **a** jolly **one.**

Mammas were particularly larky on that **day**; papas leaned forth like sun-flowers, and the spinsters occupied a carriage **by** themselves. Luncheon hampers were very visible **about** the vehicles, and none were sad but the horses. It **was a** three hours' drive, leading first through the City, then over the Nile, and along an avenue of acacias planted all **the** way out to the desert; a partially cloudy day favoured us with a delightful atmosphere, heavy with odours of the luxuriant clover and grass. While **crossing the** valley of the Nile, with the Pyramids in front **of us, some** grew enthusiastic over the interest of the view; but **for** me, the soft natural beauties of the drive possessed **an equal** interest; and certainly the Arabs' shapely, snowy tents, pitched in numbers on the long grass, where their horses grazed, and children played about; the yellow mustard fields blending almost imperceptibly into dark green meadows, and the full ponds and regularly cut rows of canals dividing the picture by silver lines of perspective, were elements not the least interesting among the many attractions of the spot. Strings of camels—scores of them—could be seen bearing their huge burdens of fragrant clover to the city. The stately ibis stalked unharmed beside us, and the sober donkey held his head above the flowers, as if to rebuke us for our levity on approaching the Tombs of Ancient Greatness.

A few English sportsmen, with their dogs and beaters, were tramping about, blazing away right and left, but with no great success; accounts being heard when we returned to the hotel of "an awfully jolly day, birds *rawther* shy though." When about a mile from the desert the Arabs from the village of the Pyramids met us, each selecting the "best good man" for his prey, and endeavouring by much flattery to induce him to make the ascent with his assistance. At Florence I met a thorough old Yankee, who he "guessed was the only man of seventy-five who had come across and clumb them *Purmids*," and he said "there's no use a' talkin', they're a *big pile o' rocks*." He was about right, they are a big pile of rocks. As it is always said to be impossible to ascend without aid, several of us did it for the sake of the feat. The ladies came up bravely with the aid of the supple Arabs, who quite enjoyed helping the daughters of England to the top; and many of these dusky children of the desert spoke very fair English.

Engineers were surveying the country from the top by order of the Khedive, who sends to America for surveyors; and a better spot could hardly be devised for taking observations. While resting after our exertions, as the fellows were immortalizing themselves by cutting their names on the stones, and while having at my feet, Cairo and the wonderful Nile valley on one side, and the boundless Sahara on the other, I felt that my position at that moment was a very strange and even enviable one. Was I not realizing what had always been a part of my fondest dreams? To view Rome from the top of St. Peter's, and Cairo from Ghizeh, had been cherished hopes with me always; and having satisfied the former, it was a proud moment when I realized the latter.

We made a purse for an Arab who was to descend and reach the top of one of the other Pyramids in ten minutes. Down he skipped and bounded till he seemed like a white flea in the distance; he reached the bottom, scoured across the sand, and commenced the ascent. With our watches in our hands we followed him with interest as he crawled up and up, like an insect on an elephant, till he reached the top, having a full minute to spare, and we cheered back to his signal to tell him he had won the stakes. The going down is far more dangerous than the ascent, as the ledges are not broad, and are of unequal height; to get started head first by the heel catching, would ensure one's being an interesting mummy in about two minutes. On entering the interior it is necessary to take two Arabs, who guide the feet and hold the candles. First we slide down an inclined plane through massive rock, then ascend another polished slide where notches keep the feet from slipping. The Arabs keep up a responsive chorus, alternately singing "Allah, Allah, oh! Gentleman! very good! Backsheesh! Satisfy Arab!" This is a gentle hint to tip them while the sheikh at the entrance cannot see them receive the money. One place to be crossed is a ledge about fourteen inches wide; an apparently bottomless abyss yawning beneath. In the centre of the Pyramid is the chamber where lay the sarcophagus of some ancient "nob," and beneath was the so-called Chamber of the Queen at the end of another long, low passage. The faint light of the candles but partly disclosing the rugged interior, and the dust of ages raised in the ascent filling the nose and eyes, it was not a place for comfortable reflection; a short scrutiny of the shapened boulders being quite sufficient for us all. We emerged covered with dust, almost stifled, and dripping with perspiration; each one's appearance creating a fresh laugh from those who had not ventured in. After luncheon which washed a good deal of dust into our systems we adjourned to the Sphynx. Shade of Osiris! Fancy *adjourning to the Sphynx.*

Standing aloof from the party, I viewed her from a more enchanting distance. The wondrous beauty was not, however, apparent to my undiscerning eye; the head is the shape of a large flour barrel, and the nose being entirely gone, its absence increases the resemblance. True, it may be said that there is character in the face, and from the set appearance of the jaw, she is evidently determined to stay there as long as she likes. The head and back are above the sand yet, but the excavations, between the fore-paws, of the immense temple, made by Caviglia, have long since been filled up by the sand. About the time the Prince of Wales was here, another large tomb was discovered, whose pillars are now visible close by.

How pleasant were the fields on coming off the desert, and how many a drooping traveller, taking the Pyramids as his landmark, must have rushed down this slope to dash into the clear ponds abounding in the valley. When all mirages were past, when the camels had safely carried the precious dust, ivory and feathers across the desert, when the mosques of Cairo burst upon his view, how he must have revelled in these limpid pools, and laved his aching eyes and blistered feet.

The return was enlivened by a number of native boys who followed the carriages most of the way for backsheesh, in a state of utter nudity; so modest reader, even if you have accustomed yourself to all the statuary in Italy, you must throw off entirely the mask of Pudentia before entering Egypt. Take for instance, the poorer classes; the women wear a long blue garment which covers them from head to foot, gives them the appearance of large sloping bottles, and the face is all concealed except the eyes; while a cumbrous brass or wooden arrangement joins the upper and lower parts of the *yashmak.* Thus while the face is well concealed, the bosom is often quite nude, and whether any other garment than this is worn is doubtful. According to the ideas of modesty, entertained in the East, it seems most essential that the face should be covered. A little Arab girl, if she *has* a rag of clothing, coquettishly covers her face with it. The wind generally produces indescribable effects upon the poor half-clad women, among the young disclosing forms of matchless symmetry, while in the aged exposing only hideous deformity.

The days pass by quietly, and are full of interest as we see the sights of Cairo; the evenings are equally pleasant, passed in the drawing-rooms or on the balcony of the hotel. The plague has never been quite removed, that is to say, there are *some* insects in Cairo yet, and though I am tolerably pachydermatous myself, I cannot help perceiving the well bred wriggle of those less fortunate and more afflicted. A breezy morning saw us at the door of the Grand Mosque, where we had to take off our boots or put on slippers before entering the walls. Tying on the huge slippers, reminded me of the Canadian snow-shoeing parties, often enjoyed at that very time of the year. In the centre of a large paved quadrangle, first entered, was a dome with taps and stone seats underneath for the worshippers and pilgrims to wash their feet before entering the carpeted mosques. The strange shape and vast interior is as striking at first as St. Peter's. Imagine a huge dome, with about twelve other segments of domes supporting it, the ceilings adorned with every device of rich embellishments. Imagine, the whole interior of pure alabaster, and a few enormous supporting pillars of the same material; picture the effect of seven thousand lamps suspended by chains from the domes; cast over the whole the varied lights from the coloured windows, and an idea may be formed of the Grand Mosque of Cairo. The huge gilt tomb of Mehemet Ali is in one corner, and immense silver candelabra surround his honoured resting place.

"Egypt is the gift of the Nile," said Herodotus, who was bewildered by its antiquity before our history was born. A bountiful gift it was that the "strange, mysterious, solitary stream" bore down in its bosom from the luxuriant tropics to the desert. "For many an hour have I stood," says Warburton, "upon the city-crowning citadel of Cairo, and gazed unweariedly on the scene of matchless beauty and wonder that lay stretched beneath my view; cities and ruins of cities, palm forests and green savannahs, gardens and palaces, and groves of olives. On one side, the boundless desert, with its Pyramids; on the other, the land of Goshen, with its luxuriant plains, stretching far away to the horizon. Yet this is an exotic land! That river, winding like a serpent through its paradise, has brought it from the regions unknown to man. That strange and richly varied panorama has had a long voyage of it! Those quiet plains have tumbled down the cataracts; those demure gardens have flirted with the Isle of Flowers, five hundred miles away; those very Pyramids have floated down the waves of Nile. To speak chemically, that river is a solution of Ethiopia's richest regions, and that vast country is merely a precipitate. We have here a whole kingdom, risen like Aphrodite from the wave."

It was here the well-known slaughter of the Mamelukes took place. Entrapped through the treachery of Mehemet Ali into this place, they fell under the pitiless storm of bullets, from which there was no escaping; horses and men soon covering the ground in one hideous bleeding mass. All bit the dust, save one—Emim Bey, with one short glance perceived that escape on all sides was cut off, but through the smoke he saw the rampart above the plain below was yet unguarded; he knew his trusty Arab could clear it, and at once "sheer o'er the battlements," took the frightful leap. A moment more, and far down he was extricating himself from his dying horse; a short fond caress to the friend that was faithful to the last, and through a storm of bullets, he reached a temporary refuge in a sanctuary. Ultimately as a fugitive, and alone, this survivor of that band which Napoleon acknowledged to be the finest cavalry in the world, escaped to the deserts of Thebaid, where it would be hard to catch a Mameluke.

Close by was one of the old Pasha's palaces, which we

wandered through, throwing **ourselves** on the rich **divans** to test their luxury; then a dusty drive took us to Joseph's Well. We groped down the quadrangular descent, feeling for every footstep **in the** darkness, and often slipping down two or three steps at **a time. At** the bottom of the first shaft, 200 feet down, we **emerge at** the top of **a second** shaft 200 feet deeper. Donkeys **work** the large wheel over the lower shaft, and a grass rope **to** which pitchers are attached, **runs** in a groove over the wheel. The pitchers fill below **and** carry the water to the top of the first shaft, **where, in turning** round the wheel they empty **it into a trough; then** a similar contrivance elevates **the** water **from the** trough to the surface. **It was** amusing to find on my return **to** Canada, that this contrivance, which is as old as Egypt, had been there lately *patented*. The Citadel, and the Mosque of Hassan were visited, but no great amount **of** information could be elicited from old Yousoof our guide. **On** some of our rambles, we entered an old Coptic church, a strange old relic of Christianity, with odd carving and paintings like many churches at Rome; said to be built upon the site of the house where Joseph, Mary, and the Babe dwelt. In the crypt, stupid old Yousoof showed us the place where Mary **washed** the babe, **or** Moses washed Joseph; but whether **they** washed each other, or got somebody to do it for them, or whether they washed at all, I can't say, for Yousoof **was very** "mixed" in the legend, which at **any** time should **be taken** *cum grano salis.* Next we **entered** what our guiding **star** called the "amorous mosque," which caused us to think of harems and that sort of thing, till somebody suggested Omar's Mosque, which calmed our apprehensions. Then we crossed the Nile in a ferry **to** the Island of Rhoda, to see the Nilometer, which, since **the** Eighth century, has recorded that most interesting **of** all events to the Egyptians—the annual rise and fall of old Father Nile. And truly if any nation might be forgiven for worshipping a River God, they ought, when we remember that their very existence depended upon the flow of its waters for the irrigation of their land. But all these fancies were put to flight by the announcement of the guide, that on this Isle, Moses was found in the bulrushes by Pharoah's daughter. We had been shown the Coptic church built on the site of the house occupied by the Holy Family during their flight into Egypt, and although we had all our lives read the biblical accounts, we again turned to them with renewed interest, noting the fact that the Founders of the two great dispensations—the Law and the Gospel—were sheltered here, so close together that we passed from viewing the site of one, into the enclosures where the great and similar coincidence is reputed to have taken place. Moses the young Law-giver of the Jews, escaping from the cruel Pharoah, and the infant Jesus, the Saviour of the World, fleeing from the wrath of blood-thirsty Herod, were both harboured in this immediate vicinity. After seeing the vast remains of ancient Egypt, and reading something of its history, one cannot help being struck with the magnitude of the self-sacrifice of Moses, when he refused to be called the son of Pharaoh's daughter, and thus, the probability of becoming king—preferring to suffer affliction with the children of God. Passing through a garden full of blossoming apricots, the ladies were conducted by Nubian eunuchs, into the Harem of the Pacha, while we were not admitted. We murmured greatly, and tried to get past a six-foot-four eunuch, with a visage ugly enough to make him sufficiently unattractive in any female society, but he laughed at our wanting to see the fair Odalisques, and still kept us out.

We crossed the Styx again in a boat just the shape attributed to Charon's mythical craft, and drove to the museum of Egyptian curiosities. It was interesting to observe the difference between Roman and Egyptian relics of antiquity, in regard to their preservation; and to note how much more tenderly the hand of Time had dealt with the woodwork and ornaments of the latter country, owing to the dryness of the atmosphere, or perhaps total exclusion from all air. The Scarabeus or holy beetle, was painted on all the mummy cases and on the sarcophagi, as the emblem of immortality; and with almost every mummy have been found numbers of these stone bugs. It would seem hard to bury the present Egyptian in this way, as their life-long experience of these friends, which stick closer than a brother, should be quite enough to secure immunity from them when this little span of life is ended. A copy of the Rosetta stone is here. It bears three inscriptions, the first in hieroglyphics, the sacred writing known only to the priests; the second in demotic, the writing of the people; and the third in Greek, being the translation of the other two texts. The event recorded is the coronation of King Epiphanes at Memphis, B. C. 196. Dr. Young, of Edinburgh was, I believe, the first to make out the writing, though our knowledge at that time, on the subject, did not go beyond the stone.

Let us now, without referring to the other sights of Cairo, come to where our dahabeah awaits us with its towering sails fluttering in the south-wind that lightly favours our course; but before we start, pause and look back on Cairo and its pinnacles now glinting in the moonlight; and mark well the citadel commanding the city like the Acropolis at Athens; then cast thine eyes eastward, and fix on thy memory the Pyramids, as, silvered by the moon, they now stand on the desert, unchanged yet, since first the Genii laid their foundations on the sand. We will glide down to the sea, between the banks where nature has written fertility in her richest, warmest colours; where the plains all teeming with cultivation to the water's edge, seem to offer up, "as from verdant altars, their fruits to the sun, while beneath us the Nile,"

———"The glorious stream,
That late between the banks was seen to glide,
With shrines and marble cities on each side,
Glittering like jewels strung along a chain,
Had now sent forth its waters, and o'er the plain
And valley, like a giant from his bed,
Rising with outstretched limbs, superbly spread."

CHAPTER V.

SOME economical tricks are practised on Mediterranean steamboats; they generally land the passengers before breakfast or take them aboard after luncheon hour, or they do not have dinner till the boat has left a harbour and has been rolling about for an hour or so; then the ladies are nearly all ill, and the men would rather stay on deck than go below, so there is little waiting to do at table and much less provisions consumed. It was a source of comfort to the afflicted to tell them the Steamboat Company had made nothing, as I had looked after the interests of the whole party at the dinner-table. The picture of a party of people trying to stave off the inevitable by laughing and pacing the deck is most comical. Everybody keeps up the jollity till he feels that his latest meal is unsettled and can be dispensed with; then saying melodramatically, "my hour is come," he makes a rush for the lee-rail, and comes back smiling and relieved. The ladies lie in heaps on the deck rolled up in shawls and sucking lemons, shrieking with laughter as each white-faced man comes up from the dining-saloon looking dubiously inward.

All this was enacted after a short stay at Alexandria, and a fine sunny day saw us running along the shore before a fresh breeze with all sail set, passing the Bay of Aboukir and Rosetta, and *en route* for the Suez Canal. We had bid our farewell to Egypt and its mysteries, and its strange people, who had become so familiar to us. We had engraved our last views of Alexandria in the mind's eye as we swept out of the matchless harbour, and waved an adieu to the mute old Obelisk still watching from the shore. Too beautiful for sacrificing to sleep was the night, and it was not till long after our chorus on deck was over that I retired; even then, lying at the large window of the stateroom, my thoughts flew about from Egypt to Canada in a wonderful way. But as the view, by the rolling of the ship, alternately sunk from the starry sky to the sparkling horizon and down into the blue depths, the two countries became confused—the Sphynx somehow got into a Toronto croquet ground, where a fair one was watering its dusty countenance with the garden hose.

Next morning the huge lighthouse of Port Said was looming in the distance, and we were soon running between the breakwaters which stretch far out into the sea. These are made of large blocks of stone piled carelessly together, so that the sea will not wear out the barricade as quickly as if built compactly. Excellent seamanship was shown in the turning of the ship in the harbour where there was hardly room to spin about; and better handling I never witnessed than on these Austrian Lloyd steamships. It was a pleasant sail in small boats up that international highway; and on stepping out to wander on the desert of Arabia, it struck me that this was another strange country entered; another experience well worth having, despite the monotony of the view.

No description of the canal is necessary; to say that it is "water between two sandbanks" would be almost too profuse; but in speaking of the interest of the spot, one might fill a volume. When we looked at a map and saw what was gained by these operations; what time, money, and lives had been saved by cutting off the long and dangerous Cape voyage; when we saw the vessels of all nations passing through, bearing the luxuries of China and the Indies, to our homes in the West, we felt that our visit here formed one of our most interesting wanderings. The cargo was being taken in all the afternoon, and the donkey engine was shaking the whole boat while I was scribbling an addition to my endless letters about the odd sights before me. Beautiful as well as novel was it to see the frigates of all nations side by side in this friendly way; each with their national colours floating at their peaks and mast-heads. The Portuguese beside the splendid English man-of-war whose masts and web-like rigging towered majestically above all others: the Russian, Turkish, French, and all the rest, dressed in their holiday bunting, with the lines of claws drawn in peacefully and scarcely shewing a sign of war, except, perhaps, the marine guard pacing the deck. Though their anchors ranged together there in the neutral sand of a public thoroughfare, who could tell when these same vessels might range together again for a different and less peaceful purpose. Inspecting their latent power conveyed to the mind but a faint notion of what their meeting would be on that day.

When I awoke the next morning, we were rolling again at sea, and all day we were "tossed about in Adria," the wind increasing till the waves rivalled Atlantic's worst. A few passengers occupied the saloon, where they propped themselves between cabin sides and tables, while the chairs and everything moveable made clean sweeps of the floor at every roll. The crockery was rolled out of the racks and occasional crashes added to the fears of the ladies, while a few sat out on deck where the gentlemen arranged ropes to prevent them from sliding into the scuppers. We were now rolling till the boats in the davits nearly touched the waves, and the sun peering occasionally over a storm-cloud made the scene more wild and beautiful in its madness. At dusk, like Columbus in the shrouds of the tall Pinta, when discovering the New World, we were peering for our first view of the Holy Land, where the Judean Range was faintly showing its outline.

There being no harbour at Jaffa, it was useless to approach any nearer to the coast, so the captain turned the ship's nose to the nor'-west gale, to ride it out till daylight, with the engines at half-speed, whilst the bowsprit seemed first to pierce the zenith, and anon, plunge into the nadir of the depths. Three hundred and fifty pilgrims, on their way to Jerusalem, lay huddled over the fore part of the ship, the seas coming over the bow causing great discomfort amongst them. Next morning we drew near to Jaffa, but it was impossible to effect a landing, so we had the aggravation of seeing our ship steam on to Haifa, sixty miles up the coast; and when we arrived there the Armenian pilgrims were compelled to land, in small boats, through more than a mile of heavy sea, rain, and darkness, to find what shelter they could on holy ground.

In the morning a picture greeted my waking gaze through the porthole—more lovely than the round painting of the Holy Family designed by Raphael on the end of a wine cask. I was on deck in an instant. We were still anchored off Haifa, the wind had changed softly to the south and the sun shone pleasantly on the swelling waters of the Bay of Acre. Haifa, built of square white houses, nestled at the base of Mount Carmel, looking in the distance like a block village a child might have built in the nursery; fishing boats rolled about in front of the town on the subsiding waves of the previous night. On the opposite side of the bay, lay Acre or Akka, which Napoleon deemed the key of Palestine—where Sir Philip Sydney distinguished himself, and which was the last possession of the Crusaders in the Holy Land. Rising behind Acre appeared bluish mountains, and above all, Mount Hermon reared its snowy crest full seventy miles away; to the east lay the Plain of Acre, and to the west stretched the boundless Mediterranean.

The great question now, was how to get back to Jaffa, as the boat had to take her regular trip around the Levant, and no persuasions could make the captain return. I thought of Byron where he says:

"Mammon wins its way while seraphs might despair."

So I proposed giving a couple of sovereigns each to the captain, and also bring the speaking eyes we had with us to bear upon him, and thus induce him to return to Jaffa. He could not resist the united persuasion, and when his decision was announced to us a British cheer broke out, rivalling those often echoed by old Acre in the time of Richard Cœur-de-Lion. Again we headed south, sweeping down the coast past Mount Carmel, in a close view of the cheerless tracts of bald country unchequered by a single village and unenlivened by a single tree; and soon Cæsarea appeared, the huge pillars of the mole built by the Romans still standing high in the sea.

The whole coast of Palestine may be said to be extremely inhospitable; the only protection I ever saw was at Sidon, where a few rocks rising from the water some way from shore offered scanty shelter to small boats. Exposed as it is, to the fury of the westerly storms, there is no natural port of shelter to the vessels resorting to it. "To remedy this defect, Herod, who, though an arbitrary tyrant, did much for the improvement of Judæa, set about erecting, at immense cost and labour, one of the most stupendous works of ancient days. He threw out a circular mole which protected the port of Cæsarea on the south and west, leaving only a sufficient opening for vessels to enter from the north, so that there was protection to be had there in all weathers."

Joyfully we hailed Jaffa, like most oriental towns, looking better in the distance; and built up a high hill, till the houses seemed almost to topple over each other. A fleet of small boats rushed at us as we cast anchor, and we soon were bearing towards the Holy Land and dashing through the rocks just wide enough to admit our small boat, where the breakers surging over the sunken rocks showed how impossible it would be to land in heavy weather. We were lifted out of the boat and carried on the backs of natives through the shallow waters, who dumped us like flour bags—in Palestine, and in one of the dirtiest holes in the world. Talk about Naples being unclean, and having a smell or two! why Naples "is'nt a patch on" Cairo, and Cairo is clean when compared with Jaffa! From stone to stone we picked our way through the filthy bazaars, dodging laden camels and **donkeys, till** we suddenly came upon a surprise that took us all aback. In a lovely orange grove where the fruit literally gilded the trees were our snowy tents, prepared **for our** reception **with** gay flags floating from their **tops; we** entered **the** enclosure, and stood spellbound at the **scene** of **enchantment;** we wandered through each tent **and viewed the** luxuries within, **beholding** iron bedsteads and **bed clothes** made up neatly **in each;** washstands, **real tin jugs and** basins; a table **forsooth! the** ground carpeted ! **and the** whole tent lined **with scarlet and** gold chintz **with gaudy** Arabic devices on **a blue ground.** In another **large tent** was **a table laden** with **fruits and silver,** and **a cloth such as had** not been seen for many **a day. I was uncomfortable** among such splendour. **I felt as if I ought to have** had my Sunday clothes on and I remonstrated **with the** dragoman for such Sybarite preparations, **telling him that** in camping in the backwoods of Canada **we were accustomed to** sleep under **a** canoe.

Ernest and **I had a** tent **for** three persons **which gave** us more **room than** others had, and **our luggage being** deposited in **our** newly leased domicile, **we strolled out to** the house **of** Simon the tanner and **mounted the roof.** The house itself is pretty well plastered and white-washed, and might, possibly, **be** a hundred years old; **and** on this flat roof Peter is **said to** have had **the** strange vision of clean and unclean **beasts.**

Here Napoleon **in 1799,** when **a** breach was made by the cannon, and **after the offers** of peace had been accepted, seized nearly 4000 **disarmed** people, and while they were bound massacred them **to a man.** We visited Miss Arnott's schools. **No** missionary work ever attracted my sympathy **as** did **hers, at** Jaffa, so **near to** the birthplace of Christianity and yet so far removed **from the** spirit and truth of it. On entering the precincts, **the clean** intelligent appearance of the children caught **the** eye at once, some being very handsome ; the enlightenment of Christianity marking their faces with **a** beautiful calm, which was but a reflection from Miss Arnott herself, wherein they formed a great contrast to the other children of the town. She received us kindly in her little parlour off the top of the house. According to the general acceptation of the term, Miss Arnott is not pretty, but a sweeter, or more benign expression never lit up the face of any one I have had the pleasure of looking upon. Her converts were apparently numerous, though she was very reticent as to her good works; but surely working for 15 years in this cause—a stranger in a strange land—has rendered a long account to her credit in a more celestial world than Jaffa.

Threading the labyrinth of convents, khans, ruins and rubbish, by means of wretched lanes, we emerged by the fortifications overlooking the coast. Far out from shore lay the reefs of sunken rock, inside which the lateen-rigged small craft were fastened as a partial protection from the waves. The rocks were brown and slimy, covered with long green seaweed, in the clefts of which the rusted anchors of the boats nestled. It was here, Jerome says, he saw the chains, that bound Andromeda to the rock when Perseus came to save her from the sea monster; and here Hiram, King of Tyre, sent the cedars of Lebanon for the building of the Temple. Picturesque and dark-eyed maidens displaying the most graceful attitudes as they bend to fill their water jars or balance them on their heads, may be seen by the public fountains, and the same bazaars and yellow, mangy dogs are to be witnessed in Jaffa as in Cairo; but the oranges piled up like coal for exportation in the market square, formed a sight never seen elsewhere. This luscious fruit here attains the size of an ostrich egg, and is of the same oval shape, while, oddly enough, the lemons are round, and nearly as large as croquet balls. We had groves of both fruit around us, protected by high cactus fences, and although it was almost cheaper to buy them than rob the orchards, we preferred to steal them for "auld lang syne." After a very comfortable dinner we had a few songs, accompanied by Mr. John's guitar, while seated among the tents in the balmy evening air. How delightful it was to feel that we were fairly in Palestine! every fragrant wreath of smoke that curled from our tchibooks adding to our sense of satisfaction with ourselves and **all** men.

Tintom at six! With sackbut, psaltery, dulcimer, and three stringed gridiron, accompanied **by the** big dinner bell, innumerable tin cans and **some** old horns, our Arab servants rushed though the camp in the morning like maniacs. Nobody has ever been known **to** sleep through tintom! half an hour is given to dress, **and** if the sluggard waits a few minutes too long the tent may raise from around him discovering him *en deshabille*. Breakfast was had in the same *recherche* style as dinner, **then our** horses were chosen for the journey. Ladies had first choice, **and** I picked out good ones for two ladies who entrusted to me their selections, which afterwards gave every satisfaction. My own choice **was** almost the last, and I was looking despairingly about **for a** respectable mount, when a stout lady, getting frightened of hers, wished to exchange for a more subdued animal, of which sort there were plenty to be had. I was never so ready with my assistance, and as soon as she reached the ground I clapped my English saddle and myself on his back in a moment. Allah hu akbar! he was a splendid little Arab, and his paces satisfied me at once. I found that the reins should be scarcely touched, then only with the lightest hand possible, as the atrocious Arab bit used for all the horses gave mine great discomfort unless allowed **to** remain quite loose. Choosing a horse to ride through Palestine, requires a few hints from those who have gone through the mill themselves, and the better way is to get the dragoman to do it. Of course the animal should **be** sound in all his limbs, but instead of looking for **a good** shoulder in front, as is customary with us, it is **more** necessary that he should be brought up strongly behind the saddle, and notice should be taken that the hind legs are muscularly developed. Because in descending the break-neck paths which are generally full of ledges and falls, the whole weight of horse and rider is thrown back on the haunches, while he feels his way carefully with his fore-feet for his next footing. A small horse is better than a large one; they are more catlike on their feet and regain themselves quicker if they lose their footing on a shelving ledge of rock, besides being easier to mount and dismount, which sometimes has to be done many times in a day in the bad places; and horses that might be vicious should be carefully avoided as they often fight terribly with each other. They are trained to turn by the movement of the reins to either side, and it is easier to use the halter rope in ordinary travelling, which will afford a great support in ascending steep places.

While we were engaged in selecting the horses our snowy village had vanished; beds, tables, camp stools cuisine, had all gone off on the backs of mules, who, with their tinkling bells stepped off gaily on the long journey before them. Had they known the hardships they were about to undergo, I think they would have remonstrated as did their ancestor belonging to Balaam. All Jaffa turned out to see our circus depart—men, women and children, cripples and beggars (which latter class would include all), hung around us, showing their deformities and whining for backsheesh, while the little children, scarcely able to walk, lisped out the same eternal cry. Not one in a hundred expected to get anything. They do it from pure force of habit, acquired before they can say "mother," relinquished only when their ebbing life cannot utter the word their lips would form. Some of the gentlemen rode in the Syrian saddles, which is like sitting on a saw-horse covered with a hairy sheepskin, while the flat, shovel stirrups protruding behind the foot serve as a goad to score the horses sides. Many of the ladies were very timid at starting, and having no idea of riding, implored us to keep our horses perfectly quiet; and it seemed odd to me how they could have come to live in the saddle for weeks, without previously knowing a horse from a haystack. Though several professed to have been previously accustomed to riding, they neglected to have their saddle girths tightened on starting, and when their horses wished to canter to the head of the party, they did not check them, but clung to the saddles, which, on turning, left them hanging, like Mahomet's coffin 'twixt heaven and earth, and yelling worse than the prophet ever was known to.

The road out of Jaffa lay for three miles through high cactus hedges, enclosing orchards which **were** literally breaking down with their golden **fruit**, the richness of the view creating favourable first impressions of Palestine that took a good **deal** of after experience **to erase**. Soon we emerged into the plain of Sharon which reminds one of the Campagna, though more varied **in tint**; on the sward stretching across the valley, the **colours** blending in delicious harmony, were brightened in the foreground by the scarlet anemones, the iris and wild tulip, the narcissus **and** marsh mallow, the asphodel lily and meadow saffron. The celebrated Rose of Sharon could not **be** found. Dismounting **anywhere a** bouquet could **be** picked without taking a step.

It would seem that the Plain of Sharon **has been** nothing but a wilderness for ages, for in Isaiah it **is said**: " Lebanon is ashamed and hewn down, Sharon is like a wilderness," and certainly it is not owing to the barrenness of the soil that it **is**, or has not been cultivated; the rich sandy loam showing that it **is** upon the inhabitants, not the land that the curse lies. Here **we met a** soldier, well mounted, and decked with all the gaudy trapping the Arabs delight in, driving **two** prisoners bound securely together in front of him, along the road from Jerusalem. He saw us admiring his horse, so leaving his captives, who were too footsore to run away, even if unbound, he put his horse through the Arab manœuvres on the plain beside us, dashing along with his long spear upraised, stopping, swerving, striking **at** an imaginary enemy, and finishing with the peculiar and picturesque trick of throwing himself clear out of the saddle **on** to his spear, his horse stopping instantly, thus giving support for his feet from the saddle. At first this seemed **an** insecure way to transfer prisoners from **one** town **to** another, but with a fellow like this behind them they **had** little chance of escape.

We lunched in an olive grove, and a spirited scene it was when the horses were being tied to the trees, the ladies riding in and dismounting with their faces glowing after the morning ride, and the dragomans and camp servants in their Syrian costumes rushing about, spreading carpets for our luncheon. While the hobbled horses and mules grazed about, we sat down to a pic-nic repast of sardines, cold chicken, eggs, cold meat, Jaffa oranges, &c., &c., and picked the drumsticks in a truly primitive way. After lunch, we strolled off through this lovely garden in parties. Mr. Johnes read Byron's "Lara" to me while lolling among the olives—the only literature in harmony with the essence of poetry we were breathing. The bugle sounded "to horse" at two o'clock, and we started again to reach the camp at Ramleh, taking in our way the old village of Lydda.

It bore in Hebrew the name of Lod, and is now called Ludd. It is mentioned in several places in the Bible briefly, and apparently was built by the Benjamites. In the New Testament, Lydda is mentioned as the scene of Peter's miracle in healing Æneas before going to Joppa to stay with Simon (Acts IX, 32, 35). It was called Diospolis under the Romans, and is said to have given birth to St. George who became the patron Saint of England, and after his martyrdom and that little affair with the dragon, he was buried here, where a Church was erected in his honour by Justinian. Saladin, in 1191, destroyed this church, parts of which we found still standing, built into a large mosque, whose lofty minaret, visible for miles around, forms the landmark of Ludd. Soon after leaving here we reached our camping ground on the eastern side of Ramleh, situated on a broad, low swell rising from the plain. We rode through the town to the tents already erected in a fine grassy place close by one of the large pools which are so common in the East, and, swinging out of the saddle, we found our tents by the numbers painted on them. There our luggage was already placed, and, a few minutes sufficing for changing our clothes and the light spurred boots for heavy ones as a protection from the night dews, a few of us sallied forth to view the wonders of Ramleh, or, as is explained below, the ancient Arimathea.

I gleaned some information concerning it from different authorities. Arimathea, the birthplace of the wealthy Joseph in whose sepulchre our Lord was laid, is called by St. Luke the "City of the Jews," which may be explained by Demetrius who writes, "We have ratified unto them (the Jews) the borders of Judea with the three governments of Aphereum, Lydda and Ramathaim that are added unto Judea from the country of Samaria." Eusebius and Jerome regard the Arimathea of Joseph as the same place as the Ramathaim of Samuel, and place it near Lydda or Diospolis, hence it has been identified by some as the existing Ramleh, because of the similarity of the name to that of Ramah, and because it is near Lydda or Diospolis. Professor Robinson, however, disputes this conclusion because an ancient writer (Abuleda) alleges Ramleh to have been built by Sulieman, after Mohammed, about A.D. 716, and because Ramleh is in a plain, while Ramah implies a town on a hill. To this it might be answered, that Albulfeda's statement may mean no more than that Sulieman rebuilt the town, which had previously been in ruins, just as Rehoboam and others are said to have built towns which had existed long before their time; and that the Moslems seldom built towns except on old sites and with old materials, so there is not a town known in all Palestine to have been founded by them. In such cases they retained the old names, or others resembling them in sound if not in signification which may account for the difference between Ramah and Ramleh.

Interesting—isn't it?

Like Jaffa, we find it surrounded by olive groves, gardens of vegetables, and delicious fruits, with occasional palm trees and sycamores. A few mosques are scattered through the narrow, dirty streets. The hovels in which we see the inhabitants living are built of stone and mud, while many of them live by the manufacture of soap for exportation. They don't use the article themselves. The most conspicuous object is the Tower, to which we naturally wend our way, where, outside the town, in a stone quadrangle, we find it wholly isolated.

What its original destination was I don't know, in fact nobody gives a very well authenticated account of it. It is about one hundred and twenty feet in height, of Saracenic architecture, and built of well hewn stone. The windows have pointed arches which give it a Gothic appearance, and the corners of the tower are supported by tall slender buttresses, while the sides taper upwards by several stories to the top. An Arabian author (Mejr ed Jin) reports however the completion at Ramleh in A.D. 1310, of a minaret "unique for its loftiness and grandeur," by the Sultan of Egypt, which seems to allude to the one we now ascended by a stair through solid masonry, and having withstood all the earthquakes for centuries, it still looks strong enough for another little thousand years or so. Continuing our walk, passing through the plantations which surround the town, we come upon dry wells, cisterns fallen in, and vast reservoirs which show that the city must in former times have been, according to an old writer, upwards of a league and a half in extent.

While sketching the camp at Ramleh, I received a welcome bundle of letters sent by courier from Jaffa, which were the first I had received since leaving Florence, and the eagerness with which I tore them open to see whom they were from, may well be imagined. The letters having been directed afresh by the banker in England, were sent to Milan, where I had expected to be, then sent to the bankers at Venice, and by them addressed to Jaffa. Owing to the mails not effecting a landing they were carried on to Egypt, where they received the post-marks of Alexandria and Cairo, and had also gone through the Post-office at Beyrout, and finally, Jaffa : so that there was not a speck of the envelopes without a post-mark or direction, and I had to pay a nice little sum for their tour. That night I wrote in my tent till very late, bringing my letters up to date; the following remarks I quote from my letter. "I cannot describe the wonders and dirt of Ramleh and have but half an inch of candle to go to bed by. My back is nearly broken sitting so long on a camp stool, and everybody is in bed but the mules, which are tethered just **outside** my tent and let fly their hooves at it and have a general free fight among themselves every now and then, braying continually, which performances relieve **the** monotony of the occupation." In the morning I lay in **bed** after tintom had **sounded** so that on dressing I had **not** yet packed my clothes, and in a moment my beautiful abode floated away from over **me**; **my** bed collapsed, my **washstand** and table evaporated, **and** I locked my portmanteau in an open field. The Arabs understood the work so **well** that the village melted away while we breakfasted, **and** the mules **got off before us, so that** at the end of **the** day's journey everything **was the** same as we left in **the** morning. Seven o'clock saw us all **in** the saddle, **and** having crossed the valley of Adjalon we came to the mountainous country where **new** ideas of Palestine were created; the mountains were for the most part mere masses of bluish rock, with no trees **upon them,** our bridle pathway being very rough; after **some fifteen** miles we were glad to have a rest and luncheon under the olives. So tame and docile was Timoleon (my horse) that I could always cast him loose and let him graze about from place to place, the other horses having to be tied to keep them from fighting. They always rolled over on the ground when **we** alighted, **a** habit not improving to saddles. While **we** were lunching here, several of the horses broke away **and a** terrible fight ensued. They bit and kicked at **each** other, stood up and struck out like boxers, or charging, knocked each other over and over.

I climbed the mountain **to** bask in the delicious sunlight and read my letters over again, when I was struck by the formation of the hill side, which, terraced as if by human hands, was yet **so** utterly barren that it was difficult **to** believe that it had ever been cultivated. Many mountain sides had so attracted my attention before, and convinced me that these were the ancient terraces which had been unused for ages, and my conjecture was correct. The whole land must have had very much the appearance that Italy has now, when these terraces, which are fronted and supported by stone, like Italian ones, were covered by trailing vines; bearing fruits, sometimes for the Cæsars, sometimes for the Christian Knights, or for Saladin; which might have furnished at last, refreshment for Napoleon, and now lie bare and barren under the Turkish neglect and misrule. While on this summit, I had valleys on three sides of me; the rugged mountains opposite cut their outline gratefully into the whiteish blue sky, and over their picturesque sides, flocks of black long-haired goats nipped the scanty herbage between the rocks. Between two peaks, the Mediterranean, full thirty miles away, stretched blue and misty into western space; the Plain of Sharon lay before me, and the Valley of Adjalon, where Joshua commanded the sun and the moon to stand still till he defeated the Amorites, was spread at my feet; while the sound of neighing horses and the tinkling of mule-bells came dreamily up the mountain side. Had I seen the vision of Mirza at that moment of reverie, it would have been but fitting to the locality and in unison with my feelings.

The horn to mount calling us together we wound round the mountain, clambering over the stones, and riding down short cuts on the precipitous descents over rocks, which for roughness I can compare to nothing—scarcely fit for goats to climb. The village of Abu Gosh, the ancient Kirjath Jearim was passed through. Kirjath means town or city; and Kirjath Jearim signifies "City of forests," an appellation not very appropriate now, as there were no trees in sight except a few straggling olives. It was from this place that the Ark, having remained during twenty years, was carried by King David to Jerusalem (II. Chron. I. 4.) "A few years ago Abu Ghaush the Sheik of this town was the most powerful *baron-robber* in Palestine, and made this spot the scene of many robberies and murders: he was the terror of the neighbouring Pacha of Jerusalem and his submission was at length bought by the Turkish Government for a large sum of money."

Every step we take now is Holy ground and the great difficulty is in trying to realize the events which took place in the scenes around us. Here is Emmaus and the remains of a Gothic church said to be built on the site of Abinadab's house, where the Ark of the covenant was kept by Eleazar (I. Sam. VII. 1.); but the church, whose gloominess is oppressive, is now an enclosure for cattle and is unproductive of religious sensation. It is also considered to mark the spot where the Saviour appeared to the two disciples after his resurrection.

At this Emmaus we find the ruin of the Castellum Emmaus of the Crusaders, commanding the approach to the glen on the road to Jerusalem. Here the Maccabees lived and were buried. After a while we come to the valley of Elah, and Shocoh. Here now, we could picture the combat of the brave young Israelite and his huge antagonist from the neighbouring Gath. "Now the Philistines gathered together their armies at Shocoh, and Saul and the men of Israel were gathered together, and pitched by the valley of Elah, and set the battle in array against the Philistines. And the Philistines stood on a mountain on one side, and Israel stood on a mountain on the other side; and there was a valley between them."

The two armies seem to have stood a long time looking at each other, and though Saul and all Israel hearing the boasting taunts of their champion for forty days, "were dismayed and greatly afraid," yet the Philistines made no attempt either; they cautiously preferred to send their monster man to fight with a single Israelite, and thus decide who should be the servants of the other. This was their crafty proposal, for who in all the land could combat with the man of Gath who gloried in his size and rejoiced in his strength whose armour's weight was enormous, and who had been brought up to the use of arms from his childhood? In those days when length and strength of arm were not yet superseded by skill and precision, no man of Israel cared to gloriously deliver his brethren from the insults of the Philistines, at the imminent risk of his own life—save one. David was sprung from a warlike family, three of his brothers were in the ranks with Saul, while the

D

gallant boy who had killed the lion and the bear in defence of his flock was kept at that ignominious occupation, probably, because no person could defend the herds so well; and Jesse wished perhaps to keep his youngest son by him, as he "went among men for an old man in the days of Saul." David was fired with all the impulses of youth, moreover, past adventures had led him to firmly believe that he bore the armour of the Lord alway; hence his confidence, which was more than a boy's foolhardiness —as Saul evidently considered his proposal to be. There were brave men in Israel, yet they were discreet; not being imbued with the spirit of implicit faith, they had only man's natural courage, and that tempered by discretion—better to live under a cloud than be cut down like a dog, they reasoned.

David my son! take for thy brethren this parched corn, these loaves and cheeses; and look how they fare, lest they need aught in the camp, said Jesse one morning; and David brought them in the carriage to his brethren, but while conversing with them the champion came out to give vent to his daily invectives and taunts. The boy enquiring about the giant, was rudely questioned by his eldest brother as to the cause of his presence there, on the eve of battle; cruelly reminding him of his humble occupation before all the people. His significant reply was "Is there not a cause?" Saul heard of it and summoned David; who quietly, as his beating heart would let him, answered, "thy servant will go and fight the Philistine." Attempts at dissuasion were useless, and when Saul induced him to change his purpose, it was only with a father's interest, while his eye kindled with admiration for the boy. It was a proud moment for David when the warrior gave him the parting blessing of a *brother-at-arms*. Armour he scorned, for it only hampered him; and taking a few stones from a brook and his sling, he goes forth to meet Goliath. As we sit on the edge of the same brook does not a thrill of pleasure and admiration stir our hearts as we see David drawing near to the Philistine? he is only "a youth yet ruddy, and of a fair countenance;" but he has within him the true warrior blood, brave to the last, with the fear of God ever before his eyes.

Need I continue such a well known narrative? No! We must push on!—ere the night closes in we must see Jerusalem—Jerusalem the Golden, the Holy, the Sanctified, the Eternal. But what means this excitement—this evident enthusiasm? I had never longed to be at Jerusalem; it never has been the cherished desire of my life; I came here in search of warmth, for a ramble, and here I am spurring forward with all the earnestness of a Christian Knight. Azekah and Gath are close by, but fail to attract me; the caves into which Joshua chased the Amorites, interesting as they may be at any other time, are now lost in the one concentrated wish to view the spot, which once attained, brings us closer to heaven than if we scaled Pelion piled on Ossa.

An emotional spirit, however undemonstrative, who has passed the time and travel necessary to arrive at Jerusalem with some sober reflection, cannot fail to experience new thoughts, new hopes and aspirations which he never felt before. After his meditation in the lovely mountain defiles, so conducive to serious thought; after, perhaps for the first time in his life, he has read the Bible for knowledge at every opportunity; while Jerusalem, though near, is still in the imagination, and incidents, sermons, miracles and remembrances crowd upon the brain—like the rock on the tempest-torn shore, which, accustomed to the music that seemed monotony, ever resisted the blandishments of the waves, he may by a sudden succession of these floods of recollection find, all at once his hard barrier broken down, while the soothing, laving waters ebb and flow through the heart of stone. Press on brave little Arab! Choose your own path, for I am ignorant of it! This muleteer says there is but a mile more, and surely thirty miles of rock-climbing has not tired *you!* Even now the wilderness looks less wild! I see a high rampart, and a large tower surmounting! I hear a voice say, "*Ecco, Signore! La Gerusalemma!*" 'Tis the City, and the Tower of David!!

CHAPTER VI.

IT is always better to indulge in any romantic or religious fervour, concerning any oriental town, either in sight of it or while it is altogether unknown, certainly before entering its immediate precincts. One might, and indeed will, grow enthusiastic over reminiscences connected with the localities sometime after departure from them, and after one begins to view them more in the abstract, when revolting connections seem less real, while the interests, divine or otherwise, swell out again to their normal size : but while actually *in loco*, it requires the sight of the blind to enjoy the surroundings and the imagination of the enthusiast to sustain the ideas conjured up about their appearance. Jerusalem is no exception to this rule, in fact, it is the leading example ; better would it be for those not thus endowed to refrain from approaching nearer than the summit of the Mount of Olives, from there to see everything in the city with the naked eye. It would be a sanguine mind, a mind, too, brought up and fed exclusively on the æsthetical language of hymn books, that would picture and expect a more glorious view of Jerusalem than is seen from this point. It was not my lot to at first approach and view the city from this sacred eminence ; but not expecting such a sight, it was as great a surprise when I did enjoy it, as if it had come at first. I

FIRST ENTRANCE TO THE CITY. 53

entered Jerusalem on the evening of my arrival, but it was only to wander among the dark and dirty bazaars, to pick my way in the stony, crooked streets, over lean mangy dogs, and to cry "impshee" to the cringing, whining lepers who thronged the path, holding out for backsheesh hands worn to a stump by disease. Judging by other towns, I had made a very low estimate of the internal appearance of Jerusalem, but the first actual experience was a little worse even than I had anticipated. I retreated to the camp outside the Jaffa gate, there among the tents to read up something about the city from a book or two that we had with us on the subject. The gloss of the ideal created on my approach was somewhat washed off, but still the knowledge of the place to be seen awakened a new interest, which was, for a few days, the interest of the antiquary, rather than the theologian, of the sightseer, rather than the devotee. Arm-in-arm with half a dozen companions, one is not apt to warm to the scene of interest, with that zeal and fervour which a Christian is ordinarily supposed to be imbued with; and of which some of my friends had such an ample share. On our first invasions of the city we went with guides and ciceroni, who explained everything and gave us an idea of its ins and outs, so that in future we could ramble about, either alone or in meditative companionship, and then arrange impressions of the credibility of the different locations and the legends connected therewith. The number of places to be seen is so great, and the scenes are passed so rapidly, that it may be better to give part of my letter written in the tent, about the first of our guidance, and then speak of the impressions they created—not at the time, but afterwards —when I had ample time to revisit the spots and ruminate upon their authenticity. First, on entering the Jaffa gate, on the right is the foundation of the Tower of David, with a more modern superstructure, dating perhaps from the Romans.

Out in this ancient land we think of the ruins and monuments of the Romans as comparatively modern. At Rome the same date is deemed very ancient, and anything of the mediæval structure too modern to look at; in fact, the guides say, with a contemptuous shrug, " it is not for to see, *c'est le douzième siècle,*" whilst in England a *douzième siècle* wonder is looked upon with perfect awe, and in young Canada a block-house a century old is considered almost worth a visit. Josephus makes a tower the commencing point in demonstrating the track of the ancient walls of the city, and from the fact that the historian makes mention of a similar tower to this, under the name of the "Tower of Hippicus," many and long controversies have arisen as to its identification, which are still undecided. Near by are some pines, said to have been planted in Herod's time, and opposite is the Armenian convent containing the supposed head of St. James, and built on the site of his martyrdom. In this large edifice, which has been rebuilt under several religions, hundreds of ostrich eggs hang suspended from the roof supporting lamps. The theory of the ostrich eggs is unknown to me, and though I have seen them in a great number of mosques and different places of worship, no good explanation of their use has ever reached my ear. One of our party suggested that as the ostrich buries its head in the sand and trusts to be saved, so those worshipers rest their head in the faith and indulge in the same hope.

Then we are led through odoriferous alleys, around several stone flat-roofed dwellings, through a few backyards reeking with decayed vegetable outthrowings, and up a rough stone stair to where the Cœnaculum is shown. There is a look of age about the room, which is supported by two rows of chipped and mutilated pillars, conveying the idea that it might be the real upper chamber where the Last Supper was eaten; but there is also another tradition that this spot saw the miracle of the cloven tongues at the meeting of the Apostles on the day of Pentecost. Should this *be* the room, I have been where He "rose from the table and laid aside his garments, girded himself with a towel and washed his disciples' feet," and while exhorting them to humility and charity, performed this most excellent example of his practising what he preached. Beyond the chamber and

THE LEPERS.

in a higher room is the entrance to the traditional tomb of David which is far down in a cave, the descent guarded by a screen, which we look at through an iron grating. I would give some credit to the spot on account of the total exclusion of all people enforced by the Moslems, for they guard in the same way the cave of Machpelah at Hebron, which is admitted by the most learned travellers to be the veritable resting place of the patriarchs. So insurmountable is their fanatical zeal, that there are many things in the country that no man ever sees, not even a Moslem.

One feels a creeping sensation and a great desire to depart when he finds himself in the portion of the city allotted to the lepers; when one sees the wretched beings surrounding him and hears their inhuman cries, knowing that to enter the habitations he is passing would be madness doubly distilled; when he sees men, women and children hobbling towards him in all stages of the disease —their hands and feet eaten away, their noses gone, their voices going also with the back of the mouth, which is generally attacked first—he does'nt want to stay there long. Is there anything more awful than hereditary disease? And such an one too, as is witnessed among the lepers of Jerusalem. It is a frightful subject to dwell upon, that these beautiful babes and young children must ere long break out with the first symptoms of the scourge, and from that time forth spend a life of exile and pain, shunned by all their fellow creatures, and only allowed to marry some one perhaps more hideous than themselves. Man seems always to have been intended to be born into the world beautiful, and even these unfortunates have as fine children as any other people on earth. It must be the happiest moment of their joyless existence when the parents, who doubtless have loving hearts within what is left of their mutilated bodies, see their offspring beautifully modelled and, as we are told, in the likeness of their Creator. But it is a brief joy; they know what to expect. In a short time, like the inherent sin of human nature, the fatal eruption comes out on their darling's body, and all the horrors described so fully in the 13th chapter of Leviticus make their appearance. All the hair falls off; the nails drop also; hands, feet, and teeth become wanting, the facial organs and the palate share the same fate—till death relieves them from their agonies. There is no cure but the act of God; no amount of research or experiment has ever been able to check leprosy, and it constantly breaks out among the natives without any apparent cause. Damascus has still the descendants of Naaman "the captain of the host of the king of Syria, who was a great and mighty man of valour, but he was a leper." When this soldier came to Elisha and was told to wash in the Jordan, he "went away in a rage saying, 'are not Abana and Pharpar, rivers of Damascus, better than all the waters of Israel;'" but having tried the Jordan, "his flesh came again like unto the flesh of a little child, and he was clean." Well might he exclaim, "Behold now I know that there is no God in all the earth, but in Israel," and well might all other sufferers from the leprosy of sin become confirmed in their belief as to the Omnipotence of the Deity who with a word "couldst cleanse the leper."

Forget now these remarks about the lepers, as I try to deaden the hideous sound of their voices ever ringing in my ears, and ascend this eminence to the top of the wall to have your interest changed. Gaze for the first time on Olivet, as it rises on the other side of the Valley of Jehoshaphat, and let the eye rest on the refreshing foliage of the garden of Gethsemane nestling at its base, where the old Kidron in the rainy season is still wont to take its rambling course. To the south lies the Hill of Evil Counsel, crowned with the house of Caiaphas, where they communed together before putting Jesus to death; below us lies the Pool and Village of Siloam and the fountain of En Rogel, and far away towards the Dead Sea rise the blue mountains of Moab. Do not stay there too long, for this, as I said, is a working day, and the guide speaks of Robinson's Arch, which we find in a wilderness of rankly-growing cacti. A pile of immense stones which, measuring with my handkerchief, seemed more than 30 feet long and seven feet thick, lay bevelled as if the bridge led in the direction of Mount Zion. It is the spring of an arch whose foundations lie 60 feet below the surface of the earth, and which once spanned the now almost indiscernable Tyropœan Valley from Zion to Mount Moriah." "It leads nowhere now," says one writer, "but it *bridges over* a great deal that was once looked upon as a discrepancy in the writings of Josephus." How the bridge was destroyed is unknown, but the excavations disclose the bevelled stones lying where they fell, far down in the bowels of the earth, showing plainly enough how much below the present City lie the streets where the Saviour walked, and how much the height of Zion and Moriah has been diminished by the disintegration of ages. There was also an old disused cistern found, where running water was discovered, and Stoughton says, "There is a tradition among the Jews that when flowing water has been discovered three times under the Temple walls, the Messiah is at hand; now according to their accounts, it has been found twice before, so that this made the third time, and the Rabbis came down to look at the discovery with cries of joy and thanksgiving."

But the spot of greatest interest—the Holy Sepulchre—has not been mentioned yet, nor would it be at all if I firmly believed in its identity. Surrounded as it is with all the gimcrack sideshows, where the sites of nearly all the acts mentioned in the Bible, and several that never were mentioned at all, are crowded under one roof, my mind revolts from connecting His last resting place with such a panorama of buffooneries gotten up by the priests. Warburton, the poet traveller, and many others, have given us their belief that it is the real site of the Tomb, and it is not for me to pass an opinion on such a matter; but I may merely say that I was unable to join them in their happy belief. It would be a great pleasure—a lasting remembrance to me—if I could have indulged in the faith of the pilgrims who worshipped here, but as it is, let it suffice for all those that need stronger proof, to feel that they must be *near* the Sepulchre prepared by

Joseph; breathing the same balmy air that He breathed, standing in the City He loved so well, and foreseeing this present day, wept over, and for whose salvation, and that of all the world, died within its very walls. And yet, on approach, I would tread lightly, lest it might be the holy spot of earth—like the pious Moslem, who will not tread on a piece of waste paper, " lest forsooth the holy name of Allah might be inscribed thereon."

The church itself covers a large area of ground, and the vast pile was partly burnt down in the early part of this century, though no trace of the conflagration can now be seen. Every person may enter the church except a Jew, who is allowed as few privileges, and is persecuted more here than in other parts of the world, for the Mahommedans detest the Jew for being the murderer of their revered Prophet, and even the Christians shrink from him as being the destroyer of our Lord. As nearly as I can recollect, the church must be almost on the lowest ground in the City, which fact may be adduced in proving the identity of the Tomb. All the way from any of the gates we descend to it; from the Jaffa gate we go down the Street of David, which slopes considerably; then turning to the left, and again, further on, to the right, the stony path sinks rapidly, till we find ourselves in the quadrangle by the portals of the edifice. Thinking over this as a probability in favour of the long-disputed question, and trying to persuade ourselves that it is in truth the Tomb, let us enter and see as many of the sights as we can before becoming nauseated, and having to burst out into the air, that seems alone, of all Jerusalem, to be without falsehood or fabrication.

Near the entrance is the Stone of Unction, on which the body of Jesus was anointed after his descent from the Cross; the real stone is not seen, but the one that covers it has been worn quite hollow by the kisses of pilgrims. Another stone, from which inlaid pieces of marble radiate, marks the station of Mary at the time. Now we enter a large, circular dome, mosaiced and inlaid, where some paintings are hung about, and the eye is at once attracted by the numerous beautiful lamps of gold and silver suspended from the dome and faintly burning. In the centre of the floor rises the chapel, canopy, or house, containing the sepulchre, having the appearance of the *baldacchino* of the churches at Rome. The entrance is handsome, embellished with much marble carving, and, with the gorgeous lamps, would be beautiful, if it were not spoiled by a lot of tawdry **tinsel** trumpery displayed in the midst **of it.** The entrance is **built quite** low, to convey **the** idea of entering a tomb such as **is** described in Holy Writ; and now, having entered, analyse your feelings **as** you behold the interior, and stand **where** millions of devotees would **give the** remaining years **of** their life **to be** permitted **to worship,** from which thousands of **Jews are** yet excluded under **pain** of death, and about which rivers of blood have **been shed.** If you can now kneel by that marble sarcophagus, feeling that at last your hopes are truly realized, and say, "My Father, I thank thee for my presence here," do so by all means, and enjoy a happiness that the sceptic never can; but if on seeing a little chamber all built of marble, and illuminated by dimly lighted lamps of priceless treasure; **if that poor** painting of the Virgin and other miserable ornaments detract from the ideal you had created in your mind, driving back the prayer your lips would gladly utter, do not rail or scoff, for there *is* **a** sanctity about the spot whence ten million prayers have winged their way to Heaven. Even if your interest descends **to** that of the mere observer of the world, **you cannot but** say "it is well for us to be here."

Next to having **the** Tomb exposed to view, under the pure air of Palestine, which would be most in accordance with my ideal, they might at least have shown some of the rock naturally connected with the **old** description, which would go a long way **to** convince the incredulous; this, however, is against all the principles of the priests who have thus worked upon the imaginations of poor pilgrims for all ages, doubtless agreeing that a gorgeous abode is only fitting for what was mortal in the Son of God. What can the Saviour think! He who spent nights of prayer and anguish exposed to the elements on the bleak side of yonder Mount! Can he feel honoured by this, His reputed resting place! Or does he feel that it was better to have risen, body as well as soul, and to have left not even a garment among such a collection of impostures?

Taking lighted candles, we go through a passage to the Tomb of Joseph of Arimathea, where, crawling through an opening we descend into a hole hewn in the solid rock, which has every appearance of being a sepulchre, and makes us think that this might be the real Tomb of Jesus, but not the burial place of Joseph. In different recesses like chapels, in the rambling edifice, the following curiosities are shown; but with the vitiated air, and smell of greasy candles, incense, and pilgrims' boots piled in the corner, we long for some fresh air, so a short survey of this museum will suffice.

Behold the spot where Mary met Jesus in the garden, when she thought he was the gardener, and he said "touch me not, I have not yet ascended to my Father." The Pillar of Flagellation, built in a hole in the wall, which can be felt by the stick that Moses struck water out of the rock with—the stick is neatly turned and brass mounted En passant, let me remark that the late newspapers of this November, 1874, speak of the probable removal of this Pillar of scourging by the Latins to Rome. It seems that some alterations were found necessary, and the pillar which had to be displaced, was in the meantime, boxed up and sent to Rome. The trick was suspected, and another fracas similar to many witnessed before on the very spot ensued. The Latins have stoutly denied the accusation, and have since got another pillar in its place, which may be felt in the hole by future pilgrims with the same amount of satisfaction I experienced myself.

Godfrey de Bouillon's spurs, cross, chain, and immense sword, presented to the church by some prince from his collection, were really interesting; but Christ's stocks, which are shewn, have a different charm, as I never heard that he ever was in the stocks, but am open to any enlightenment on the subject; there is also a picture of His undergoing this punishment, taken "instantaneously" in oils upon the scene which it is said to faithfully portray. The tomb of the good centurion. The place where they drew lots for the clothes. In a cave under the church, the place where the Empress Helena, the mother of Constantine, found the *true* cross; odd too, that it should be called the Chapel of the *Invention* of the Cross. The column Jesus sat on when they crowned him with thorns. Another crown of thorns. (I wonder how many crowns I have seen.) Then up a stair-case, about 20 feet, the top of Calvary is reached, which is but a few yards from the tomb; here a silver plate shows where the cross rested, and two holes, one on either side, for the two criminals, disclose faintly some pieces of rocks in the darkness below. The fissure made when the veil of the Temple was rent at the Crucifixion. Adam's grave, and where, when the rent opened widely, our great progenitor's head leaped out. Godfrey de Bouillon's tomb. The Greek church richly gilded, actually containing in the middle of the floor "The Centre of the Earth," marked by a little marble pillar. They seem to have "mixed up" Adam a great deal about this church, and from here the dust was taken for his creation. The place of the Holy Fire in one of the walls of the Sepulchre, where, on Easter Eve, fire descends from heaven and lights all the candles. The priest hidden in the Sepulchre, produces fire through a hole in the wall, while the multitude light their flambeaux from holy fire. On these occasions the people often become so maddened with religious excitement, that they not only fight desperately to reach the holy fire, but trample upon and kill the weaker ones that have mingled in the performance. Such a great loss of life generally ensues, that the authorities always have armed troops on hand now to maintain some show **of decorum.** Such scenes occur almost annually, about the reputed tomb of our Saviour, and such are some of the impositions that surround the spot, which, if true, would be most hallowed of all others to us. But as it is—let us get out.

It will always be a subject of great regret to me, that the unusual severity of the weather so impeded our progress while at Jerusalem, that the intended journey to the Pools of Solomon, and to the tombs of the Patriarchs at Hebron had to be abandoned. After viewing all the doubtful sights in and about the Holy City, the mind turned with an intense longing to something about which no imposition seemed possible—and writers in all ages point to Hebron as the one place quite beyond the reach of doubt or scepticism. Josephus states that the sepulchres of the patriarchs were still in Hebron, built in marble and of elegant workmanship. Jerome and Eusebius speak of the monument of Abraham, and in the twelfth century, Benjamin of Tudela, a Spanish Jew, gives the following description: "There is a huge temple called Saint Abraham, and that place was the synagogue of the Jews at what time the country was possessed by the Ishmaelites. But the Gentiles, who afterwards obtayned and held the same, built six sepulchres in the Temple, by the names of Abraham, Sarah, Isaac, Rebecca, Jacob and Leah, and the inhabitants now tell the pilgrims that they are the monuments of the patriarchs, and great sums of money are offered there. But surely to any Jew coming thither and offering the porter a reward, the cave is showed with the iron gate opened which from all antiquity remayneth yet there, and a man goeth down with lamplight into the first cave, where nothing is found, nor also in the second, until he enter the third, in which there are six monuments, the one right over against the other; and each of them are engraven with characters and distinguished by the name of every one of them after this manner: *Sepulchrum Abraham patris nostri super quem pax sit;* and to the rest after the same example."

In 1601 Sanderson visited Hebron, and although he was not allowed to enter, he agrees with the Jew in describing the tombs as in a *cave* under the church. The fanatical prejudices of the Moslems have for several centuries excluded both Christians and Jews from this most interesting place. On referring to the twenty-third and following chapters of Genesis, how touching is the account of Abraham's sorrow on the death of his beloved Sarah—that Sarai for love of whom even the "Father of the Faithful" descended to prevarication and deceit (Gen.12.13.)

How perfect a picture of the manners and customs of the East does the Biblical account furnish us with: as true are they, in the present, as when 4,000 years ago, the Ishmaelites fed their flocks and herds, and sat in the doors of their tents before Mamre. What a perfect pastoral do the lives of the patriarchs compose. On reading it, we cease to wonder that the early masters so often portrayed the vivid scenes by which they immortalized their names. For manly and dignified sorrow what could surpass the venerable figure of Abraham bowing before the children of Heth, and exclaiming, "I am a stranger and a sojourner with you: Give me possession of a burying place, that I may bury my dead out of my sight." Witness also his anxiety to procure a wife of his own race and not of the daughters of Heth for his son Isaac, which resulted in the finding of Rebekah, so that "Isaac was comforted after the death of his mother." Reading on, we come to the deception practised by Rebekah to obtain the father's blessing for the second son. Confessing that this had often been read as an almost incredible story, after seeing some of the hairy, rugged sons of the desert, the perfect feasibility of such a subterfuge dispelled all previous doubts. Then we come to that most perfect idyl—Jacob's love for Rachel, her sad death and burial on the way to Ephrath: then Joseph's departure into Egypt and extraordinary success there, his magnanimous forgiveness of his brethren, and the touching scene where his father Jacob blessed his two sons, Ephraim and Manasseh, again preferring the younger in a marked manner; and finally his pathetic appeal to be buried with his fathers "In the cave that is in the field of Machpelah which is before Mamre in the land of Canaan. There they buried Abraham and Sarah his wife, and there they buried Isaac and Rebekah his wife, and there I buried Leah."

How often in the present day have we read of the

wonderful success of young men in the gold fields of California or Australia, or the diamond fields of Africa. But do any of the narratives compare with the life of Joseph? Carried as a slave into Egypt, he was advanced to the highest post of honour, till at the death of his father, we find his position so exalted that "all the servants of Pharaoh, the elders of his house and all the elders of the land of Egypt, and all the house of Joseph, and his brethren, and his father's house went up with him, both chariots and horsemen; and it was a very great company. And they buried Jacob in the cave of Machpelah, and Joseph returned into Egypt." Assuredly, "The Lord was with him, and that which he did the Lord made it to prosper."

Like Damascus, Hebron seems to have been a city of note from the earliest ages. We read that it was built "seven years before Zoan in Egypt," and it was in the field of Zoan that those mighty acts were performed of God before Pharaoh would permit the children of Israel to depart. After this we find that "Kirjath-Arba, the same as Hebron," became one of the six cities of refuge, to which the manslayer might flee for safety. Many generations afterwards, all the elders of Israel came to the king at Hebron, which was the accustomed place of anointing the kings of Israel, and David made a covenant with them and was anointed king over Israel. It is very evident that it was a place of greater antiquity than Jerusalem, because David, after reigning 14 years in Hebron, took the castle of Zion, and *built the city round about.* It was the Winchester, more ancient than London, or the Scone, far older than Edinburgh, whither Saxon and Scottish kings resorted to be crowned. As recounted in II Samuel, David made Absalom judge in the gate of the city, and for forty years he "stole the hearts of the men of Israel" by his kindly plausible manner, till the time was ripe for his rebellion against his father; when he obtained David's permission to go and perform his vow in Hebron, being told to "Go in peace." Peace not being in his heart, he immediately "sent spies throughout the tribes of Israel, saying, as soon as ye hear the sound of the trumpet, then shall ye say Absalom reigneth in Hebron;" evidently hoping that being proclaimed king, where the kings were customarily anointed, he would be more likely to succeed in his rebellion. And looking at Absalom's career for a moment, we all know that although at first "the hearts of the men of Israel were with him," he was not allowed to prosper in his rebellion, but came to an untimely death while fleeing from the battle; and we feel how great was the love of the father he had outraged, whose first cry, on hearing the tidings was, "Is the young man Absalom safe?" and whose pitiful tears and heart-broken ejaculations when the worst was told him, have been sympathetic words for many a disappointed parent since. From that day to this, Hebron has been built and rebuilt; it is now a town of about 9,000 who are notorious for their fanaticisim.

The Pools of Solomon lie a few miles to the south of Jerusalem, on the way to Hebron, and quite within the range of a pleasant afternoon's ride, constructed partly of large hewn stones, and partly by excavations in the solid rock. They are three in number; the one leading into the other, and all fed by the same fountain, three hundred feet further up the hill. Many writers have striven to throw doubt upon their being really the work of Solomon, but why they should thus try to stifle the voice of tradition, I am at a loss to conjecture; unless it be that there are so many things to call into question, that the mind, which begins with a certain amount of discrimination, merges at last into a chronic state of doubt. The very fact that the water from these pools was carried by aqueducts along the hill-sides, and over the valleys, till it reached the site of the Temple of Solomon, ought to be ample proof, because a king of such wisdom would never leave so magnificent a structure without a supply of water adequate for the sacrificial rites. Even now, it is said that a moderate expenditure would enable the pure stream to again find its way into the city.

For several years the rain-fall in Syria has been much greater than formerly, causing these reservoirs to constantly overflow; and the hill-sides thus watered in the

E

spring, exhibit great verdure and beauty; so that it is no difficult matter to imagine them the site of the gardens spoken of by the preacher. "I made me great works; I builded me houses; I planted me vineyards; I made me gardens and orchards, and I planted trees in them of all kinds of fruit; I made me *pools of water* to water therewith the wood that bringeth forth trees."

CHAPTER VII.

JERUSALEM has from **the** time of the Crusaders, been called **in Arabic** El Khuds, the holy, and for a long **time** before went under the appellation of Elia, **so named in** the hope of perpetuating the name of the Roman general Elius.

Its history is a succession of stories of its captures, stormings and massacres **by different nations**; but it would now in spite of the frowning battlements fall an easy prey to a modern army; a few cannon placed on the Mount of Olives would lay in ruins the stone-built city in a very short time. Yet, although **it** has been so repeatedly destroyed, it does seem strange that the prophecy should be so literally fulfilled, and that of the old city not one stone seems to lay upon **another**. The fields of grain on Mount Zion wave in **the** breeze and the plough furrows the ground as the prophecy foretold, and outside the wall foxes may roam unharmed. Of all the books within my reach written on Jerusalem, the fruits of many learned travellers' researches, I can find no mention of a single foundation (much less an edifice) nor even a stone lying above ground, except perhaps Robinson's arch, and at the Jews wailing place, that is certain to have existed at even so late a date as the time of Christ. Nearly all the old nations have had a hand in the taking and government of the City, and as far back as A.D. 614, the Church of the Holy Sepulchre is mentioned as suffering partial destruction from the invading Persians, who then overcame the emperor Heraclius, whilst the streets ran with the blood of thousands. The reign of Constantine saw the first pilgrimages to the Holy City, the sainted Helena, the mother of the Emperor, making a remarkable journey hither at the advanced age of eighty years, when she spent enormous sums of money in building the Church of the Holy Sepulchre, the Church of the Nativity at Bethlehem, and many others, besides making valuable discoveries, in finding the place where the cock crowed to Peter, &c. &c. About this period it became the heartfelt desire of the early Christians to visit these holy places, and for many centuries they did so in great numbers. The Moslems, with their innate thirst for money, exacted a tribute from all the worshippers who yearly visited the city, and about A.D. 1090, the insults to which the pilgrims were subjected—who were generally well to do, and frequently of the highest rank created a great ferment among the nations of western Europe ; and, excited by the preaching of Peter the Hermit, and encouraged by Pope Urban II, they determined to wrest the Holy Sepulchre from the hands of the Infidel. Before long, an army headed by Godfrey de Bouillon, was drawn up in battle array before the walls, when after a seige of forty days, Godfrey was made King of Jerusalem, and soon became master of the greater part of Palestine. But this success was not of long duration ; in all its endless history, Jerusalem saw but eighty-eight years of Christian government, which ensued after Godfrey's coronation. Then in 1187, Saladin was ensconced within the battlements as victor, and the crescent floated where the cross had adorned the sacred dome, the holy places were purified with rose-water brought from Damascus, and the muezzin's call to prayer from the minarets again sounded over the sacred hill of Zion.

The houses of the present city are built of rough hewn limestone, in which material the country abounds. They are neither large nor commodious in any way, and no sign of comfort is seen on looking into the interior, the inhabitants having no beds; and feather or hair mattrasses among the poor, being quite unknown, they are supposed to sleep on a mat or some clothes, but the generality find a great deal of refreshment in sleeping on the soft part of a stone floor. They never renovate their houses; ricketty staircases may be propped but never repaired, and they will live in a house as long as it affords shelter, or till the vermin drive them out of it. Wood is too scarce to waste for any domestic purpose, and is only used for doors and window sashes, for it is brought as in the days of Solomon from Lebanon. As a rule there are no windows facing the streets, and the few that may be seen have no glass in them, but are merely made of a close lattice-work admitting a few rays of light into the apartment, and being closed at night, leave the streets in total darkness. Nobody is allowed to move about the town at night without a lantern and a good account of his object and destination, and after eight o'clock, the gates are all shut, except the Jaffa one, which is left open for pilgrims arriving late from the sea-coast.

One pitch dark night I left the camp to visit some friends quartered in the city, taking with me a lantern, without which it would be impossible and illegal to enter the walls. It was raining, and the holes in the road were filled with water which thoroughly wet my feet over the rubbers; the large native dogs, very wild and even dangerous at night, suffered me to pass unmolested through their groups, only about a dozen snarling unpleasantly behind my heels till I reached the gate of the city. Here it was more gloomy than outside the walls, and a tall figure of a man following a short distance behind me all the way did not render the solitude more desirable. The streets were deserted, no light of any kind pierced the opaque blackness of the night, and through the long vaulted arcades, so busy in the day, there was no sign of life, save when a dog or a vagrant Arab rose startingly under the light of the lantern and fled into the darkness. Still the mysterious figure dogged my footsteps round each turning and through each alley, and I must confess to a feeling of satisfaction in having brought out my pocket revolver; for what would have been easier than to strike me down in the dark, and in a moment take my money and clothes! However I reached my destination, and returned home much later the same night, without having a hair-breadth 'scape to record here, but enabled to speak feelingly of the delights of Jerusalem's streets at night.

Surrounded by all this poverty and degradation, and in the midst of houses so devoid of all ornaments. nay, destitute of all the common conveniences of life, it is difficult to realize that these thoroughfares have been lined with the summer houses and ivory palaces we read of in the Prophets. "I will smite the winter house with the summer house, and the houses of ivory shall perish." (Amos iii. 15.) Yet thrones, beds, benches, vessels, and horns of ivory are mentioned in the Bible, so there is no occasion to doubt that their houses were so adorned with the same material as to warrant the expression of "houses of ivory." And although the great Mosque of Omar is one of the most majestic of Allah's shrines, how far it must fall short of that temple upon whose site it stands. "That most wonderful of buildings, whose cost who can compute? whose glory who can picture? whose carvings and sculptures of infinite variety, in precious woods, costly stones, and solid gold, who can number?" and around whose old foundations we now see a crowd of wailing Jews. By Constantine, the edict excluding the Jews from their father's temple, was so far repealed that they were allowed to enter once a year to wail over the desolation of their holy and beautiful house; and ever since then it has been the custom and forms part of their education to mourn and weep in the small quadrangular area beside the immense old stones which are believed to be part of the foundation walls of the Temple of Solomon. It was on a Saturday I first visited this spot, so the place was well filled by many Jews, both male and female.

Having a spot fraught with such interest as this within its walls, Jerusalem cannot be regarded with the same feelings as Athens, Ephesus or Rome. About the Jews there hangs an indefinable mystery which proceeds from the isolation in which, as a people, they have always existed ; and apart from their being the most interesting race on the face of the earth, which they undoubtedly are, in their virtues and vices, wisdom and folly, customs and prejudices, **is** seen a height and depth which man cannot fathom. Here they face the wall which is worn **by their** kisses, and while reading their Book of Lamentations they cry and wail lowly as the tears roll down their faces copiously. Jews from **every** quarter of the globe, **rich** and poor, cripple **or** whole, assemble at this their **centre of** the world, than which, **to** them, **there** is no more **holy** spot this side Heaven.

It is worth while to come and consider where these mourning mortals all come from, and what hardships, privations and trials they have endured ; **to** come and meditate upon the thousands of this blighted race, who, before travelling was simplified and rendered more secure, have toiled over the trackless snows of Siberian steppes and burning sands of African deserts to reach **this** hallowed spot.

It is a touching sight to see the old men tottering to the wall of the dishonoured and desolated sanctuary, realizing for the first time the dream of their lives ; burying their faces in the niches and uttering their lamentations, while their tears drop **on** the oft-moistened stones. In the words of the Psalmist, they may well exclaim, " Oh **God the** heathen are come into thine inheritance ; Thy temple **have** they defiled : **they** have laid Jerusalem on heaps. **We** have become a scorn and derision to them that are round **about** us. How long Lord ? wilt Thou be angry forever ? " Among the congregation assembled may be witnessed the rich Polish and Russian Jews in their long coats reaching nearly to the ground, and wearing the costly fur hats of the Northern climate, mingling with the poor sallow-faced Pharisees **from** Tiberias with their light, floating curls hanging to **their** shoulders from under square-topped felt hats. How **little** we think while gazing on the Coliseum and its neighbouring Arch of Titus, that the massive stones, piled and shaped to withstand an eternity, were the handiwork of thousands of these outcasts taken by Titus to Rome. It is the handful of Jews still remaining in the modern city that makes it interesting as regards the population, and not the turbaned devotees of Allah and the harem who have command over it.

One of the oddest excursions I ever undertook, was with a few of the young fellows who procured with me an Arab guide, and started off on a wild night to explore the tombs of the kings and the quarries of Solomon under the city. It was a strange adventure, and the novelty of it attracted several others who joined our party. Following the guide, who by his single lantern lighted us along the break-neck paths, we left the camp, making the old battlements ring with unaccustomed mirth, and reverberate with the heart stirring strains of "John Brown's Body;" and after stumbling about a mile, we descended to a low doorway, seven feet thick, leading into a court about 90 feet square, and very deep. To the left of the court was a spacious vestibule, the entrance to the tombs being by a low hole through which we crawled. Now at this entrance was a curious piece of ponderous mechanism, devised to prevent the tombs from being rifled; an occurrence very common in all ages, and which the utmost precautions were taken by the ancients to guard against. Originally the door could only be approached by a subterranean corridor, ten feet long, the descent to which at one end was guarded by a trap-door, closely covered by a flag stone. The landing place in the corridor beneath the trap-door, was on the brink of a deep well, but which the robber might avoid if careful. The circular stone door, not hanging on hinges, but resting in a socket, might be rolled up a groove with the aid of levers:—even supposing the marauder escaped falling down the well, and pryed up this door, he was sure to be caught by a hidden slab hung on pivots behind him in the corridor, that turned, fell down and shut him in for ever when the pressure of prying up the circular door was brought to bear on it. The first chamber we entered was higher and better hewn and smoothed than those at Thebes, several persons who had just come from there declaring, that if not so extensive, these tombs were as fine as any thing up the Nile. We passed through several chambers, dripping with the damp of ages, with tombs cut in on every side as in the Roman catacombs. Down some stairs we crawled through mud and slime to where sarcophagi of white marble have been found, one of which, said to be that of David, is now in the Louvre. Unlike other important discoveries, there are no hieroglyphics or marks about the locality, to aid in its identification or to determine for whom the operations were executed, and the name can only be said to be as good as any other. We emerged hot and begrimed, and extinguished our candles, till we reached the entrance of Solomon's quarries outside the Damascus Gate, where they were again lighted.

We descended a steeply inclined cave, till we came to a dome-like vaulted cavern, which loomed up whitely on all sides from the light of our many tapers, the stalactites glistening and dripping with the damp hanging down from the roof, and the stalagmites tripping us under foot. On we went, descending from one cavern to another, and on all sides were seen the marks of the chisel, and the places where huge stones that the world has ever wondered at, were hewn out. In the sixth chapter of I King's, where it gives a profuse description of the architecture of the Temple of Solomon and all its beauties, the seventh verse says, "And the house when it was in building, was built of stone, *made ready before it was brought hither;* so that there was neither hammer, nor axe, nor any tool of iron heard in the house, whilst it was in building." Undoubtedly then, this was the spot where some of the stone was prepared by measurement, before being fitted to its place in the Temple; but we are not to suppose that all the masonry was prepared here, for Solomon had four score thousand stone-hewers in Lebanon. The vast caverns may not have been altogether the work of human hands, though this is open to doubt, owing to the damp eradicating in the progress of ages, the chisel marks on the ceilings.

And now the guide placed lighted candles in the inches,

for fear of losing the way back, for even he would not trust himself in the labyrinth which has never in modern times been followed to the end; we left our coats, fezes and staffs beside one of the candles, as it was intensely hot. How far we went under the city and into the bowels of the earth, I know not, but far down here were immense square stones and unfinished pillars, just wanting a few strokes of the chisel to set them free from the bed they nearly left 3,000 years ago. What appliances the workmen used to get them to the surface, and how they placed these stones hundreds of feet up on walls, laying them to a hair's-breadth, is a pleasant subject for speculation, and likely to be a lasting one. We rested far away down and gazed into the bottomless pits, yawning on every side, which reminded the Americans of the Mammoth Cave of Kentucky, and several broke off bits of rocks for mementoes. The white walls seemed almost translucent as we ascended, and a wholly unnatural picture was formed by my friends trooping up from the gloom, with fire in their hands, bare headed, and looking more like the inhabitants of a worse region than adventurers from the beautiful world above. All the romantic, wondrous stories in the Arabian nights of Genii and endless caves, seem to have been concocted after wandering through the ramifications of this world of eternal darkness, and after the narrator had had an experience of the weird scene in which we were now actors. Fresh and sweet the night breeze seemed to us as we emerged into the air, and cramming on our fezes and buttoning up our overcoats for fear of chill, we stumbled home, well satisfied with our night's experience, and quite ready to sleep for at least two days.

Sunday in Jerusalem and Service on Mount Zion! How gratefully my mind will always revert to that memorable day. We all repaired, in the morning to the English Church, a neat little building, near which is Bishop Gobat's School, and the boys were all coming out of the Sunday School, looking very neat and clean, and as glad to get out as any other Sunday-school children.

On the quiet, beautiful Sabbath mornings, how prone

we are to indulge in those delightful meditations and recollections that are always nearest to our hearts, and which await but the relaxation of a moment to present themselves afresh! And here on Mount Zion, with the old Prayer Book open to remind me of home, and the scene outside the window to remind me of where I was—could there be any association of incidents moreproductive of reverie than this? Though we had the regular service of the day, it seemed as if it were arranged by design to impress upon us the complete appreciation of our position; in all the lessons and psalms were allusions to Mount Zion and its many connections; the sermon was eminently calculated to, and did fully convince us of, our situation on that day. There are certain times in every man's life, no matter how far he has fallen away from good, when the religious spirit, by force of circumstances, or without apparent cause, breaks out, or struggles hard to do so, and if the spirit be not resisted a multitude of sins may then find forgiveness. They are rare illuminations of our lives, and if quickly forgotten, resemble flashes of lightning whose momentary effulgence serves but to redouble the succeeding gloom. And even if forgotten there is still the recollection of how bright the landscape appeared for those brief periods; how white a light it cast upon all earthly objects, and how clearly the narrow way could then be discerned which afterwards became obscure and hard to follow out.

That afternoon was passed the most pleasantly of any spent at Jerusalem; mounting our horses, with our Bibles in our pockets, Ernest and I quietly set off on a ramble. My friend possessed one of the most admirable characters I ever knew, and was, I think, a sample of many of England's young men—thoroughly good, without being sanctimonious, he could ride a horse with any one, which, in my opinion, much enhances the perfections of any Christian. Making a detour of Jerusalem, we crossed the Valley of the Kidron, and encircling the Mount of Olives, we came near to Bethany: and there, where "they found a colt tied," we rested and read aloud. The fragrance of the blossoms filled the air, and the beauty of the wild flowers which damasked our resting place, gathered new enchantment from the bright sun and gentle breeze. After the Book was closed we lingered long on the slope of Olivet; there was a sweet tranquillity pervading both earth and heaven; Bethany lay in sight, the Dead Sea glistened in the distance, while the Mountains of Moab, rising in many shades of blue and purple, limited the view, which in the peculiar transparency of the air might have continued on to Mecca. Separated from all the mummeries exhibited in the city; wandering on the paths where He had often wandered, enjoying the same view He knew so well, we instinctively felt a closer communion with Him than ever before, and silently, as the shades of night grew long and dark, we were yet tarrying and waiting as if for a Friend.

CHAPTER VIII.

OUR camp was pitched outside the walls of Zion, on the edge of the Valley of Hinnom or Tophet, where in ancient days the hideous sacrifices to Moloch were enacted. In the nineteenth chapter of Jeremiah he speaks of these heathen rites, and accordingly utters the denunciations on the Jews which were fulfilled to the very letter when Titus besieged Jerusalem. "And they built the high places of Baal which are in the Valley of the son of Hinnom to cause their sons and daughters to pass through fire unto Moloch." (Jer. xxxii. 35.) Therefore "I will cause them to fall on the sword before their enemies, and by the hands of the men that seek their lives. I will cause them to eat the flesh of their sons and the flesh of their daughters, and they shall eat everyone the flesh of his friend in the siege and straitness wherewith their enemies and they that seek their lives shall straiten them." Anybody who has read any detailed account of the sacking of the City by Nebuchadnezzar or Titus, must see how this frightful doom came to pass. The children of the fanatics used to be set on the red-hot hands of a huge idol, their agonizing shrieks being drowned by cymbals and the shouts of the frenzied worshippers.

On winding down the stony path below the Zion walls we enter the valley which now is called Gehenna, a word synonymous with "Hell," on each side seeing ancient tombs in the rocks which now show no signs of the awful slaughters the place has witnessed. Passing eastward to the junction of this valley with that of Jehoshaphat or Kidron and the old Tyropean valley, we come upon the well of En Rogel. This was the scene of Adonijah's attempt on the kingdom at the close of his father David's life, in opposition to Solomon who was proclaimed King in Gihon. (I. Kings. I.) It is now called *Bir Ayoob*, Well of Joab, by the Arabs, probably from Joab who was Adonijah's chief partisan. The well is 125 feet deep and overflows in the rainy season, forming a brook which after traversing the valley of the Kidron empties into the Dead Sea. It is also called the Well of Nehemiah, as it was from this well that Nehemiah recovered the sacred fire there concealed by the priests before the captivity of Babylon. The water is said to be good, but as several Arabs were swimming about in it we did not feel thirsty just then; the ladies that accompanied us could not look into the well for these fellows being there, and when the dragoman told them they must go away, instead of dressing on the platform inside the well,—Lo, and behold! they came outside and dressed in the sun.

The Potter's Field is passed and we reach the Pool of Siloam, where Christ healed the blind man on the Sabbath day (John ix. 7.) There is little doubt as to this being indeed the Pool, and late discoveries show that the same spring from which the Pool derives its existence, supplies also the Fountain of the Virgin further on. Josephus describes the waters as sweet, and Jerome describes it more precisely, mentioning the irregular flow, which confirms its identification, so I need not give the numerous texts relating to it in the Bible. Further up the valley of Jehoshaphat are the three tombs of Absalom, Zachariah, and St. James, cut out of the solid rock at the base of the Mount of Olives. They are of very peculiar construction, that of St. James having four short columns in front of it, and an entrance leading around through the rock from near the Tomb of

Zachariah; but the great interest which they created in my mind was that they are the only objects that we are certain Jesus must have known, **and that** he must have passed many times just as we **were** then doing. Absalom's is **a** huge monolith about **forty** feet high, and in shape is a square surmounted by a pointed dome supported by Ionic **pillars**; it is a good deal battered, for Moslems throw **stones at it as** they pass, **and** spit at it, to show their disapproval **of** the conduct of Absalom. Although it has **become** customary with most writers **to** throw doubt on **these tombs,** imagining that chance alone has assigned **to them the** names they bear, there seems to be good reason **to** believe in them, for we are distinctly told (II. **Sam.** xviii. 18.) that "Absalom **in** his lifetime **had** taken **and** reared up for himself a *pillar*, which is in the king's dale, for he said, I have no son to keep my name in remembrance. And he called the pillar after his own name: and it is called unto this day **Absalom's** Place." And if Time has dealt so gently, and **Tradition so** faithfully, with Absalom's pillar, we might **also** believe that the others are correctly named.

Then the horses clamber up the Mount, and among the myriad graves of Jews we find the Tombs of the Prophets, where we dismount and enter by a very low and muddy hole. It doesn't amount to much. It is only one of those large hewn excavations traversing a considerable distance into the earth, and lined along the sides with receptacles for the dead, to which no name can be given or satisfactory explanation made.

I hurried out of the hole before **the** rest, and selecting a nice looking stick **among** the branches of one of the olive trees, I got up **and cut it** in as short a time as possible, not wishing to be seen cutting a memento from the sacred **Mount** of Olives. It still forms one of my relics which were too often acquired by vandalism. On the top of the Mount is the small Church of Ascension with a minaret rising from it, which **can be** seen from a great distance. The Church itself **is** uninteresting, but supposed to be built on the spot whence Jesus ascended to heaven, which is possible, though much doubted. The attraction however, lies in the view which is commanded from the top of the minaret.

It may be safely said that there is no natural picture in the world so eminently interesting to all mankind as this; as a landscape it may with difficulty be excelled in beauty, so that it has almost as many attractions for the artist as the Christian. It embodies, in its vastness, all that is delightful to the historian, to the antiquarian, to the theologian, to the general or engineer. Philosophers, moralists also have ample scope to let their imaginations run riot over the scene. Self alone is forgotten in the remembrances it calls forth, and whatever point of the compass is faced the perspective opens up a field of thought that is boundless in extent.

Below us, to the west, lies the precipitous valley of Jehoshaphat, and crowning its rocky heights on the opposite side rise the walls of Jerusalem, while within, the city that never could be entirely crushed out of existence, still rears its head majestically among the cities of the world. There is a want of colour in the appearance of most Eastern cities, arising from the fact that the houses are built of dull coloured limestone and clay, and, to an English eye, this forms at first a great drawback; but in Jerusalem there are certain bright spots which relieve this monotony, and while the campanilé of the Holy Sepulchre Church and the minarets of other edifices brighten up the general appearance, the huge dome of the Mosque of Omar, standing well in the foreground, looms up like a huge balloon, as if only waiting until fully inflated to float up and off with the whole city.

Hundreds of small domes form the roofs of the ordinary dwelling places, this style of architecture seeming to be peculiar to Judea and the country to the East, as I don't remember ever seeing it north of Nablous. Owing to the scarcity of all wood, these dome-roofs of mud and twigs, which, on account of their convex shape, support themselves, have to take the place of rafters necessary for flat roofs; so that as we approach the more wooded country in the north they disappear. Turning to the south we look down upon all the villages, pools, tombs, fountains, some of which I have mentioned, and over all the country in the direction of Bethlehem and Hebron; while, on directing our sight more to the east, we overlook Bethany, and far in the distance, and 4,000 feet below us, the Dead Sea sparkling in the bosom of the barren hills. Though about seventeen miles away, that azure sheet of water only seems to lie behind one of the neighbouring hills, while the course of the Jordan, still further off, may be distinctly traced twining towards the mysterious and poetic sea that covers Sodom and Gomorrah. When from the dizzy height of St. Peter's dome we gaze over Rome, marking its old ruins and churches, its hills and yellow Tiber, the boundless Campagna, divided by lines of aqueducts and roads leading to Tivoli, Albano, or enchanting Frascati, we are apt to think it is *the view* of the world. Not so! Come to the East, and stand on this minaret, and gaze upon the pages of the Bible, rather than Gibbon's Rome, upon Zion rather than the Palatine, upon Jordan than Tiber.

Again mounting our horses, a winding path leading down the eastern slope soon brings Bethany into notice. It is merely a collection of poorly-built stone houses, and probably, since its first mention to the present day, no great change has ever taken place in its dimensions. The tomb of Lazarus is shown. Why it is selected from all the other tombs abounding in the neighbourhood, I really don't know, as any of them might be that of Lazarus. The house of Mary and Martha is exhibited by the priests, but what is the use of going into another of these show-places? Let us encircle the Mount till we reach the *present* Garden of Gethsemane. A few very old and gnarled olives have been lately walled in and turned into a neat garden full of flower-beds by the priests, who distribute flowers among the visitors to be pressed as mementoes; and at stations about the paths are pictures representing the Bearing of the Cross. For those who think it is better to believe too much than too little, this spot forms one of the

F

pleasantest retreats for meditation in the locality, and under the shade of the ancient olives, "that wreath their old fantastic roots on high," the heat of the day may be passed agreeably even by the incredulous. Now we have encompassed and scaled Olivet ; touched at Bethany on the east of it, and Gethsemane on the west, which Mount, says Dr. Thomson, " has witnessed the most affecting and stupendous scenes in the history of our blessed Redeemer. It was in connection with this spot that the God-man—the Divine Logos—chose to reveal more of his *human* nature than anywhere else on this earth. How often after the fatigues and temptations of the day in this wicked and captious city, did he retire in the evening to Bethany to enjoy the hospitality and affectionate sympathy of Lazarus and his pious family ! There He laid aside the awful character of Prophet and Teacher divine, to rest his hard-tried energies in the gentle amenities of social life ; and such was the freedom of intercourse between these social friends, that Martha could even come to him with little domestic troubles. Alas ! how many Marthas there are, careful and troubled about many things ; and how few Marys, anxious to sit at Jesus' feet and hear his word."

After enjoying, for some time, beautiful weather, which was unusual for Jerusalem at that time of the year, the westerly storms came upon us at last with all the condensed fury of the elements generally vented on old Palestine. One evening the premonitory signs showed themselves in a way that unmistakably boded the approach of some great tumult in the atmosphere. Many of us were gazing at the dark, waving bank of gloom stretching up into the sky, appearing like a tremendous sandstorm driving towards us, but as it held off during the evening, we forgot, in the merry tents, the sword of Damocles hanging over our heads ; and it was not until after I had slept for some time that I became conscious of the raging of the storm. The shouting of the camp servants and muleteers, assembled to keep the tents over our heads, sounded at intervals above the howling of the wind as they dashed about from one tent to another, driving down the pegs and placing large stones upon them to prevent their coming out of the ground. Luckily for me, my tent was to leeward of all the others, so was somewhat protected, yet from the way it swung about and tore at its ropes we thought every instant would see us unhoused. Two ropes had yielded on my side of the tent, which the storm beat upon, the tent had sagged in far enough to touch the bed, thus wetting everything; so the first thing done was to move the bed, strike a light, and collect and pack up all clothing and writing materials, to spread a mackintosh over the bed, and put the portmanteaus under cover. This was the work of a few seconds, and we retired shivering to bed again, to wait for our canopy **to** float away, while we listened to the shouts of the unfortunates whose tents **had been** blown down. Female cries and even laughs were heard too, but our gallantry was at a low ebb, and **we** rightly conjectured that the Arabs knew their work better than we could shew it them. All night the poor servants were at work, in hail, rain, and wind, yelling continually, as Arabs must do; and in the morning when we had put on our damp clothes we heard at the breakfast-table everybody's experience of the night. Several had been awakened by the cold soaking tents laying on top of them like a clammy contact with a ghost (if a ghost be clammy), while others had been left reposing in bed unprotected as Jupiter Pluvius wreaked his utmost upon them. But the most amusing anecdote was told by Mrs. ——, who related how "all her nice back hair was found plastered against a stone wall in the morning." The storm, however, had not abated one iota, and preparations for a continuation of the same were made. Sellers of waterproof leggings and rubbers found ready buyers in the camp, while some began to try to get quarters in the city.

We congratulated ourselves upon having seen the interior of Jerusalem pretty well before the **bad** weather came on, but some of it we can splash through again in the rain, as it is more dismal in the tents than anywhere else. Suppose we go along the Via Dolorosa, where the Saviour is said to have borne the Cross. This street was first heard of in the *fourteenth* century, but, nevertheless, has some *highly interesting* marks along its course. One of these is the location of the stairs Christ ascended to the Judgment Hall of Pontius Pilate. These stairs, which all pilgrims ascend on their knees, may now be seen under the name of Scala Santa in San Giovanni in Laterano at Rome. The mark in the stone caused by the falling of the Saviour when He bore the Cross along this street is shewn, and where Simon the Cyrenian assisted Him in carrying it. Also where Jesus consoled the maidens of Jerusalem, saying, "Weep not for me, but for yourselves and for your children." The Church of Ecce Homo, built on the site of Pilate's house is seen, and a stone bearing a fancied resemblance to a human face, much worn by the osculations of Pilgrims. "If the people would stop shouting Hosannah," Christ said, "the very stones would cry out," and this is pointed out by the guides as one of the stones that would certainly have cried out. Here is the pool of Bethesda, resembling many other old reservoirs and much crumbled away at its sides, which has been dry for about 200 years. Dr. Robinson is very dubious about it, thus casting doubt upon almost the last of the localities shewn in Jerusalem that I shall mention. But I have kept a tit bit for the last—a raisin or two after "worrying down" the duff—Jerusalem's beauty, the Mosque of Omar.

The Mosque stands in a large area containing thirty-five acres called El Haram, and as it is all holy ground, we have to put on our slippers as usual before entering the enclosure. Until lately, it was almost impossible to gain admission here, but the backsheesh of English and American travellers has satisfactorily dispensed with the scruples hitherto indulged in by the Moslems, and now Christians may enter by paying the fee and getting the necessary permission. Groups of cypresses and rows of arches are interspersed about the grounds, and here and there we see a pious Moslem going through one of his daily devotions, kneeling on his outer garment spread on the paving stones, and facing towards Mecca, where all his aspirations as to travel concentrate. He does not notice our approach, but continues on muttering and bowing his head to the ground with an energy and activity that would give stoutish Christians a good deal of trouble, if they had to pray that way. The enormous dome rises in front of **us,** but we are almost too close to obtain a correct estimate of its magnitude, and outside the entrance is **a** smaller edifice called the Judgment seat of David, supported by pillars said to have been in the Temple of Solomon. Here, the belief is, that all liars have places allotted for them to hang at the last day, the smallness of the place speaking well for the Moslems' idea of the veracity of **the** western nations. The interior which has been very beautiful in marbles, is now much faded in colour; and scaffoldings were erected for repairing the roof which detracted from the general effect, whilst much rubbish was scattered **over** the floors. The dome is supported by four gigantic piers, and in the centre of the **floor** the native rock of Mount Moriah rises in a large mass, and it does not seem **to** be disputed among authorities that this is the last summit of the ridge of Moriah.

I was unprepared to see such **a** strange ornament as this **in** the body of the edifice, and rather expected to have to feel it through **a** hole in the wall, like many other celebrated localities, but here there **was no** attempt at deception, nor was there any polish or ornament about the unsightly mass—save the gilding **of** interest in **the** beholder's mind. Moslems are particularly wanting in taste as to decoration of their places of worship, and in this respect differ very much from most occidental religionists. The High Churchman looks in vain here for pretty decorations of flowers and wood-carvings, and even the Low Churchman feels bound to confess that the Moslems have exceeded the barrenness of adornment he approves of so highly. The rock is well defended from attacks of vandal pilgrims by the railings that surround **it,** for it would soon disappear in mementoes if left unguarded.

We cannot fail to look upon this mass of ugliness with great interest, when we remember that it is the site of the intended sacrifice of Isaac by Abraham, and also as being the probable spot where all the ancient sacrifices of the temple were performed. But the Moslems have an additional interest, inasmuch as they believe that Mahomet ascended from this spot to heaven. Moreover, this rock, forgetting the laws of gravitation in its attraction for the Prophet, essayed to ascend with him, which it would have done, as the tradition says, but for the Angel Gabriel, who was near by and arrested its course; and ever since, it is supposed to be suspended in the air. To demonstrate clearly that it is yet so suspended without any support, there is a cave cut underneath, into which we descended. We saw there too much *foundation* for the theory, and were inclined to think that the walls of the cave yet sustained the rock. There seems to be a slight contradiction in the tradition, which however, none of us quarrelled over, *i. e.*, that Mahomet was once down in this hole himself praying, which must have been before it took flight after him in his ascension, and when arising from prayer, "*horribile dictu*" he hit his head which "*mirabile dictu*," left a hole in the rock about the size of a coal-scuttle.

There is a slab covering a hole in this cave where the spirits of all Moslems descend immediately after death, and Mahomet at the Judgment is to haul them out by the lock of hair always worn for that purpose. Those who support the theory that the mosque occupies the very site of the Temple, contend that this is the hole for the blood of its sacrifices to be carried off by an aqueduct to the Kidron. Others, too, affirm that this is the actual Holy Sepulchre, to which description it certainly answers in every way. Would it not be a strange revelation if this should turn out to be the case, that the Moslems in reality hold our Tomb? Some beautiful twisted marble pillars form part of the structure of the mosque, which in all probability were, as it is said, taken from the Temple, and hence served as models for the immense bronze pillars of the *baldacchino* of St. Peter's. There was, however, one disappointment about the main rock, for in the scores of Italian pictures of the sacrifice on Mount Moriah, one always sees a goat conveniently caught in one corner of the picture, and though I could here imagine the preparations for the sacrifice, I could not "*place*" the goat.

From here we pass into the Mosque of El **Aksa,** which was formerly a Christian church, and it may **be interesting** to know that the sons of Aaron are **buried here.** There are also handsome pulpits of cedar of Lebanon, richly carved, and near by, two old wax candles, about as large around as stove-pipes, partly burnt away, **relics of** the Crusading era. Proceeding now in a westerly **direction** across the grass of the harem enclosure, we reached that part of the city walls overlooking the Valley **of** Jehoshaphat. At the top of the immense fortifications we are shown the station of Mahomet, when, **at the** last day he will judge the world arranged before him in the valley below. At his feet, **a** bridge will be **thrown** across space unlimited, for the passage of the good and faithful, the first stone of which now projects a few feet from the battlements. This stone is shaped somewhat like a cannon, and the bridge Es Sirab, as it is called, is to continue on in the same cylindrical form, while the Moslems have to walk across fettered with their sins to pass into their heaven where Houris await their advent, and where every sensual enjoyment is expected to pamper the tastes the harem cannot satisfy. Angels will support them if they have been regularly responsive to the five daily calls from the minarets to prayer and ablution, and will assist their perilous passage into eternity from the edge of this frightful precipice.

What a cheerful look out for the poor old Mahommedans! And despite their many attempts to be pious, how their faith must waver when they look at the Blondin-like feat that awaits them after death, when a single false step will dash them to atoms on the rocks below. On that last day they certainly seem to expect a most thorough "mauling." I would speak of their faith with more respect if it did not seem to be too exquisitely ludicrous to be hauled up a hole one by one by their back-hair and set to walk this impossible path.

As to the judgment, in this valley, of the nations of the earth the Jews also believe that their Messiah will come and judge them in this renowned valley (Joel III. 2), and in order to be ready at that day, thousands have for all generations, been buried over the slope of Olivet, so that there is not a spadeful of earth to be taken up but will contain some of that dust to which we all return. Thousands come to die and be buried in the valley, so that the population of Jews in the City, consists, as a rule, of old people, who, hoping they are near their last days, do not shed a very cheerful light among the inhabitants.

It must be rather a shock to the proud Mussulman to lay his bones near "the dog of a Jew," he has so shunned and hated in his lifetime; yet, to be ready at the resurrection he is compelled to have his remains laid among those of the Israelites—a striking instance of the equalizing effect the grave has upon mankind.

Very likely at the commencement of the Moslem religion, the many Arab sons of Ishmael, who doubtless were attracted (as is always the case) to the new faith, carried with them this tradition, whereby Mahomet became, as regards the judgment in this valley, identified with the Messiah of the Jewish religion. Moreover, Mahomet in the inculcation of his doctrines, reserved from the Bible, the Pentateuch, the Psalms, and the Gospel, and of course was familiar with the rest of the Holy Volume, as is shown by the similarity of the Koran to many parts of the Bible. So that nothing could be easier than to substitute himself for the Messiah when, in the successful propagation of his religion, he went so far as to proclaim himself the prophet of God.

When, then, we look down upon the myriads of graves in the valley, knowing the creeds of both religions, and recognising every now familiar object on or near the Mount of Olives opposite us, we try to stereotype the view on our minds, for it is peculiar and striking; we would lay by its treasured memory among others of the most captivating panoramas of the world. Facing the precipice, close by, is an ancient gate of large and handsome construction, which is approached from the **Haram**, by descending the depression in the earth lying before it. There is now no road or way leading to it on the other side of the wall, which is built over and around it, and for a great while it has been closed and walled up by the Moslems, on account of the tradition that Jesus entered on Palm Sunday by this gate, and that at his second advent, will enter here again. It has always been called the "Golden Gate" of the Temple, and ranks chief in importance above the other closed gates of the ancient city, which lie in different places about the suburbs of the modern Jerusalem.

If any one is in doubt whether he is to enter paradise after his demise, there is a contrivance here outside the Mosque of El Aksa, that will satisfy the uncertainty. There is a black spot, perhaps two feet square, painted on the wall, and a mark at the other side of the arcade, where the pilgrim must stand with his back to the target; now if he shuts his eyes, turns round, walks with the hand outstretched, and places it on the black spot, he may feel sure that the bridge, Es Sirab, has no terrors for him, and that his abode in the celestial harems has been made sure. We all had a few futile trials which created almost as much fun as the "cocoa-nut cockshots" on the Derby Day, at "three shies a penny;" only one of the "boys" got **his** hand **on it,** while one of the spinsters hit it fair, whereupon the boy said, he "didn't want to go to paradise now." He did not know that women, according to the Moslem faith, could never enter those realms of bliss, reserved only for their imperious lords and masters.

Then we descend under the ground into a place, whose history and original use seem as little known to any one as to myself, and whose ruins rival any constructions of antiquity yet extant. It is called the Stables of Solomon, and was used by the Crusaders for the purpose of stabling their horses, whose tying-rings may yet be seen in the stone. It **is a** labyrinth of high vaults supported by innumerable piers **of** massive size. There are about fifteen rows of these, which may be counted and reached by climbing over the heaps of rubbish **in** some places filling the whole arcade; and even in the parts most cleared away it is evident that the foundations are much below what is seen of the piers. I wandered for a long while bewildered among the stupendous complications of masonry, feeling again and again the unsatisfactory longing for the aid of some body of excavators, who would undoubtedly be able to reveal the idea of those constructions if the search were continued further than by Captain Warren.

Indeed, one gets thoroughly lost among the theories pertaining to each spot. All seem plausible, and all have more or less proof to support them. Jerusalem might be truly said to be the home of the antiquary. There are such endless sepulchres, foundations, under-ground aqueducts, unexplained heaps of ruins, ancient walls and wells, that the city awakens now a keener excitement by her mystery, than she could have done in the days of her prosperity. Enshrouded as she is like a spectre city in the robe of death, her power is only latent; the youthful splendour of her beauty is indeed gone, but those occult charms in her barren bosom still offer allurements to the wise. The voluptuary may no more seek her palaces of pleasure, but the philosopher and the sage can find that in her presence the mind is ever in the ascendant, while, forgetting her faults, it dwells upon her glories. Thus she yet holds proud dominion over the intellect of the world; she does not look for admirers among the votaries of pleasure, but where veneration and respect abide, there she is to be found enthroned in ancient grandeur.

CHAPTER IX.

THE weather still continued for days to wreak its utmost fury upon us, while we had nothing to do but wander about in our waterproofs among the sights of interest, or huddle around a charcoal fire in the dining tent. Much time was spent in the Holy Sepulchre and about the Jews' Wailing Place, where the arrivals of the pilgrims formed attractive subjects for observation.

One morning I was surprised to recognise the faces of several of the Armenians who came with us in the steamer to land at Jaffa, but were carried up to Haifa and made to land there. The poor people had had a very hard time of it—walking all the way to Jerusalem, and carrying their baggage and cooking utensils with them, and, in many cases, their children also, who sank under the fatigue of the pilgrimage. Now, men, women and children were assembled at the Holy Sepulchre; they had enjoyed a night's rest under shelter, and were again looking bright with the excitement of having reached their longed-for destination, and beamed with religious fervour on approaching the spot which was to reward them for all their sufferings.

Their first act, after a prayer at the threshold, was to take off their boots, which showed how rough their journey had been, and pile them in large stacks in different corners of the church; then tucking their trousers into a clean pair of stockings brought especialy for the occasion, they enter the Rotunda, in the middle of which the sepulchre stands, and approach slowly, praying at different stations on their knees, and bowing their heads to the ground continually.

How their eyes glisten at the costly lamps which shed a truly sepulchral light upon the scene! They have seen some adornments in the churches among their native mountains, but nothing so priceless as this; the thought seems to strike their poor ignorant minds that with all this treasure the church must indeed be holy.

So far from being ridiculed or sneered at, how enviable is their faith! Who would grudge them a single moment of rapture here, or instil a doubt in their minds concerning the revered Sepulchre? By degrees they approach and enter, and then another prayer of heartfelt thanks is added to the numbers that have here been uttered by men of all nations, creeds and doctrines; another petition ascends to the Omnipotent—The Great Spirit, who makes His unseen Presence felt by the Redskin of the far West —the Allah, at whose name the Moslem quakes—the Almighty God, who is the same under every circumstance and under any name.

Short intervals of sunshine would at times light up our camp during the day, but they were generally the precursors of a heavier storm. Let it rage as it would, some of us determined to make an excursion to Bethlehem and to the Monastery of Mar Saba. We started one morning, heavily clad and covered with waterproofs, resolved to make the journey if our horses could carry us through. As usual, we took our packhorses with provision bags well filled with the good things of life to refresh us at the Convent, and a sudden cessation of the rain favoured our departure.

In single file we descended the stony path and crossed the Valley of Hinnom, and in the ascent to the plain above we were shown the impress in the rock where Elijah rested in his flight from Jezebel. One would think

Elijah had been a hot stove and the rock made of ice, to see the hole made by him; or else he must have been very uneasy in the night to wear it out in such a manner The wind swept across the plain with great violence, when we laboured through its mire, insomuch that the horses, unable to take a straight course, were blown out of the path, and once or twice I felt moved in the saddle, as if about to be lifted from it bodily.

Presently we came to the tomb of Rachel, a mausoleum of Saracenic architecture, which, in its present state lays no claim to antiquity, but is well worth stopping at, owing to the unanimous concurrence of all authorities, that it marks the identical spot where Rachel was buried. In the thirty-fifth chapter of Genesis, mention is made of Rachel, who as her soul was departing, called her new-born babe Benoni, son of sorrow. "And Rachel died and was buried in the way to Ephrath, which is Bethlehem. And Jacob set a pillar upon her grave; that is the pillar of Rachel's grave to this day."

In the prophesy of Jeremiah foretelling the slaughter of the babes of Bethlehem under Herod, he says, " In Rama was there a voice heard, lamentation and weeping, and great mourning, Rachel weeping for her children, and would not be comforted, because they are not." There was no opportunity to search the Biblical narrative with comfort as we gathered around the ancient tomb, but a burst of sunshine came upon us through the gloom, gladdening the desolate spot, and warming our shivering bodies which were now stiffening with the exposure.

Soon we wind round a valley and enter the main street of Bethlehem. The approach is not striking, and the interior of the town is uninteresting. The houses are square-topped, and not domed like those of the neighbouring Jerusalem, and the inhabitants eke out a scanty existence principally by the manufacture of necklaces, beads and crosses, which command a great profit among pilgrims. Hawkers of carvings of mother-of-pearl surround us, hoping to make sales; their wares being often executed in a manner that would rival the best Florentine workmanship, which seems strange, emanating, as they do, from such a place as Bethlehem. The town seems never to have been much larger than it is now, and for ages nothing relieved the unimportant history of its existence or shed a pleasing light upon it, except the story of Ruth and Boaz, which is related with such beautiful simplicity.

The inhabitants, numbering now over 3,000, have always borne a character for ferocity and lawlessness, which shows itself at the annual feasts at Jerusalem, where great disturbances are created by them. The Moslem element, which was continually warring with the Christian, was exterminated by Ibrahim Pasha about forty years ago, and now they are nearly all of the Greek, or what is called Christian, religion.

The Church of the Nativity seems to be held under the Greeks, Armenians, and Latins. On entering the walls, we are shown into a reception room, and from there taken into the Greek Church. As at the Holy Sepulchre, the different sects meeting within the church, have caused the most horrible fights to take place within its precincts; both the pictures and ornaments exhibiting traces of the mêlées. We are not accustomed to see the altars of our native churches guarded by soldiery; the sight of the stupid-looking fellows walking about the church, with guns pointed in every direction, are eyesores to us; the frippery, too, of the ornaments, seems hardly worth guarding. Down a winding stair, some twenty feet, with bad smelling candles in our hands, we come to the Grotto of the Nativity, cut in the rock and surrounded by lamps; a silver star on the floor marking the exact spot where Christ is said to have been born. The star has some relation to that seen in the firmament by the Wise Men, and has around it the inscription: "Hic de Virgine Maria Jesus Christus natus est." Hard by is the Grotto of the Manger, a recess from the cave, as gaudily decorated as jewellery, lace and gew-gaws can make it.

Now how think you such localities should be approached? In what spirit should we gaze upon these reputed holy spots? Well, I would say, in spite of all the revolting adornments and improbable look **of the place,** that the greatest respect is due to the locality owing partly to the great force of argument that tradition brings to bear upon it, and of course on account of the sanctity even of its reputation. Long before the Empress Helena built the present huge edifice above, in A.D. 327, the tradition could be traced back till shortly after the death **of** the Apostle John; and remembering how faithfully traditions have **been handed down by** word of mouth, **we** must try and convince ourselves that this is the place where He who "became poor for our sakes" first saw the light of day. On several occasions I have noticed houses built in front of and including a **cavern, where the** cattle are kept, which circumstance seems to **meet** all the demands of the tradition.

Happily, about the site of Bethlehem there hangs no shadow of doubt: it is enough for us to know that this is the humble village honoured by witnessing the commencement **of our** Redeemer's life; that from this obscurity the Heavenly Light first shone out upon our lost world, whose dazzling rays, gradually piercing the ends of the earth, continue ever to illuminate the darkness of our nature, lighting us to the haven where the effulgence is all-prevalent.

In contemplating the consequences of the occurrence, what a small piece **of business** it is to harangue about the **actual** spot of His nativity. Let those who profit by these exhibitions find proofs of their identity, and let those who can, believe in them. Matthew says the Wise Men "came into the *house* and saw the young child with Mary his mother, and fell down and worshipped him." Moreover is it natural to suppose that wherever the Holy Family went, **they** dwelt in grottoes under the earth? In Egypt, **we see a** cave whither they fled and dwelt; at Nazareth is shown Mary's kitchen, sitting-room, &c., completely cut **in** the rock, and here, another similar abode is seen. No—a grotto is the only thing which will withstand earthquakes and wear of weather for all ages, so the monks know right well how to immortalize their churches by connecting a biblical event with their subterranean caves. The Jews had more materials for building in ancient days than they have now, but to see their reputed habitations one would think they were a nation of Troglodytes. A glance suffices for the Chapel of Joseph, whither the husband of Mary retired at the moment of the nativity, and in another part of the rambling passages, the Tomb of the Innocents, where it is said 20,000 babes were buried after the massacre by Herod.

Here in another low, rambling, underground cave, St. Jerome, the most learned of the Latin Fathers, after a wandering life, settled down; near what he supposed literally to be the cradle of the Christian faith; and wrote the last of his works, most of which have come down to us. Born in Dalmatia, educated in Rome, he then travelled in Gaul, and subsequently through many countries in the East. Four years he passed as an anchorite in the desert of Chalcis, near Antioch, where he adhered strictly to the most rigid observances of monkish asceticism. Again he returned to Rome, where his contemplative life and deep religion drew many enthusiastic disciples from among the Roman ladies; which influence over them exposed him to attacks upon his character, so, after visiting Constantinople, and making a tour of the Holy Land, this great traveller and priest spent the last years of his ebbing life as a recluse in this comfortless cave.

His celebrated Commentaries on the Scriptures, upon which his profound knowledge of the Greek and Hebrew languages, and of Eastern life, enabled him to throw great light, and which is still the Biblia Vulgata of the Latins, was composed in the gloom of this confined abode. Here he studied, prayed, and fasted, and here, at the termination of his wonderful life, he received the last Communion, in all the meekness and resignation that his life of self-abnegation produced over the fiery spirit which showed itself in the vehemency of his controversial works. That scene, through the transcendant genius of Domenichino, has been explained to the people of the world in a painting, whose matchless colouring, depth and rare idea are rivalled by few, and whose beauty does not wane when placed before Raphael's Transfiguration in the Vatican.

Our horses where waiting in the courtyard of the church, where a number of trinket-sellers were awaiting our departure. We all bought rosaries and bracelets from the bright-eyed children who form the most pleasing pictures in Palestine. The boys are well made and athletic, and have fine eyes and intelligent faces, and the beauty of the maidens of Bethlehem has been raved over by many a writer. Both sexes, however, soon lose all traces of beauty; the form becomes pinched and bony, and young men become gaunt, hairy, and wild-looking. Women, whose beauty is their only safeguard from desertion and abuse, in a few years have no remaining attractions, except, perhaps, the pearly teeth, which they disclose in a radiant smile as they induce us to buy their handiwork.

After a look through the streets we bade good-bye to Bethlehem, and, as we wound down the hill sides and terraces, there were many turning in their saddles to have a last look at the birth-place of our Lord. Two hours were not enough to satisfy the desire to wander about precincts so fraught with recollections as old "Ephrath which is Bethlehem," but with such weather as we were then enduring we were glad even to get a glimpse of it. While the storms of hail swept us along, the Shepherd's Field was shown, and little did I think, while singing at every Christmas of my boyhood that fine old hymn, that I would see the spot under such circumstances. How did the verse run? Everybody knows it—all the better! let's have it!

> "While shepherds watched their flocks by night,
>   All seated on the ground,
> The angel of the Lord came down,
>   And glory shone around.

> "'Fear not,' said he, for mighty dread
> Had seiz'd their troubled mind,
> 'Glad tidings of **great** joy I bring,
> To you and all mankind.'"

I forget the rest of the hymn, but, anyway, even this spot they could not leave to the imagination of pilgrims, but have it walled in, and forsooth! another adorned grotto! where the shepherds watched their flocks. "*C'est très drôle, n'est-ce pas?*" A grotto is always such a lively stimulant to my mind now in thinking of any Biblical event, that I may picture vividly its surroundings by imagining it in a gaudy cave. Why, of course, it cannot be expected that the shepherds were going to stay out in the cold all night—shepherds never do—they were down here, sitting round a fire, having a *quiet rubber*.

And this is the field where "Boaz said unto Ruth, Hearest thou not my daughter? Go not to glean in another field, neither go from hence, but abide here fast by my maidens;" and by way of reassuring her, in her timidity at working among the young men, he told her that he had cautioned them against paying her too much attention, adding, perhaps, a caution by way of graceful compliment, "Let thine eyes be upon the field that they do reap, and go thou after them." When he emptied the six measures of barley into the *vail* which she wore, it was not into one of the flimsy witcheries that form part of the modern girl's head gear; it was into a useful and graceful garment, still worn by the Eastern maidens. These beauties always manage in some way, even in the smallest hovels, to have a clean white linen vesture to put on when emerging into the streets, which covers them from head to foot, serving the purpose of a veil as well as gown if they wish to hide their faces. This, however, they will generally not do, unless some of their friends are looking on: their innate curiosity and love of admiration often affording us pilgrims fair glimpses of rare faces.

I think we plunged through the field of Boaz itself on the way to Mar Saba, and a hard journey it was both for horse and man; the fields being so soft and loamy, it was a comfort to reach the stony bed of a stream where the animals had not to plunge so heavily to move along. Sometimes we crept along the brinks of precipices, where the horses hugged the wall of rock rising beside them; sometimes we passed under the grateful shelter of some over-hanging crags; anon we were on the hill tops, **where** the full blast of the storm often carried the horses dangerously near some yawning gulf, while they struggled hard to keep the path.

It was with unspeakable satisfaction that we at last **beheld** the towers of the monastery, **after three** hours in a wet saddle. As we assembled outside the court-yard gate, **and** were dismounting, all feeling rather stiff and benumbed, a distressing accident took place to an elderly gentleman of **our** party. He dismounted on a stone platform raised about three feet from the ground, but on attempting to stand his legs failed him, and he turned backwards in his fall, striking his head heavily on the rock below. I was standing by him when he alighted, but could not aid him in any way. The mackintosh was torn open and animation restored; and, after the ugly gash in his head had been attended to in the monastery, he so far recovered as to be able to ride home.

Before entering the huge stone portals which would bid easy defiance **to** anything but gunpowder, a basket is lowered from **an** aperture in the wall by the monk on guard, into which the letter of introduction is placed, and soon we are admitted to the yard where our horses are tied. Now, in descending into a sort of porch, where the wounded man is attended to, we catch a cursory glimpse at the world-renowned monastery. We see a rambling, massive edifice, built **to a** great height up the face of the precipice, so amalgamated with the native rock that it is impossible to tell, in many places, where the architecture is natural or where the work is of human hands. We see some parts castellated with turrets and battlements, other parts have the appearance of portions of chapels—cupolas, queer looking ledges, odd holes or windows in the face of the cliff are seen—while a large palm tree grows out of one of the nooks far away up, shaking its funereal plumes over the sepulchre where the living are entombed for ever with the dead. Below us we see more courtyards, and around us winding stone stairs, leading everywhere and nowhere, up and down, in and out and through the labyrinthine maze of inhospitable-looking rock. Such a formidable place takes away the idea of receiving entertainment and kindness within its walls; the feeling is rather to look back at the gate to see whether retreat is cut off, lest, through treachery, we should happen to be entrapped.

Bunyan never imagined his hero arriving at a fortress so peculiar as this—a stronghold that fire won't touch, and which laughs at earthquakes. Yet there are warm hearts beating within the frowning chilling mass; natural, loving men here crucify themselves into apparent apathy to all affection, in the belief that by leading the half-performed life of celibacy, they better the hereafter. They try hard to kill their nature, but I doubt whether they ever do more than stagnate the fondness that shows itself pitiably in the caresses of their pet birds. This man wearing a high felt hat with the brim on the top, and a long black coat reaching almost to his unsandalled feet, has a face that might be taken for that of the Christ, only it is too fined down by indoor life.

Almost every picture that I ever saw of the Saviour was very erroneous as to colour of complexion, for nobody can live any time in the Holy Land, remaining much in the open air as he did, without becoming as brown as a berry, and the representations of Him are either pink and white, like this Greek monk, or else they are sallow, like Carlo Dolci's Virgins. But to return to the monk, there is tenderness of expression about his mouth, and a fountain of benevolence welling forth from his eyes that indicate well his character; the way he helps to wash the wound, to separate and cut away the hair, and apply the bandages, shows some knowledge of surgery too; how much good he might do if he were to go abroad in the world as a great *Hakim* for all weaknesses of the body and soul?

Instead of waiting here in the wilderness of the Kidron, where his chance to act the good Samaritan might happen but once in his lifetime, if he would go where his opportunities would be many—go where he could rejoice with them that are joyful, and mourn in sympathy with them that are sorrowful—how great might be the **result?**

Having divested ourselves of all waterproofs, whips, **and** heavy clothes, we **are led** over a few more passages and into a divaned **room, floored** with such clean matting that we appreciate **the custom, in** the Oriental etiquette, **of** taking off **the dirty boots before** resting on its easy cushions. Here where **we repose** in all the *abandon* of luxury, like Great Moguls: our luncheon is served by the attendants brought with us, and Bass' Ale seems strangely fitting, yet thoroughly exotic, in this old convent. We receive, too, some delicious coffee, prepared at the hands of the monks, and some native wine resembling in flavour the vintage of Cyprus. Then the inevitable cigarette is rolled, the ordinary accompanyment of every act in the **east,** and while the wreathing curls of fragrant smoke mingle with the aroma of the coffee we are sipping, Mar **Saba** does **not** seem such a bad spot after all.

Odder still were the internal retreats of this vast construction, than the exterior predicted. Winding flights of gloomy stairs led us to the cave of Saint Sabas, the founder of the convent, **who, in the** fifth century, chose to come and live in this spot, to enjoy the great resources for meditation and prayer which the wild gorge offered. Many others followed his example, and we **were** told that many thousands came and lived around him in similar holes, forming a colony of cave-livers which looked up to St. Sabas as their leader. On his first coming to this cave he found it inhabited by a lion, which, it is said, he told to evacuate the premises; and this the animal kindly did, **but** was allowed to remain as a tenant-at-will in a small den adjoining, in consideration of general good behaviour, and occasionally mounting guard over their home. The beast could not have been very large, as the entrance to its den would hardly admit of the passage of a man's body,

We noticed all over the walls and low ceiling of the cavern, innumerable little crosses scratched by pilgrim visitors to the place. Each pilgrim did not paint his name with boot-blacking in large letters on the wall, as modern travellers often do; and no quack medicines were advertised there either; every worshipper at this saint's abode was content to make another little cross upon the rock wherever he could find an inch of clear surface.

There was another descent, and then a climb up to several chapels that have lost many of their peculiarities to me now, except a remembrance of their gorgeous adornments, which in Greek churches are often very costly. The pictures were the most amusing part of the spectacle, having about as much perspective about them as on a Chinese plate. Art had been at a low ebb when they were painted; the men were nearly as tall as the trees, while the houses in the back ground would reach about to their shoulders; the roads had been filled in afterwards, and great difficulty had evidently been experienced in the endeavour to get them around the houses; so that the thoroughfares stopped on one side of doorless houses, then commenced again on the other. As they generally represented persecutions, the eyes of all the people in the picture, except the saint, had been gouged out by the pilgrims, to show their abhorrence and abomination of the cruel men, and their extreme sympathy with the saint. Although this detracted considerably from the general beauty of the pictures, Jimmy drew aside one of the monks and stood gazing at one of them in rapture, telling him in Italian how he admired them, while the monk acquiesced vehemently with "Si, Si, Signore!" but when Jimmy said *ma che belli occhi!* (but what beautiful eyes!) he turned from him with a pitying look, and still thinks we had an idiot among us.

From the chapels we emerge on some roofs and battlements, where the view into the valley below was grand and most striking. Very rarely had the Kedron, which is generally dry, been known to be so deep and rapid as was its flow after the continual rains of the previous days. Far away down, between the wildest and most rugged of precipices, a river now foamed and dashed along its tortuous bed, lashing the bases of the rocks hundreds of feet below us, gathering fresh impetus **every** moment in its rapid descent to the motionless waters **of the** Dead Sea.

And it struck me, how much the lives **of some of** these monks might resemble this very stream over which they live. Take this man beside us, and the stream so typical of **his career.** Born, perhaps, in a high position, life may have **been a** succession of rebuffs received on all sides from cold shoulders, or it may have been the whirling blind **descent of the prodigal** and the profligate. Having **taken a** few **downward** steps carefully enough, **a** rapid succession **of** falls ensued, each adding more desperation **to** the wildness of the current. The race is run, in spite of all obstacles, and many a miller profits thereby; fine old rocks offer obstruction, **but are** overwhelmed and passed by; at length, when its strength is nearly spent and ended, the stream suddenly begins to flow on more evenly, deeply and quietly. Tired of the madly-rushing life, and not evaporating, **as** many waters do, at this point, the **resolve** is made to take the **last,** and, perhaps, more fatal step for happiness, it enters the Dead Sea—the Mar Saba from which there is no outlet, save underground—there to taste the bitterness of its eternally motionless waters—there to **let the** old sparkle of life die out and become a **recollection.**

But, unhappily for my little comparison, the monk does not look as if he **ever** had done anything wrong **in his** life, and when **a** number **of** them are seen together, **the** idea comes to us, that we **never saw** such a collection of handsome and *good*-looking men. The younger ones have a beautiful look of purity in their faces; they seem to remember their Creator in **the** days of their youth, and the fine patriarchal old men appear to have kept up their good lives from their childhood. One thing lessens their trials to be good **and** tends to perpetuate the tranquillity of their lives, and that is because no woman is ever allowed inside the gates. Many **a** lady traveller has been turned away when seeking shelter and rest within the walls, but the hinges have ever refused to creak for their entrance, though well lubricated with the oil that makes the world run smoothly. And **rightly too**! Woman, with all her beauty, with **all the happiness she imparts to** man, brings a corresponding and a **greater amount of trouble** with it ; as these **poor fellows must never** know the happiness of a **married life, even if** they would take the rough with the smooth, like thousands of others—why should they risk their peace **of mind by ever** seeing a woman ? Yet there may be a treasured **lock of hair** lying somewhere in those rocky **clefts, that has witnessed** many a time the outbursts of a passionate **soul long pent up**—**a fair** ringlet, culled from the **waving harvest of some Haidee on** the Grecian shore, from **which the curl may** have departed, but where the words on the **faded ribbon** αληθης καί νημερτης (faithful and true) may seem more deeply **fond than ever**.

No price is laid down for **the hospitalities** of the monks who treated us **so** humanely, nor **is the** question **ever asked** of the pilgrim, **whether** he be **Jew or** Gentile, **Roman or Protestant, or whether he has** provided **scrip** for his journey. Whoever he be, rest and **shelter here await** him, and **he is sent on his** way rejoicing.

We left a purse for the support of the noble institution. I call it *noble*, for I see only its good works before me ; it is not for me to criticise the aimless lives of the dead men who people its walls. If they retired to this seclusion after a sorrow that could not be forgotten, if they could **not face the world and deaden** anguish by struggling **with the multitude, for their country, for** science, and for **themselves ; or if, by mortifying the flesh** and abstaining **from all good and lawful happiness, they** hope to see God, mine is not the pen to blame or to praise ; but one thing I know is, that whenever I **dwell** upon the lives of these monks, unspeakable pity for them fills my heart. My **best wish is that their peace of mind** may equal the tranquillity of the region **they dwell in**.

Out again in the storm **we faced the** blast, now full in our **faces, on** the return **to Jerusalem**. We took the valley of the **Kedron, where** in the gorge we were somewhat sheltered from the furious wind. Bending over the saddle-bows, while the rain poured off our hats by the bucketfull, we pressed on, impatient at the pace when the horses had to pick their way carefully, and rattling along at a good rate when the ground would permit of it. Many times we had to ford the raging stream swollen higher than the saddle-girths; often a path only a few inches wide was the only footing between the precipices uncovered by the **flood**. Often it seemed doubtful whether we could press **against** the torrent as **it swirled** round some angle of the valley.

Several hours thus passed **and** dusk settled down upon us before we ascended out of the valley to the heights where we got the wind again. It was perfectly frightful. The hail stung like slugs from an old Queen Anne musket, so that the horses that were not perfectly under command would not face it, but stood cowering, with pain and fright, with their tails to the storm. Our path was discernible only by the rushing stream that flowed in it, and the danger was doubly increased by the horses being unable to see where to place their feet. Darkness came on and no sign of any habitation gladdened our view; we were miles away from Jerusalem and still among the mountains; there was nothing to do but ride it out, following our dragoman, in whom we placed implicit confidence.

Floyd—by far the best dragoman in Palestine—has made a study of every thing connected with the land, his instructions and information being invaluable to **the** traveller. He was one of a party of American emigrants, who, attempting to found a colony at Jaffa, for the most part either died or returned to their native country; and since then he has gone again and again through the country, knowing every path and by-way. He is a fine, noble-looking fellow; in my opinion much too good for his work, but **even** *he* must have been somewhat bewildered that night, when sight was almost useless, and the instinct of the horses **more** to be relied on than any knowledge. None of us said **a** word, for the desolation struck us dumb. I tried to get up a chorus, but the wind drove the sound down my throat. Every half-hour or so, Floyd would stop and pass the word aft, to see if we were all following him, his voice ringing out full of determination and unflinching bravery. In such a time true manhood shews forth, when the elements conspire to create awe in the chilled heart and tired frame. It is no place for the frock-coated dandy, who canters from twelve to two in Rotten Row, and we could not but follow in silent admiration of our dragoman.

Again, we were in a valley, and on looking up saw a straight line dividing total darkness from partial light. It was the wall of Zion rising above us—Jerusalem lay within, and the tents at last were near, the horses clambering out of the valley of Hinnon, with their ears pricked forward pushed along more briskly, and after all the day's work recounted in this chapter, shall I say they were not tired? It seems incredible, but I certainly saw little sign of it. Soon we arrived at the welcome lighted tents, where the ladies and others were anxiously awaiting our return, and with dry clothes on, and a good dinner *in*, were relating the day's adventures, surrounded by eager and sympathising faces. My ride from Mar Saba will not soon be forgotten. It eclipsed all that I ever experienced in the saddle, but may all hardships terminate as satisfactorily, as when I then reached home—*home at Jerusalem!*

Next morning I got up feeling very cold; as usual, the servants had been up all night attending to the tents—they were rapidly losing strength, being always soaked through and through, both night and day. But what was my surprise when, unhooking the canvas door, I let in a flood of snow! "Snow! snow! beautiful snow!" as the poet says, I never hated you so much as at that moment—why could I not have stayed in Canada where I had a house to cover and fires to warm me? I dressed in all my remaining wardrobe and went to breakfast, there to hear such loud complaints, that I felt the merit of making light of our hardships. We tried that day to get warm in the dining-tent around the charcoal fire, on the ground, which could only be fanned into glowing coals; several endeavoured to write letters with benumbed fingers, but went to bed at last in the endeavour to get warm.

Another night passed—the servants were completely used up. Accustomed to fiery heat and having no preparation for cold, they suffered agonies. The boots we had given them had become so soaked, that it was impossible to get them on, and they worked with bare feet in the snow. One by one they came to Dr. —— who was with us, saying they were dying. This could not go on for another night, and there was no accommodation left in the city. A house was bargained for after much difficulty, and we were enabled to move into it for a few days. Everything was taken from the tents and brought to our new home; the beds were set up, a fire kindled on the stone floor, and soon many of us nearly got comfortably warm. Of course, leaving Jerusalem was out of the question, as the horses could not take a step on the mountain sides in snow, so we spent the time in playing games, writing letters, or eating the capital dinners our cook never failed to provide. The house had five rooms, two of which the gentlemen occupied, one the ladies took possession of, another for the cuisine, while the large centre one served as dining-room, parlour, and store room; also, as bed-room for the servants.

It was certainly a glorious and rare privilege to see Jerusalem from an eminence, clothed in the spotless robes of snow, but I could have survived without that pleasure. In her palmiest days she never could have looked more beautiful. Her numberless domes, both small and large, appeared to be made of purest alabaster, her walls were iced with the delicate frost-work of a wedding cake; we realized at last the ivory houses of the Scripture. No heaps of rubbish marred the beauty of the view, no noisome lanes offended the senses, no life was to be seen in the streets. There she stood, proud as ever, though the uplifted gilded cresent flashed profanely o'er the scene; there she stood enrobed in splendour—the splendour of the lily —immaculate, pure and undefiled, she lay before the eye as a transient vision—the unpeopled city of the brain; or as a sight of heaven flashes through the dying mind, ere the spirit leaves the clay to there abide.

Snow is somewhat akin to Death—Death equalizes man, and snow his habitation. As death often smooths away the furrowed lines from the careworn face and presents it to the fond gazer with a smile of youth upon it; so snow, at the expiration of the old year, often offers the earth, having now ended one of its lives, smiling and radiantly shining in the shroud in which it leaves our view forever. It makes the trellised cot of the humble peasant as beautiful as the massive mansion of the rich. As it covers each projection, and fills each nook and cranny, as it settles on each twig of the clinging vine, and hides all evidences of poverty in the purity of its feathery touch; can man erect any edifice that may not be embellished still more highly by its fairy finger?

CHAPTER X.

WE have bid a long good-bye to Jerusalem. We have mounted our horses refreshed by their rest, and have skirted the walls past the Jaffa, the Damascus and St. Stephen's gates. We have descended and crossed the Valley of Jehoshaphat, and looked into the garden of Gethsemane for the last time, and when winding up and around Olivet, we have halted at the spot where Jesus wept over Jerusalem. It was a fitting station from which to take our last long view. In that moment of farewell the old city seemed all at once unfamiliar to our eyes; its aspect seemed eccentric, its position appeared odd. Was it that we viewed it from a different spot? Surely, we had been near here before?
No! it was Jerusalem passing again into the ideal. Even before losing sight of it, it took the form of the mind's fancy before ever gazing on it. We thought we were familiar with its every hole and corner, but not for passing pilgrims, such as we, was it to comprehend and know Jerusalem over whose head nigh four thousand mighty years had rolled. It seemed strange and unlike its reality. The snow had disappeared and the sun was again beaming over our heads, yet in that moment, when we would have impressed its memory upon our minds, a singular unreality seemed to hover over its site. Perhaps it was owing to the momentary forgetfulness of the lepers, barefaced mummeries, questionable sites and filthy

streets within its walls! Regardless of all the prejudices which were created in our narrow minds by these detractions while among them, a broader view, more comprehensive and more searching into ages past, seemed to be felt at that moment. Again, we seem to hear that mournful cry, "O! Jerusalem, Jerusalem, which killest the prophets and stonest them that are sent unto thee; how often would I have gathered thy children together as a hen doth gather her brood under her wings, and yet ye would not." Perchance He saw that unfamiliar and ungrateful city look thus coldly down upon him, He who for peace had to take refuge on this hillside, who, foreseeing the calamities and downfall of the city He loved so well, wept exceeding bitter tears; and here perhaps we may ascribe its fancied strangeness to a blurred eye that was tardy to turn away *forever*. A hard word to probe, that word forever—it is a hard word to get over, and there's another little word which causes a like sad vibration among the chords of the heart, the apparently insignificant word "once." One feels small, and very powerless, and very melancholy when dwelling upon the word *once*. We can, nevertheless, comprehend *once* better than *forever*. We are born once, we are once children, we love once (?) and we die once, and in some things the mind can easily be reconciled to the word; but it applies more to the things of this world than the word *forever*—which stretches both ways into the Past and Future of Eternity. We grasp at the meaning of forever, while looking into the future, as for a sunbeam or shadow, and we know not whether our Forever may be in sunshine or in shade.

No mention has yet been made as to our destination on leaving Jerusalem; the fact is my pen, instead of going quietly and carefully down to the Dead Sea, wanders off, like Borack (Mahomet's camel), on extraordinary aerial flights from Mecca to Medina and elsewhere.

The feeling of exhilaration at being once more in saddle and out in the pure air and glad sunshine soon diverted our minds from all heavy thoughts, and we felt that we might, without regret, exchange the highly problematical exhibitions of the city for the lovely hillsides and rocky defiles down which we were so rapidly dropping to the Bitter Sea. It was no funeral procession that wended its way **down** the steep declivities on **that** memorable day. We **felt** far more like jovial wedding guests, or gay banqueters summoned to the "Feast of Roses," for Flora had with such a lavish **hand** bedecked our path with her most gorgeous gifts, that **we** rode through endless masses **of** flowers, covering the ground with indescribable variation of colour. While the bright **birds** were skimming about in every direction, and the bees, like sparks of light, buzzed from tulip to hyacinth, from anemone to daisy, and the sky arched cloudless and **serene** above us, we ambled about among ourselves, chatting and laughing, and under constant orders to dismount and pick some fair one a peculiar flower for pressing. Who wouldn't be **a** pilgrim? Who wouldn't be a flower?

Our mounted guards were the "toughest" specimens of the genus ever seen. They were regulars under the Turkish flag, but seemed more like some sort of local volunteers. One of the two was called the Sheik, being "a man under authority;" he rode in front of us and the other brought up the rear.

Of course, on leaving Jerusalem for the dangerous spots about the Dead Sea and Jordan, where the attacks of the Bedawin are most to be feared, no protection is really expected from these Don Quixotes, who, unlike the gallant knight, invariably run away at the first approach of danger. The object, then, in taking them is that they form a sort of insurance policy granted by the government, which is thereby responsible for all loss and damage occasioned by the attacks of the robbers. They constitute a sort **of** floating policy which the authorities afford, and indeed compel travellers to take out.

They were mounted on sagacious looking Arab screws, trained to all the manœuvres which, as the old books say, the free and roving Child of the Desert delighteth in. Their nags, adorned with shabby tassels, were guided by rope halters, while the bits, kept safely in their riders' pockets, were only put on when an exhibition of skilful riding demanded their use. The noble knights sat in their hairy native saddles with their knees up to their chins, their feet crammed in the square shovel-stirrups, with which they kicked their horses' ribs to keep them awake; and in this situation represented a combination of an ancient armoury with a depository for old iron. To say that they were armed to the teeth describes but faintly their formidable appearance. Their heads were covered by the ordinary richly-coloured silk *keffieh*, held on by a camel's hair rope encircling the brow like a fillet and tightening behind, while its graceful folds, dropping over the back of the neck, protect it from all weathers. Slung around their backs were flint-lock guns, about six feet long (warranted not to go off) with very thin stocks of rotten-looking wood; while in the sash were numerous gaudy old silver-mounted pistols, more for show than use, as one of them confessed, saying at the same time that he trusted more than anything else to a fine revolver he had concealed in his voluminous garb. Small comfort the revolver would have afforded nervous travellers if they could have seen the ancient pattern on which it was made; and of all the murderous array, the waving daggers, placed in convenient places about his person, were perhaps the best weapons he had. A huge curved sabre and scabbard of ponderous dimensions completed the attire of these gentle creatures. No wonder their horses looked dejected! Encumbered as they were, the wisest thing the riders could do would be to run for it if they scented a foe—I should certainly do the same thing under the circumstances, and would throw over-board, while "running free," some of that iron ballast.

Dropping from one mountain to another, perhaps two thousand feet in half the way to the sea, a momentary glimpse of the sheet of water and valley bursts upon our view; then nothing is seen but the quiet undulation of the neighbouring mountains. As we ride along the paths on precipitous declivities, a look below and above us is something I wish everybody could enjoy—such a vast bed of flowers could not be made by human hands—it is no exaggeration to say that it rivals the gorgeous tints of an Eastern sunset. The scarlet anemones and yellow marigolds predominate, combining to make a richness and warmth of colour which the lighter flowers save from being too gaudy—blending the whole into one huge bouquet.

On every side lie immense grey rocks with heather and flowers filling up the crevices, while large leaved **plants** grow here and there to give more luxuriance to the verdancy. Among these crags browse vast herds of nimble goats, careless of their narrow footing while turning to gaze upon us curiously; and the active shepherd bounds up the rocks from the valley below **to inspect our** peculiarities and to ask possibly for backsheesh **or tobacco.** These fellows have most pleasing countenances **and a** smile as free and open as the air they breathe. They will follow along with us cheerily, not generally bothering for money like the beggars of the towns, for they are in **no** particular want; their only business is to mind the herds and amuse themselves by playing **on** reed-pipes, whose tremulous strains, floating dreamily over the pleasant hillsides, often betoken the presence of a neighbouring flock.

Most graceful and winning are they in their movements. Here we **see** one stop for a moment in mute admiration of the faces in **our** party, which are enchanting to his eyes as well as ours, and darting off to cull a hyacinth, or perchance a rarer flower, he presents it, with a sunny smile to the belle his unerring eye at once detects. It is an action full of native grace. Though, perhaps, he never saw the ribbons and adornments of our ladies before, he bows in the natural homage which all men pay to beauty. Mightily pleased will he be if you take some notice of him. Tell him **he** is good-looking and he will blush and show his pearly teeth; ask him if he has any tobacco, "*andak douhahn?*" **and** his eyes will glisten still more in the hope of a cigarette as he replies, "*lah! douhahn mafeesh?*" (no, it's all gone). A deal of fun could be had out of these fellows, and many an hour have I beguiled in the day's ride teaching them English words in exchange for Arabic.

The rascals would always be looking back at some lady; in great confidence and friendship, declaring his admiration, using the words "*yah yuni*," meaning, I think, " she is my very eyes."

When we had descended about four thousand feet over the last few incinerated hills bleached with glaring suns of summer, we passed through the jungle waving above our heads on the plain, where the jackals and other beasts occupy their lairs undisturbed—a few minutes more and we dismounted on the beach of the Dead Sea, our horses rolling over at once in the sand, regardless of the saddles and the umbrellas strapped on their backs.

All thought of cold and snow was now forgotten, and a protection from the sun, made of driftwood was erected for the ladies to take their luncheon under, and while they wandered about, we bathers started off in another direction, and in a few minutes were floundering in the wonderful Dead Sea waters. I had not been acccustomed to bathing in the Dead Sea. I never did it before; consequently I was considerably enlightened and very much fooled. Instead of going in quietly and keeping my face and lips out, I went in the old way with a run and a " header."

I didn't want to dive any more that day.

The brine seemed to enter every part of my face and eyes like needles, smarting till I howled again. The greatest surprise was, that in my dive I didn't get under water, but only got my head and half my body below the surface, then floated like a nautilus on the top. When striking out, my feet flew clear of the water; it was an effort in such a position to keep the mouth out of it, so the easiest way was to lie on one's back and kick. Progress, owing to greater density, was much slower than in ordinary sea water—a great deal of propulsion going for nothing—like the screw of a steamer when it gets out of water in a storm. It would be perfectly practicable to rig up a small sail to the feet, lie on the back and cross the lake without a motion—fast asleep if need be. When immersed up to the chest, it was impossible to stand on the bottom, as the feet would rise to the surface, and the trial felt like endeavouring to tread down a life preserver in fresh water. After getting full of salt we did not feel the smart so much, and tried swimming under water but found it quite impossible. After enjoying this sport for a long time we dried ourselves reluctantly on the beach, feeling no enervating result from our prolonged bath.

We did not perceive the fetid odour of the air spoken of by travellers, which **is said** to be caused by exhalations of sulphuretted hydrogen from the neighbouring springs. We did not see the birds that flew over the water drop lifeless **into it, as** ancient popular credulity would have us believe, under the influence of the supposed destructive properties of the atmosphere to animal life. We could not peer down through the waters and **see** the submerged cities, as Josephus maintains could be done in his time. The heat was not oppressive, but, on the contrary, we revelled in the genial warmth after the cold weather in the high lands. No sticky feeling was experienced after bathing, and no saline incrustations on the bodies discomforted us in any way. One would think that the people came out perfect pillars of salt, to listen to the narratives of different writers concerning the waters, **and I** am inclined to think most of them took other people's stories rather than their own experience. The water was perfectly transparent, and chemical analysis, which I forbear to give, shows that the Dead Sea **is** not saturated with common salt, as is generally supposed, but contains more largely the salts of lime and magnesia. The taste, which **is** bitter, saline and pungent, owes its caustic qualities to **the** presence of bromine, and the taster generally suffers from excoriation of the palate after making his first and last experiment.

No doubt our visit was made at the most propitious time of the year; many of the drawbacks to enjoyment, which are felt during the summer solstice, being thus escaped. The enormous evaporation which takes place must then be very oppressive; the locality must be like **a** vast chaldron, boiling fevers enough to kill the world.

Enclosed by lofty mountains, and placed so much below the ordinary level of the land, where no cooling breezes can penetrate, the atmosphere must be as deadly to life as the exhalations of the fabled Upas tree. It has been estimated that the Jordan alone empties over 6,000,000 tons of water daily into the sea, and the stream which in some seasons rushes down the Kidron valley, and several other tributaries add considerably to the volume of the lake, so that some idea can be formed of the evaporation going on from this huge boiler. The officers of the American expedition of discovery found the lake to be forty miles long and eighty-nine wide, and their observations and soundings dispelled many of the delusions concerning it.

Instead of being bottomless they found that its greatest depth was only 1,300 feet, and they discovered no trace of any ford, which supported the theory concerning the flooding of the cities of Sodom and Gomorrah. It was supposed that this ford, or belt of land rising from the bottom of the lake, formed the barricade, and was one of the limits in ancient days of a lake much smaller than the present one; and that the overflowing of this bank caused the cities of the Pentapolis, built on the plain below, to be submerged. They made no discovery of any outlet to the lake, and its being much lower than the Mediterranean or the Red Sea dissipated any ideas about subterranean canals or the like. Lieutenant Lynch, who commanded the expedition says:—"We know that the Almighty usually operates with secondary causes; and it may be that volcanic agency, as has been presumed, was the physical instrument employed by Him in this case; that the salt sea was formed by the subsidence of the plain, or from the damming up of the Jordan by a current of lava, or both combined; and that the showers of fire and brimstone were occasioned by the fall of volcanic ejections. But the most reasonable supposition is, that, simultaneously with the fire and brimstone rained out of Heaven upon the doomed cities, volcanic eruptions took place; that the slime pits, or pits of bitumen according

to the version of the Septuagint, **with** which the plain
was filled, were inflamed, and that the combustion of the
soil on the underlying strata was followed by the subsidence of the plain."

That seems to be the cleverest and most probable
theory I have ever heard of, the volcanic appearance of
the country, the peculiar formation of the hills and the
abundance of igneous elements to be seen in the region
fully supporting the supposition.

After lunch a fine galloping ground lay before us for
miles on the plain where the ground was dry, whilst in
places, where covered with low bushes, it sometimes became muddy **and** slippery.

Game abounded in all directions **where** the water lay
upon the ground from the recent rains, and to "flush"
the birds it was necessary almost to step upon them. As
our popping revolvers did very little damage among the
feathers, and feeling desirous of examining the brilliant
plumage of the birds around us, we offered the guard **a**
franc to fire his gun at them. He "fixed it up" for about
ten minutes, arranged the flints for five minutes more,
wrapped himself timidly around the gun, and took aim
for an **eternity**, but no report followed when he pulled
the trigger. **He** tried **it** again and aimed longer to make
sure of its going off, but **to** be short, after trying nine or
ten times he gave **up**, saying it was a very fine gun, but
Allah wouldn't let **it go** off.

Along the flats **we** passed the saline incrustations and
flakes of bitumen lying on the surface in the moist ground,
and saw footprints of some beasts, probably jackals, or
possibly panthers, which are said to infest the wild
ravines and desolate places of Palestine. Now the wild
geraniums were growing in rich luxuriance up to our
knees as **we** rode through their pathless beds, the broad
leaves clinging **to** our leggings and the horses tearing
away large mouthfuls of the juicy herbage growing so
temptingly under their noses. In this locality, close to
the Jordan, the robber bands of Bedawins, crossing the
river from the land of Bashan, generally make their

attacks upon unwary travellers, and no better spot for an ambush could be imagined than here, where a whole army could be concealed under the bushes. In my ignorance of the fact I was enjoying a swinging canter through them when Floyd came behind and told me to keep a bright look out or I might suddenly be minus everything; and that he had come forward himself as an advance guard to make sure of no attack being made from concealed enemies. While we pioneered the way, there was an exhilarating spice of danger about it as he told of two encounters he had had with Bedawin in taking other travellers through; and that on one occasion the very guard we had with us proved his courage by galloping off to Jerusalem, after which, the party he was then prorecting saw him no more.

So concealed was the river by the thickly-growing trees that it was not till we were actually upon the banks that this most interesting of flowing waters burst upon our view. There, swirling past the willows hanging gracefully over the stream, shadowed by the weeping branches that gently tipped the rippling waters, reflecting its grassy banks in mingled hues of brown and green, flowed the ancient Jordan; honoured and most blest of waters, sole river of the land, whose unchecked course has, ever since the Saviour of mankind was laved between its banks, murmured on and on through all the ages past! No changes wrought upon its banks, no desolation by fire and sword, no scenes of sorrow, woe and death did aught to mar the sparkle of its flow; beautiful now, as when Moses from Pisgah's top, let his desert-weary eye rest gladly on the silvery wandering stream, threading its way through the Land of Promise, to which tantalizing Elysium he was ever to be a stranger.

For ages it has rivalled the Nile, both as to mystery of its source and the annual overflow spoken of by Joshua irrigating its banks. Disappearing from view in one place, bursting from a rocky cave in another, swiftly following its tortuous path past its banks of waving flags and oleander, its fields of mulberry and olive, of vine and waving grain; lingering about Bethsaida and Capernaum, kissing the foundations of Tiberias, again it takes its rapid course and passes wild and gleeful at our feet, careless and heedless alike of its grave in the Dead Sea each moment drawing nearer.

The spot on which we stand shows no trace of man, save a few charred sticks, where the Arab's kettle has simmered on the beach; not even a broken vessel marking the spot where thousands yearly come to cleanse themselves in the holy waters.

They appear as by magic at the banks on the anniversary morning of the Saviour's baptism. Every nationality is suddenly seen; all at once every tongue is heard on the silent banks; they come down by torch-light over the hills, "dwellers in Mesopotamia, in Judæa, in Pontus, in Asia and in Egypt, strangers of Rome, Jews and Proselytes, Cretes and Arabians," as, "when the day of Pentecost was fully come, they were all with one accord in one place." Here they rush into the water together in their long white dresses; men and women both dipping themselves three times in sign of the Trinity, and carrying their offspring between them to let their sins be borne away on the rushing stream, so that they may start in life unburdened by sin and regenerated by the purification of the holy waters. As soon as the dipping is over, all gather together their things and disappear in the same mysterious manner in which they came, leaving nothing more than footprints on the sand to mark their flying visit. It is said to be generally the scene of much trouble and fighting, as one would naturally expect from the congregation of thousands of Christian fanatics; each sect having, at that time, their religion uppermost in their minds, and ready to fight at any time in their zeal to maintain their own creeds and opinions.

As to the source of the Jordan, which was long in doubt, Josephus makes the following remarks, which need but little further comment:—" Now Panium (Banias) is thought to be the fountain of the Jordan, but in reality it is carried thither in an occult manner from the place called Phiala, which indeed hath its name Phiala (vial or bowl) very justly, from the rotundity of its circumference as being round like a wheel, and as the origin of the Jordan was not known it was discovered when Philip was Tetrarch of Trachonitis ; for he had chaff thrown into Phiala, and it was found at Panium, where the ancients thought the fountain head of the river was, whither it had been carried by the waters." (De. Bell. Jud., cap. IX.)

My fellow pilgrims were determined to bathe in the Jordan, so the ladies were accompanied by dragomen and attendants across the plain of Jericho, while one of the guards and Mahomet, the head waiter, stayed to guide us to the camp after the bath. We had yet a long ride before us, so we made as much haste as possible in getting in and out of the water. For my part, I had had enough bathing for one day, and it was only to keep the others company that I went in. It was very shallow and rapid, and the banks and bottom were composed of slimy mud, which oozed up around the feet unpleasantly ; we could not help thinking that when the thousands of pilgrims waded in here, the mud stirred up must have been very disagreeable to those a little way down the stream. As it was we came out very much dirtier than we went in, the refreshing effects of the bath in the Dead Sea were neutralized, and the pores filled with mud instead of salt. Many brought away tin bottles of water for baptisms and other ceremonials, but I contented myself with retaining a large quantity of Jordan mud, which was easier to take than to leave behind.

Ten miles stretched between the river and the camp at Jericho, whither our course lay. A farewell glance at the meandering stream, half secreted by the waving ferns and osiers, where, whispering softly to the white fringy asphodel, it gurgled on past the grassy floating tresses and water lilies that would fain join in the merry ramble over the shallows before us ; a last review of the place where the Children of Israel* "passed over right against Jericho,"

---

* Joshua iii. 16.

with Joshua at their head, when the river was divided for the dry passage of the ark of the covenant, and the waters were heaped up beside the City Adam, near Zaretan, and then we went off.

We looked high and low in vain for all the cities and places named as being near here, and conjectured that this was probably the place where Elijah clove the waters with his mantle, whilst in company with Elisha, previous to his ascension in the fiery chariot,* for it is the nearest part of the river to Jericho.

The great plain of Jericho is an expansion of the plain of the Jordan, the name including also the Plains of Moab, on the east side of the river.

The soil is evidently very rich, and its fertility has been described in every age. Josephus calls it a divine region, and speaks of its groves of palm trees and beautiful gardens; and Jericho is spoken of in several places in the Bible as the City of Palms. A solitary remaining palm tree, shown to travellers of late years as a relic, and the sycamore tree that Zacchæus climbed into to see Jesus pass, have also disappeared with all their kind. You remember that Zacchæus was the chief among the publicans and a rich man, and when he could not, on account of the press of the multitude, see Jesus, for he was short of stature, he mounted into the branches, where Jesus saw him and told him to come down, for he would abide with him that night.

No cultivation is ever attempted here, as the marauding Bedawin would always take the harvest when it was ready to be gathered in, and the only production of the soil is a thorny bush, the myrobalanum, which the Arabs call *Zukkum*; and no regular road now leads across the plain, the mountains of Benjamin forming the land mark to guide the traveller to the site of Jericho through the sinuosities of the prickly paths.

After borrowing some tobacco and a pipe, which he never returned, our valiant guard put a bit into his horse's

---

* II. Kings ii. 84.

mouth and showed his manœuvres, which were rather tame, as the animal he bestrode was tired with the day's ride; then he got very confidential and pleasant, and tried to borrow a few more things, after which he disappeared altogether; so we were left to "go to Jericho" our own way. Mahomet, who had crossed the plain a long time before, still was with us, but it was getting very dark, and the mountains seemed to be getting further away than ever. We forded a stream that was descending from the highlands with a rush that nearly carried our horses away, and soon after we came upon the Arab village, which is identified with the ancient Gilgal. It was a wretched place, built of mud huts, and lighted up by a few fires blazing about, from which a number of Arabs sprang up suddenly on our approach, shouting among themselves and brandishing their guns in a way which was more fantastic than terrifying. However, Mahomet explained that we wished to reach Jericho, and promised a reward to any one who would conduct us there. We numbered about seven or eight, all young and well mounted, and after thinking it over they concluded that they would get more money by serving us than by attempting an attack; so several started off in front with their guns slung over their backs, to guide us to the camp.

In truth, it was a strange ride we had that beautifully soft night. We had come into thickets of flowering bushes and blossoming plants that emitted, in the evening air, an indescribable aromatic perfume that fully realized for us the "spicy breezes" of poetry. Once or twice we passed encampments of Bedawin, with their black tents pitched among the trees, their camels and horses grazing about in the light of the bonfires, forming rare and richly-coloured illustrations of the wandering Arab's life. The women could be seen gathering fuel and preparing wheaten cakes for their evening meal, and the men, ever on the alert, had sprung up on hearing our horses' feet in attitudes of defence, while the children crept frightened into the tents. Moreover, we knew not ourselves whither we were being led; we were aware that the inhabitants of the region bore a bad character, and when the fellows, after answering peculiar signals, led us into an open space, where a score of gaunt rascals, all armed with guns, were standing, it behooved us to keep together and prepare for treachery. Our suspicions may have been groundless, but it must be said, that the appearance of this large armed band, far from an encampment, without any ostensible purpose for their being there, seemed decidedly mysterious. When we reached the camp the tents were all glowing like huge Chinese lanterns with the "bedroom" lights inside of them, the horses neighed in responsive chorus, the mule-bells were tinkling drowsily at the neighbouring fountain, the ladies beamed a welcome in the fire-light, and Mahomet got the dinner bell and dashed around like a maniac to summon us to the banquet in the canopy. Even after our long ride there were few fatigued; the amount of endurance which came to all of us seemed marvellous, and before the journey was ended no one thought anything of eleven or twelve hours in the saddle, and a large part of this chapter was written in the tent that night, in a letter to be sent home.

CHAPTER XI.

OF all the enchanting moments of a traveller's experience, there are always some recollections that stand out as landmarks while he takes a retrospect of the general landscape of his wanderings. There will be some spots over which the pale moonlight of recollection seems to fall with greater brilliancy than over others, some moments of happiness brought about by various circumstances and attributable to numberless secondary causes, when for a moment the soul seemed perfectly content, when the present seemed to fill the future and blot out all the memories of the past. But to these ephemeral periods the mental eye ever reverts with such undiminished clearness of vision, to these enjoyable spots the perception returns with such vivid intensity, that instead of the luminous but shadowy radiance of the night into which the whole has passed, we rather discern every feature in the view with the gorgeous sunlight of the day, that not only shows all the elements, but penetrates the obscurity of the minor fillings in of the picture in the mind. So transient are these feelings of fullest content, these instants of great quiet happiness that in their utter peace seem almost to approach ecstasy, and so begotten are they by apparently trivial circumstances, that we sometimes scarcely realize their presence before they have slipped away into the past, eluding the analysis we would subject them to; and **we** know not whence they came, but merely feel the void left by the fleeting luxury we would fain prolong. This momentary state of mental felicity is perhaps the truest and most unalloyed happiness we are permitted to enjoy in this world, evidently but a glimpse **of the** bliss contained in the **next,** given to us to feel **the** unfathomable depth of the pure happiness we are heirs **to, and** to make us sensible of its superiority **over** the pleasures **of** the senses with which man would seek to beatify life.

A strain of music wafted through the aisles of **a cathedral will** often arrest and hold fast the listener's attention, and may, while he connects it in some way with his own thoughts, transport him far from all surroundings. On the solitary midnight watch of a yachting cruise, when the vessel, obedient to the power he wields, foams through the heaving waters, straining under her canvas, and leaving a seething streak of white behind her; when the moon, shining out from behind a fleeting cloud, lights up both boat and snowy canvas, and the toppling crested waves pursuing, one may feel this sense of utter happiness. But, when we awake in the gaily decorated tent at Jericho, and find the flowers growing up and blossoming profusely around our bed, and while lying at the canvas door gaze down upon the vast plain, seeing Pisgah and the peaks of Moab tipped with the roseate hues of the rising sun, we are apt to feel it again. The limits **between** the dreamland and reality seem vague and **undefined.** Yet, we are not sleeping. The misty clouds **of** slumber have passed away with those arisen from the plain now clearing the heights of Benjamin behind us, and the body and mind refreshed and invigorated, drink in the scene with the dewy fragrance of the morning air.

It is a matter of minor import to us whether we are encamped upon the site of old Jericho or half a mile one way or the other. We know that there are no extensive ruins here to identify the place, and rejoice in the very fact that there are none. We know that the locality is marked by its proximity to an overhanging cliff, as described by Josephus, and that it is so many furlongs from Jerusalem and so many stadia from somewhere else, but there is no inclination to get up and try to change the supposed site by personal discoveries. We would perhaps drop off to sleep again, but for the ominous and hated sound of a tin pan being struck, announcing the approach of "tintom," and we get under the bed clothes to escape the din created by the servants as they rush around the camp, having a deep set presentiment that soon, at the tooting of another horn, our present snowy Jericho will have fallen to the ground, as it did in Joshua's time, and vanished so that its site should not be known.

After Joshua burnt the city, the Israelites pronounced a curse upon it, "Cursed be the man upon the Lord that riseth up and buildeth this city Jericho, he shall lay the foundation in his first born, and in his youngest son shall he set up the gates thereof." But we find it rebuilt by Hiel the Bethelite in spite of the prophetic malediction, and, as recounted in Kings, he laid the foundation in Abiram his first-born, and with the gates thereof perished his youngest son, Segub. It is also known that several towns were built so near that the advantages of the old Jericho could be enjoyed, without incurring the curse connected with it.

The Arab village of Rihah, lying down in the plain which we came through last night, is supposed to be the Gilgal, where the Israelites made their first encampment in the Promised Land under Joshua, and where the Ark and the Tabernacle remained for so many years after the conquest. Near by, springing from the mountain side, is the fountain of Elisha, which was sweetened by his cruise of salt; its course through the rock, where we see it, seeming to have been cut by hand. Doubtless, the ample water-power has turned many an ancient mill long since disappeared from here; and in this sharpened cleft the waters gained new force to turn the wheels of those further below. Doubtless, the vast stores of golden grain, that supplied the great cities of the plain, for ages found their way up here to be crushed between the revolving stones of the ancient mills; and if again "the wilderness and the solitary place shall be glad for them; and the desert rejoice, and blossom as the rose," this very fountain may be re-utilized. How different would be the appliances and machinery used if ever the land was repeopled and cities flourished as of yore in the plain below! How incongruous would the rattling thunder of modern steam-power seem with all our ideas of the quiet land of Bible story, and how impossible it is for one who has been stricken with its intense stillness and solitude to associate in his mind the bare idea of such events with the country he has passed through.

We were entertained by a Bedawin dance late at night while at Jericho. While writing at my portfolio I heard some strange noises, and left the tent to find a troop of wild-looking creatures assembled for their barbarous native dance, which, in the pale moonlight, seemed unnatural and even weird. I suppose they were the same rascals that we had seen on our approach, who now had come into the camp, under this pretext, to steal anything they could lay their hands on; but whether they were the real Bedawin or inhabitants of Rihah I cannot say. They were large active men, some bare-headed and others with the keffieh and the circlet of camel hair rope upon their head, while their scanty ragged "abbas" failed to cover their bare legs below the knees. Chanting a monotonous grunting song or chorus, that seemed to excite them amazingly, they clapped their hands, stamped their feet, and, formed in a semicircle, went through their antics around the Sheikh. He stood in the centre of the band with a drawn sword in his hand, and as they swayed their bodies incessantly to and fro, grunting their frenzied ejaculations, he answered them with similar sounds and motions until they all rushed in upon him, while he threw himself into a crouching and picturesque attitude of self-defence. This was repeated several times, and so amused the Arab servants, who understood it, that several joined in the dance.

To our ears the chorus **was** discordant, guttural and monotonous, like the sounds emitted by some beasts, and, in fact, all Arab **songs are** completely wanting in harmony and variation **of melody.** Eastern nations altogether lack appreciation **of our music,** while the nasal discordances and squeaking sounds of their's stir them into rapturous ecstacy, and strains that are excruciating to our nerves affect the deepest fountains of feeling in their hearts.

Music always seems to keep pace with the degree of civilization of the country from which it emanates; the more refined the religion and habits of a people, the sweeter are the outpourings of their elevated souls and ennobled minds. I believe that music is the gift of God to His people, and that as Christianity progresses harmony will increase, till it reaches nearly to that excellence which we hope some day to hear from golden harps and winged choristers.

There are many things by which the progress of nations, and even individual men, can be judged—music is, perhaps, among the greatest of these. The barbarians will have barbarous instruments becoming less degenerate as civilization makes its inroads upon them; even two sticks knocked together satisfying some of the most degraded of them, and, I think, the man who has no appreciation of melody in his heart should be watched, if not shunned altogether. We can in this way reconcile ourselves to the appellation of David, when he is called " the sweet singer of Israel." He sang the praises of the Most High, and was favoured of all men in His sight. The country was more densely populated in his day, and though we do not learn that the ancients were more enlightened than the present inhabitants, yet we are led to suppose that festivals and performances of worship which naturally called for music were scenes of greater refinement than at present. Otherwise we would be compelled to believe that David **was as bereft** of the elements of music as any Bethlehemite of the present day. Why, Beethoven, as an itinerant musician, would not take a piastre here, whereas a fourth-rate negro minstrel could literally take Jerusalem by storm, by "bringing down the house" of each inhabitant.

We were sorry to leave the warm climate of the plain to ascend the mountains, where overcoats again would be necessary, but up we had to go, clinging to the horses manes, and sometimes alighting where it would be dangerous to ride even an Arab. From each summit of Benjamin the retrospect became more extensive as we ascended higher and higher into the colder atmosphere. Great distances could be seen both up and down the plain of the Jordan, carpeted with flowers and feathery bushes, and enamelled with all the colours of a Florentine mosaic. Jericho and Gilgal lay at our feet, and across the undulating expanse, the Jordan shambled through its willowy banks; and the mountains of Moab, with Pisgah in their midst, limiting the view, were brightened in colour by the morning sun. No trace of those cities of the plain was seen where, to the south, the Dead Sea rippled on, scintillating gaily, as if unconscious of the story buried in its depths. One view of Olivet in the distance was seen, then a long ride over the hills followed, passing Rock Rimmon whither the Benjamites fled, and leaving it on the right-hand, we soon came to Ai, whose name is familiar to the Biblical scholar.

Now one would be supposed to linger about Bethel, the scene of Jacob's dream, the place where one of the golden calves was erected, and about which we sing loudly at home when the hymn is pitched in a key to suit our voices; but there is now little to arrest our attention among the ruinous dwellings, and when again I sing "Bethel I'll raise," I will know what a hard time of it may be expected. Yet, on looking back at it, at Bethel, the house of God, my imagination will carry me pleasantly to the spot more from the associations of the hymn than anything else.

> "When like a wanderer, the sun gone down,
> Darkness came over me, my rest a stone."

I will think of it as I saw it in the distance, couched prettily enough upon a low hill, surrounded on almost every side by shallow valleys and green hill-sides, forming a quiet little view, as Palestine landscapes go. The remains of ruined churches and the half-standing walls of ancient houses would perhaps have been interesting, but for the huts built against them, as a sort of lean-to, which, however, superior in capacity they might be to huts of mud alone, created a sort of dread in our minds that they were going to topple inwards on the nest of dirty children at the entrance, and we instinctively took care not to push against any of them in riding through.

I don't think they have any insurance offices in Bethel; they think it's a better policy not to lounge too hard against the walls; and as for fire, a Palestine Fire Insurance Company would never have a loss; there would be no "fire fiends" as in Chicago, because the houses could not be inflamed under the oxy-hydrogen blow-pipe, and they've got no fuel to speak of anyway. Why not have a Head-office for general insurances at Jerusalem, and a branch at Bethel, kept by Abdallah Moostapha, who lives by the old tower? Money you know, would be made like bricks, and if an earthquake came and demolished every structure like a house of cards, then the Head-office could just throw up their hand in the game, and shuffle off a deal quicker than they came.

On going through the first part of the country, there was an encampment made in a wild gorge at Ain el Something, (I don't want to disarrange anybody's jaw, but the Arab name means the Robber's Fountain). The pronunciation resembles the difficulty of arriving at the place itself, situated as it was in an expansion of a long wady, whose passage capped the climax of a dangerous day's ride. We had been climbing along shelving slopes of rocks, wet with occasional rain showers of the day, which rendered them more unsafe than usual, and several horses fell under their riders. One horse slid side-ways about twenty feet down the smooth mountain side, his legs flying in all directions for footing, which, strangely enough, he retained. Of course all got into the way of dismounting frequently, and crawling over the slippery inclines, leading the horses behind us; but the sure-footed creatures got over so much easier than we did, that it was doubtful which was the safer course to pursue.

When we entered the narrow defile, the horses could not be relieved by our dismounting, because the bed of the muddy torrent formed the only path, the rushing water having so washed the earth away from the large stones, that it seemed miraculous how the animals staggered through the knee-deep holes and over the sharp hidden boulders without injuring themselves. On sighting the tents, however, they again pricked up their ears and were quite ready to throw dust at the very wind in a scamper across the more level approach to the camp, where, on arrival, I attended as usual to the washing and rubbing down of Timoleon's legs, which never once failed him in the whole journey. I was getting very fond of this little craft —my ship of Palestine; he would follow me like a dog, and seemed grateful for the extra attentions in the way of fodder which I always saw that Cudor his groom gave him; and whilst beneath me, he seemed almost to anticipate my wishes as to his movements.

Hay, and oats and other grain, on which we feed horses, are unknown in this land, and a little chopped up straw is all that the animals receive, in addition to what they can glean from the rank grass and herbage about a camp. Exposed always to the storms of night and day, often tethered on broken rocks, which is not a soft bed at any time, their courage is actually indomitable; many a score of miles being passed willingly before they sink down for their first halt—dead.

A jolly dinner was finished, the last whiff of the tchibook had floated away, and the camp was hushed into slumber by the barks of the jackals, reminding me of similar concerts given by some connections of theirs on the picturesque wood-sheds of Canada, when I was aroused by hearing my name called through the camp. I heard the word "letters" too, which had all the magnetic wakening influence of cold water; but how could letters come, I bethought me, into this fearful glen, whose name we think of with a shudder; was it not a vile disappointment, concocted by the semi-somnolent brain? Was it not a dormant thought connecting ideas of home with the howl borne on the wings of the night breeze? Was it not any other nice idea? No, nothing of the kind! It was a much nicer bundle of realities sent, as the crow flies, by courier, from Jerusalem. I went at them like the fugitive tears at the throat of the blood-hound that has tracked him down (poetical again), and by the light of a candle stuck in a boot I was led through the diagnoses of various peoples' health and a large account of their small doings.

By that waning stump of light I was led through a lot of "stuffy" ball-rooms, where the arsenic from green tarletan dresses was poisonous even to think of; where young men in black clothes, toiling along with their names written in the Sahara of dust on their backs, were supporting figures divinely fashioned but humanely gotup, whose motions were evidently intended to assimilate with their own. The ladies' faces were most immodestly uncovered, and, I almost refrain from adding, they wore the most brazen-looking dresses, puffed, frilled, and furbelowed, and, I believe, those barbarian boots, instead of the demure and proper voluminous trousers, disclosing neat little spangled slippers. Many couples, otherwise goodlooking, had their appearance marred by the mental exertion and carefulness of movement betrayed in endeavouring some outrageous and new-fangled motion, which, as I found, was called the "Boston." It was edifying to find that Mrs. Somebody wore white celestial, trimmed with blue silk hallelujahs (or something else), and that Miss So-and-so wore that eternal pink silk and white cockade sticking up out of a mountain of ill-concealed hair-pads, and that she inquired after me (I always thought the pink silk was very nice). "And, by the way, do you know that she's engaged to that fellow that has something to do with the what-d'ye-call-it department—

at least they've had the most tre-normous flirtation" (on second thoughts, that pink silk *was* getting rather shabby).

Other letters carried me back into Italy, to the friends I made and left there. Once more I was with them, looking **down** from San Miniato over Florence, its huge Duomo, campanili **and** gleaming **Arno**; or, **at** Fiesole, was watching the **sun** set and the glowing hues of day deepening into **softer tints** over the city, till **the** rising moon, presumptuous **at her** warmer rival's descent, usurped the throne in **heaven**, and gathering majesty each moment **as** the other **waned**, imperiously cast long shadows in his diminished **face**, while fickle Florence, bribed with silver, when gold **there was none**, shouted, "*Le roi est mort ; vive la reine.*" Or among the **few** remaining white-clad monks, **we were** sipping their good Chartreuse out at the grand old Certosa, whose grounds, full **of** cypress and olives, resemble **some** regions of the Orient.

In a late work published here **in** Canada, upon the Ojibeway language, the dialect most generally spoken by the Indian of North America, we learn that there is **a** great resemblance between it and the ancient Hebrew.

The similarities are many, both in roots and in the peculiar inflections of the words which serve to express variations of meaning, instead of using prefixes as in our modern English. Would this go to prove any more clearly the long-sustained **theory of** the Redskin in the far West being identical with some **of the** lost tribes of Israel? Would it throw any more light **upon** the origin of the race **that** has peopled our **territories from** time immemorial? **If it** would, there may **ensue a** strange result from the author's labours. Having **some knowledge as** to the penetration of the wandering tribes into Asia, and **their** overrunning the north-eastern part of that portion of the world, it **is not** impossible for us to believe that by the aid of the stepping-stones in the Behring Straits, they may have unwittingly strayed into our continent before the man of Genoa was even prophesied.

As the course of Gipsies, and all nomadic races, is said

to be from west to east, we can, by making all allowance for constant change of climate, and different productions of the various countries they passed through, expect some change in dress and colour of skin; but what great changes have taken place in the habits? Taking the wigwam for the tent is but following the resources of the land, and to this might be traced nearly all the differences. As to religion, a glance at the present generation will suffice to show how that may change with every new creed that makes its appearance; their Great Spirit is the God of Abraham, of Isaac, and of Jacob, who, if the theory be correct, judged them here in Canaan. Where the feathers adorn the head, we may easily imagine the cowl-like covering of the Arab secured by similar fillets; and instead of the flowing "abba" of camel's hair, we have the majestic deerskin "toga" of Cooper's model Indian.

Having stood at Shiloh, these rambling thoughts occur to me. Wonderfully interesting would it be, if we could follow the history of the different tribes which were allotted their portions of land, when Joshua set up the tabernacle there, and made the division by lot of the land subdued before them, among the children of Israel, who had not received their inheritance. "And the men went and passed through the land and described it by cities, into seven parts in a book, and came again to Joshua, to the host at Shiloh," and the records of this survey, as set out in Joshua, have been of much use in determining the sites of many prominent land marks which still serve to limit the tracts given then to the seven remaining tribes.

Shiloh is a curious heap of ruined edifices and stone pillars projecting in every direction from the earth : rank vegetation springs up among the embedded stones, lizards dart in and out of the rocky crevices, and the snakes that warm themselves in the sun are the sole masters of the long-deserted habitations. No Arab builds his mud-roof here where walls of antiquity would give him the best part of his house; not a living creature is seen anywhere within the range of vision; the ground would produce abundant crops, doubtless, but the old prophecy of Jeremiah must be fulfilled. More than once has the prophet compared the downfall of the object of his prediction to Shiloh, "this house shall be like Shiloh, and this city shall be desolate *without an inhabitant.*"

It is a rare occupation to read amongst the ruins of the old city, where the spirit and voice of the Lord so many times descended ; of the peculiar birth of Samuel and Hannah's thankfulness; of the boy's progress in the Lord, and his vision when each time he ran to Eli at hearing the soft voice of Him, at whose whispers we approach fondly as to a father, at whose thunders we stand appalled. Close at hand we have Lebonah, the scene of an occurrence similar to that witnessed in the Campus Maximus, when the Sabine women were detained to brighten the desolate hearths of the Romans. There was a great number of warriors of Israel who, after their many battles, found themselves bereft of the natural home companionship which, through the cessation of hostilities, might be now enjoyed in peace and comfort ; and although four hundred maidens had been captured from the Benjamites at Jabesh Gileah, thousands were yet unmated. So the men were commanded to lie in wait in the vineyards, " in a place which is on the north side of Bethel, on the east side of the highway that goeth up from Bethel to Shecem, and on the south of Lebonah," till the daughters of Shiloh came to dance on the green at the annual feast, when they were to catch each one a wife for himself. This was very satisfactorily accomplished, and as usual, they seem to have made happy chances and choices, and are said to have departed to their respective tribes, rebuilt their cities and dwelt there.

A traveller in Palestine is bound to find out at times, the blessedness of having a shelter and home for protection from all weathers, which dwellers in cities deem nothing more than the ordinary provisions of Providence. In the hot summer he will gladly seek the scanty shadow of the olive partially intercepting the scorching rays that beat down upon the bleached earth and whitened rocks ;

and chancing upon an occasional cave, it is a great relief to be able to infuse new energy into his enervated frame and rest his dazzled eyes gratefully upon the cool sides of the rocky vaults; and in the spring-time when the land looks fresher through the continual rains, he will often look in vain for some temporary refuge, to instil life into the body suffering under the incessant down-pour. He will ride for hours through miry plain or clamber slowly over slippery hills, till the spark of life grows dim within him, before he is able to rejoice in the elysium of a mud hut, and partake of refreshment among the families huddled together inside.

I looked upon the village of Howarah, as the embodiment of every comfort known in the present age; regal were its structures of loose stone, designed of Angelo were the roofs of reed and straw plastered over with mud; altogether celestial were the abodes themselves. We alighted into the mud ankle-deep in the alleys that made some sort of connection between edifices that reared their lofty crests to the height of five or six feet. We judged of human nature more pleasantly while gazing upon a dozen heads of children and old hags appearing at the portals, and it is not necessary to dilate upon the cleanliness or the vestments of people dwelling in such mansions—for as to the former the imagination returns empty-handed from a long flight after the invisible, and the pen lacks power in describing the paucity of the latter. The Sheihk's house had an upper chamber, which was reached by a few stone steps ascending on the outside of an entrance like that of a rabbit hutch, which afforded all the light into the interior, and served as a chimney for the exit of the smoke. There was no Mansard roof on this palatial residence; the noble son of Ishmael dwelleth not under such heathen fabrications; but in one corner of the apartment sat the governor of this well populated village, with a few wives behind him, the youngest of them bearing an infant of which she was intensely and justly proud. Pharaoh, Joseph, and Mahomet, had spread carpets inside, with the lunch upon them, and as soon as we could see through the darkness and smoke, **we fell** to at the sardines and lobsters, much to the satisfaction of the wives, who were curious to know if, how, and what, we did eat. Curious compositions were eaten with strange weapons, which we never carried on our persons, sparkling liquids were poured out from beautiful glass bottles, **which we** actually didn't seem to want afterwards, and shining **cans** with real pictures on them were thrown about by young men with utter recklessness as **to** their value. I got **into** trouble by leaning **in the** dark against something **I took** to be a large pottery kind of bath, which crumbled beneath me, enabling me to take a sitting posture on the floor amid howls of pilgrim laughter. In a moment their wives were at **me,** jabbering away with the **worst** Arabic Billingsgate, and **the** Sheihk, looking to Floyd as interpreter, in a great heat, engendered by the hope **of** gain, exclaimed, " There's a franc gone." The vessel was only made of dry mud compost, but I did not enquire into its value, I only paid the shilling and got out of that window or chimney-door as fast as I knew how, to escape the infernal women ; each Hecate meriting the epithet of Triceps while talking enough for three heads and tongues.

I left Howarah without a sigh.

Mounting into a wet saddle set on a shivering horse, **I** descended into the weary mire and rain, refreshed by my rest yet fearful of its memory, and full of the moral enunciated by one of the camp servants "*guarda del tutte donne, ma specialmente del l'un Araba.*" The distance was not very great from here to Nablous, but it took us a long time to cross the intervening space, owing to the extreme heaviness of the rich loam of the valley which, in the continuous rain, had acquired about the consistency **of** "porridge," offering small support to the horses, and less to the little feet of the mules. We passed these latter poor beasts **as** they were toiling on their way under their immense loads **of** tents, carpets and baggage—heavy enough at all times, **but** when soaked with the rain, perfectly enormous in weight. Many had trunks, which were always crammed with clothes, slung three or four on each side, covered with our tent-carpets, from which burden, very little mule was to be seen; only four emaciated legs taking short quick steps, and here and there a tail could be seen under the moving masses; while in front, the head and neck appeared stiff with the position it was kept in, and the expression of the face was perfect agony. People should take it as a compliment to be told they look like mules, for they have the most expressive countenances of any animals I know; martyrs should take lessons and emulate them—when suffering, they look patient—when oppressed, they look resigned—when helpless in the mire, they look composed and comfortable. In the long string of animals thus following each other, frequent falls would occur, necessitating the assistance of several muleteers to put the beast, now covered with mud, on his pins again; for when once down he is anchored more surely than a tortoise on his back.

I know nothing of the scenery here, but my horse seemed to have a hundred hairs to the inch along the ridge of his mane, which was the only thing I saw while the rain poured off my hat as if the mill-dam of the Deluge had broken away above me.

Floyd stops at a hole sunken in the ground, with no barrier or aught to guard its brink, and as we ride past he says in sterotyped speech, "This is Jacob's well." As we can't get into Jacob's well, it has, at present, no interest in our eyes. We know Nablous is near, and that there are houses there, in which we will stay till cruising in shallow water will not be necessary as a means of progress. We now pass through a wooded valley between mounts Ebal and Gerezim, and chatter loudly through the dripping bazaars of Nablous, where the phlegmatic occupants almost look interestedly at us, and soon we are in a house —yes—in a real house.

CHAPTER XII.

AFTER wading through many a long page of the history of Nablous, and through many a controversy concerning its surroundings, I feel constrained to come back and give the little knowledge I picked up whilst in the town, and keep to my letters as I have only proposed to do. I don't care about inserting other people's opinions, and even if I palmed them off as my own, it might make my little sketch-book savour of the encyclopædia. This is to be a collection of young views of old sites, early impressions of ancient places, unformed ideas of any matters, spiritual or temporal, struggling for expression at the hands of a novice; also let it be a truthful account of what a traveller may now see during his limited sojourn in the land.

If we stop to see what coins the Arab boy is attempting to sell to us, we notice the name of Flavia Vespasian on them, and our curiosity will lead us to find out that these have been in circulation ever since the days when the town was nearly destroyed in the Roman wars, though, probably, for centuries these coins have passed more as " anticos," as the boy calls them, than current money. This old Shecem of Jacob's time was, when rebuilt by the conqueror Vespasian, termed Neapolis, and in honour of the new city and of the Emperor, the coin was doubtless then struck off, and it is remarkable that the name Nabulus or Nablûs, which is an Arab corruption of Neapolis, is almost the only name remaining in Palestine of all the cities that were renamed by the successful invaders from Italy. Situated inland, with no great traffic with the rest of the world, the queer old town lies embedded between its hills of renown, unmoved by the turmoil of other lands, content to rest in stagnation upon the antiquity of its history, and preserving oriental customs and habits more undiluted with European sprinklings than most of the Eastern towns it has been my lot to visit. Like its white-haired old heathen neighbour Damascus, which clings tenaciously to fanatical ideas of religion and custom, it cleaves as hard as ever to its ancient wells, temples and sepulchres, and is justly proud of these spots that must adorn every picture taken of its loveliness like the armorial devices of a time-honoured escutcheon. Like Damascus, it plumes itself on account of the crystal stream that flows through its streets, but its horn is more exalted than that old city's by the beauty of its surroundings. It rejoices in orchards of pomegranate, olive and fig; it gladdens the eye of the traveller as he approaches between the mountains of Blessings and of Curses, and shows well as he sees it for the first time while fording continually the winding rivulet which warbles and chirrups along through the mulberry and orange trees—rivalling the myriad songsters flitting gaily through the pendent boughs. It is one of those few places in Palestine we can look back upon as having numbers of trees about it, remembering pleasantly the rambles through the groves to Jacob's well and Joseph's tomb, and the climb up Gerizim to the old Samaritan temple on its crest.

It is a neighbourhood that exhibits the architecture of every date except the modern. From the same old temple, which, Josephus says, was destroyed one hundred and twenty-nine years before Christ, one may pass to the foundations of Vespasian's structures, or to an old church of the Byzantine style; or may exult in the handsome arched gateways of the Crusaders, built over the limpid stream that dashes through the town. There, where the cool current gushing suddenly into sight forms a useful fountain, the women may be seen washing clothes, soaping and beating them on the smooth stones and rinsing them in the reservoir where the stream dallies for a moment to view the beauties of Nablous.

The fountains, and the gates of an Eastern city, form the most interesting places for the observer to lounge. At the former can be seen the water-carrier filling his unsightly water-skin, the pious Mussulman washing himself prior to devotion, and roguish children dabbling about in the fallen water; and often will be mirrored at eventide the pensive face of some witching Zelica who *by chance* may meet her Azim here.

At the gates of walled cities we find groups of gossiping Arabs, where half the business of the city is argued, *pro* and *con*, over the tchibook in the cool, vaulted archway. If they have a new keffieh they will most likely come here and show it, and if there is a contract to be made, it will be here in open court of all the bystanders, who, by their approving voice or veto, determine the equity of the transaction. In this way, from of ages past, witnesses have been the sole means of enforcing the terms of bargains, as writing was, and is, of course, only known to the scribes. In Genesis we have a most perfect description of an Oriental purchase, when Abraham bought the cave of Machpelah. The bargain was made at the gate of the city in the presence of the children of Heth and all that passed in and out of the city, and Abraham stood up before his dead and said he was a stranger amongst them, and wanted a sepulchre to bury his wife Sarah in, to which the audience, in the usual high-flown language, replied that all their burial places were his. It is yet usual to employ mediators to bespeak the wish of the purchaser to the vendor; he says, " hear me and intreat with me to Ephron the son of Zoar for the cave." Ephron was evidently on the spot, and answers, " the cave is thine, in the presence of the sons of my people give I it thee; bury thy dead." The patriarch, quite understanding that gift, says, " if thou wilt give it, hear me, I pray thee, I will give the money for the field;" so Ephron replies, more to the point than usual, but still regarding price as of no consideration, "My Lord, hearken unto me, the land is worth four hundred shekels of silver; what is that betwixt me and thee? bury, therefore, thy dead." So the sepulchre was made sure unto Abraham by the sons of Heth after the amount "in current money" was weighed out. At the gates which form the Arabs' "Clubs," the Pall Malls of the East, one might witness a similar ordinary purchase at the present day.

Mr. El Karey, the missionary at Nablous is a native, who, having been educated in England and married to an English lady, returned here to promote a good work, which his birth and advantages give him more than ordinary ability to do. Through his innate hospitality, our ladies received many of the comforts of an English home, pleasingly mingled with the internal oddities of an Eastern domicile, and charmingly superintended by English hands. As for us, we had to find our home through a labyrinth of dirty alleys and low archways, where, in a room that served every purpose, except for cooking, which was done outside, we alternately saw the beds made at night and packed away in the morning, and the tables set up and spread with all the celerity of Genii; while at other times we were seated round a glowing charcoal fire built in the middle of the damp ground floor. There was an upper room which we endeavoured to sleep in, but the rain came through the mud roof to such an extent that it would have been better to stay outside altogether than try it again.

A handful of the Samaritans still remain in the vicinity, continuing their old religion in all its aged forms; their church, which is the only Samaritan Church in the world, is doubly increased in interest by an ancient copy of the Pentateuch. These five books of Moses, written in manuscript, and bound heavily in gold or brass formed to roll up the scroll as it unwinds from one roller to the other, have traditionally been in the hands of this sect for three thousand years; but, as Mr. El Karey said, they are probably not more than one thousand five hundred years old.

It was amusing to visit the Mahometan school where heathenism is nourished, and where the smooth faced young dogs, as hypocritical as their fathers, gabbled off their Koran in a loud sing-song tone, while slyly glancing at us they thrust their hands round the desks and lowly whispered "backsheesh;" and then to pass to the mission school for native girls, where they teach in Arabic the truths of Christianity, and try to elevate the intellect of the benighted female youth of the country, and make them more conscious of the true sphere in which woman should walk.

This is all very interesting, only it is a pity that teachers try to make them sing "God Save the Queen" and "Home, sweet home." For however animating the former may be at times, when one would chance to hear it among strangers, and however prone the latter is to dip into our wells of feeling and bring a sympathetic tear to the surface, we had some conservative ideas of harmony concerning the songs that would suffer no reform. Although far enough away from home to weep a little weep if our heartstrings got in any way relaxed, it could not be perceived that to any person's eye the unfamiliar strains fetched the drop of sorrow. Not a *fetch* did I feel as I quietly withdrew. Some other fellows came out too, but they came to see two girls who were standing in a neighbouring casement, to satisfy their curiosity as to the costumes of our ladies. They were living beings to whose beauty Byron has but faintly given expression. They wore the golden dowry given them at their birth upon their luxuriant hair, their eyes eclipsed the Genoese, their dark olive complexions were warmed by the sunset's deepest hues caught and laid upon their cheeks; the damask lip, arched as Cupid's bow, shot an unerring dart whenever a smile relaxed its tension, and flowing vestments clothed the rounded forms whose unrestrained undulation they but ill concealed. I wanted the boys to come away, but they wouldn't—so I stayed too.

Don't go to live permanently in Nablous. It had been raining every day for five months when we were there, and the houses, made of mud and stone, were falling in on every side of the streets, creating many accidents and causing considerable loss of life. The remedy adopted by the authorities, however, was almost worse than the evil of the general misfortune. If any of the houses looked as if they might soon fall, the families were turned out of them perforce into the streets to find shelter and homes elsewhere, none being provided for them. This occasioned the most lamentable street scenes; men, women and children were ejected into the rain, and the houses knocked down to prevent their revisiting them. Women were crying in the streets and leading their homeless shivering children into the arcades of the bazaars for shelter, the men fought like devils to retain all their goods, which the unsympathizing bystanders would also help them to lose; but the authority of the Sultan, no matter how far down it is deputed through officials, always wields a terrible and most effective persuasive power. The Arab woman would live in the house that had sheltered her so long, and where her children had been born and brought up, till it dropped rather than leave it, but as, in her loud remonstrance, the brutal lash winds round her tender form, she is constrained to lead away her children in a misery and anguish too utter and complete to witness without emotion.

We did not leave Nablous without remembering Mr. El Karey's mission and leaving our mites to aid him in the propagation of the seed of Christianity now sown in the jungle of Mahometanism; but as an edict, which we see has lately gone forth from the marble palace on the Bosphorus, for the prohibition of all Christian schools in the Sultan's dominions, will probably suppress this worthy object of aid and encouragement, we may now look for no further notice of the progress of the work. And after all, limited and weak as the strength in operation is and must ever be in comparison with the odds in opposition, is it not doubtful whether the mere sprinkling of the Gospel which they could only receive, would prove a blessing or a bane to the recipients?—certain it is that it would unfit them for the society of their fanatical neighbours; certain it is, that it would create dissensions and strife among such members of families as did not believe, and, isolated **as** they are from all **intercourse** with the world, their zeal would diminish through want of example and encouragement, for which they could look alone among themselves. Besides, looking at Islamism for a moment, in a **broader** light than is permitted by our church, which **denies that** a good **man** will go to Heaven if he does not believe in Christ, before we denounce entirely **the** writings of that wise man who wrote the Koran, and **afterwards took the title of** prophet, we should make **an** insight **into the** good precepts and sensible exhortations **contained in** that book which **is so** subtly suited to the minds **of** the people to whom **it was** addressed, and notice what good work **it** has wrought in overthrowing Polytheism. It has been the conclusion of one of the most approved writers in England on the subject, "That Islam will never give way to Christianity in the East, however much we may desire it, and whatever good would result to the world, it is difficult to believe; but it is certain that Mohammedans may learn much from Christianity and yet remain Mohammedans, and that Christians have something at least to learn from Mohammedans which will make them not less, but more Christian than they were before."

It is owing to the monstrous traditions, and to the overpainted legends concocted by the priests of Mahometanism, which are brought in nearer connection with our passing glances at the religion than the real benefits to be derived from it, that constitute a great part of our prejudice. We naturally judge of religions by what we see of them. Rationalists exclude themselves from all churches, seeing no **reason** for the rites performed therein; Protestants recoil from Romanism because of the ceremonies they see in the churches, and Romanists look down at the Protestants with holy horror from the ancient throne where the king is not so despotic as of yore, while many endeavour to strike the happy medium and dabble in bold religions to find an exit for their zeal. And so with

J

every other religion on the face of the earth, but can any single one be shown where the Almighty is worshipped, either in Trinity or Unity, where there is no restraining influence from evil, and where there is no encouragement to virtue and good works; where the people are less happy in their religion than in any other, or where a man cannot be a good one if he is so inclined. The bigot must be either an ignorant or a calculating man; either his views can only run in one groove, or he makes them run there for the bettering of his own ends. We cannot but see the good in every religion, no matter how different the creeds may be from our own; and while not putting Islamism on a par with our own, I think we might, at least, spare some of our commiserating pity. We submit, of course, that we have the right anchor down, but then, is there not good holding-ground every where in the broad roadstead of religion?

After taking this little sail out of our course, let us round up at that village standing on a hill like an island in the green expanse. It is Samaria. After you have climbed about six hundred feet and wound around the miserable village that now crowns the hill, just sit down on that broken fragment of pillar, and while resting yourself look over at the blue Mediterranean miles away to the west. Never mind the descendants of Gehazi who yet haunt the spot where their ancestor was stricken with leprosy, they will only sit on their haunches and beg at a distance. Of course you know who Gehazi was? but if, in pitiable ignorance, you don't, just remember that he was Elisha's servant who, when the Naaman I told you of before was healed of leprosy, thought he would exact the doctor's fee for himself. So he ran after Naaman, and said his master had sent him for some money and two suits of clothes for some guests of his. After Gehazi received them and had got them safely concealed in his house, Elisha asked him where he had been, and, like one caught after stealing garments off a clothes-line, he said he hadn't been anywhere. Then Elisha, for his sin, gave him the leprosy of Naaman (which he might have got eventually by wearing Naaman's clothes). "And he went out from his presence a leper as white as snow."

There, to your right, are the long colonnades where the pillars stand a considerable distance out of the ground, though imbedded by much accumulation of ruined cities. While walking through the interior of the temple whose proportions are so well delineated by the rows of pillars which nearly all remain, does it not strike you how mighty must have been the edifices when they were complete? You notice that the pillars are weather-beaten and have lost the capitals that would give some notion as to the style of the architecture; can you not picture in your mind the majestic roof covering your head or admitting a broken sunlight through an aperture subtly and beautifully designed by the ancient architects to shed the light of heaven on the shrines below! Or if, instead of a temple, it was the Aula Regis of Herod, who is supposed to have been the founder of all the ruins here, can you not imagine the dread Judgment Seat at one end, where the cruel king, surrounded by his still more heartless satellites, pronounced grim sentence on the culprits chained together at the other? And if I pointed sneeringly at the unadorned columns, saying that they were erected during the infancy of art, would you not reply:—then it is the infancy of Hercules where the power that crushed the serpent in the cradle is apparent in every pillar before us?

An incident is recorded of Samaria by Josephus, which illustrates vividly the sufferings the people underwent during the time when Elisha dwelt there. It seems that Benhadad, king of the Syrians, made an expedition with a great army against King Joram, who, doubting his own strength in battle, shut himself up in Samaria, and trusted to the strength of its walls. The Syrians laid siege and resolved to starve the Samaritans into subjection. While walking around the walls to see for himself that no treachery was going on, while the people were in such straitness that an ass's head sold for four score pieces of silver,

Joram was accosted by a woman, who said, "Have pity on me, oh Lord." He, having no food himself, rebuked her, but she said she only wanted his justice, for she had made an agreement with another woman, in their awful hunger, that they would live upon their offspring. She said I have killed my son the first day, and we lived upon him yesterday; but this woman will not do the same thing, but hath broken her agreement, and hath hid her son." In this, and in many other accounts, Josephus resembles the language of the Bible* so much, that one might almost think that he had "cribbed" the story as I have done from him. No doubt Joram had a hard case to decide. As he felt the pangs of hunger, he could find some compassion for the unnatural woman he might otherwise have recoiled from. Very likely the woman committing the breach of agreement was as greatly culpable in his eyes as the murderess herself, and, perhaps, if it had been anything else than enforcing a fulfilment of a bargain for human life, it would have been carried out, but however that may be, the king was exceeding wroth, and called upon Elisha to pray harder for deliverance.

Without going further into Elisha's prophecy of immediate succour, and the sudden influx of provisions which he predicted would come in and be sold for almost nothing, what a well-known reflection Joram's application to God, through Elisha, leads us into! How naturally and instinctively do we turn to God when we feel weak and "unable of ourselves to help ourselves;" when our strength is reduced on the bed of fever to that of an infant's, and the stubborn conviction that we can get on tolerably well without other aid dissipates into nothingness; when we feel that no money, no friends, no determination of our own to get up and *be* well will avail us aught—how then does the strong man, the self-sufficient atom of the world, humble himself before God! Have you not sat by the sick-bed of some man and seen that it is a hard struggle for him to feel that he is conquered, and that he cannot

---

* II. Kings, vi.

glory in his strength as before? But with the body weak, and the obdurate mind ready to yield its banner of "No surrender," the struggle is a brief one; the man of the world, whom we think has no idea **of** prayer, then finds relief in tears, bitter, bitter tears of penitence. His hands are clasped above his couch for the first time in many years of sin, his body, quivering with emotion, shakes the whole room as the long, silent, wordless prayer **of** agony, of which the pouring tears are the chiefest signs, ascends to heaven; and after that long-deferred communion with God, when he feels the tranquillity of the calm after the storm, and feels that **he** may lay his weak head upon a breast that is able and willing to receive it, when he feels that if for life and its holy joys it were blessed to to live, it were thrice blessed to die thus in confidence in God, is it not difficult to imagine how he will return to sin? We marvel at the children of Israel returning time **after** time to their iniquities, after repeated plagues and admonitions from God, but which of us does not resemble in every particular that vacillating host? Once let strength return, and with it comes the long string of passions; under the armour of resolution sin creeps insiduously; evil insinuates its subtle form under the greaves, and encircles upward **under the** breast-plate of righteousness, and though the intellect may be the last to yield, soon, through the breathing holes in the closed visor the noxious perfume is inhaled, **and** the mind too becomes again diseased, worse than before. These moments are looked back upon regretfully and with sorrow, at again sleeping after being thus awakened, when it is remembered what relief was experienced, and what happiness and contentment was afterwards felt; yet, speak with the atheist for a moment, and **he** will cleverly argue that this turning to God (which he admits **he** might do himself) is but the weakening of the mind prior to death; that it **is** but the drowning clutch at a straw, that the reason, being debilitated along with the body, thus loses its dignity and self command. An unbeliever is **too** often found to be, in many ways, a clever man; but he must either be a braggart that would hide the moments when he was weak in his own views, to boast of his consistency, or he never can have felt the peace of God pervade him when called for in the tone of a challenge to show His power. We sometimes meet men who would utterly argue away all faith if we did not cling longingly to our hope of salvation. Heaven grant that we may always find this straw to clutch, which may prove to be the raft to float us from the burning ship into the horizon we wot not of.

But I find I have got off the track again.

Let us leave Samaria for it has nothing in its history or heroes to call forth admiration. Excepting Elisha, who only visited there, Ahab, who murdered the innocent Naboth, and Herod, who, for a Syren's dance let fall the head of John the Baptist, were the chief actors in the tragedies on this now quiet hill.

But before we mount again, we must enter this picturesque old Gothic church, perched on the hill-side. Here the natives fondly imagine the tomb of John the Baptist now is; and after entering a court-yard in the precincts, we are led down a steep staircase under ground, where the tomb is shown. "John, the son of Zachariah," is engraved at the mouth of the receptacle for the dead body of the baptiser of our Saviour; but he is supposed to have been buried at the other side of the Dead Sea, and even though we see the body itself at Genoa, whither it was removed from here, we doubt a little about this spot.

After lunching as usual in a grove of olives, the weather began to return to its old abuse of us, and made the rest of the day's ride unpleasant. About here we came to a large lake covering a valley which in summer is dried up, and planted with grain and vegetables; but now the road leading through it was quite impassable. Only a few days before some travellers had nearly lost their lives in attempting to ride through it, and so close a "shave" had it been for them, that two or three mules following them never got out at all; so we did not attempt the passage, but took to the mountains, skirting the sheet of water. There was of course not even a goat path to follow; the descents over the shelving rocks made more slippery by the drizzling rain were so slow that we made very little progress towards our destination. When we descended again into the low land, to take the ordinary path as it emerged from the lake, the ground was so soft that it became doubtful whether the animals could struggle through it at all. They laboured heavily and plunged so hard that I thought somebody would certainly be unhorsed; not that this would be anything uncommon, for the pilgrims were rolling off all the time, but because the ground would make it an uncomfortable occurrence for them.

We had again to betake ourselves to the mountain sides, to secure something like a firm footing, and in this way crawled along till night came in upon us, when, after the road diverged to the left along the bed of a stream, we followed its rocky course for an interminable time. How the horses managed to pick their way in the inky darkness, I never knew, the ground was almost undiscernible, and the white splashing water beneath us was our best guide. To give ourselves up to gloom whilst in these circumstances was a natural inclination, but it had to be fought against. I endeavoured to get up a chorus, but it was feeble; so I howled myself, every song, every tune, every snatch of an opera I had ever heard, then went over them all with variations, till I found myself as jovial as a cricket. It was the only time I ever remember my singing being sufficiently appreciated, for several ladies told me afterwards that if it had not been for laughing at it they should have died. The desired effect was accomplished, though perhaps the compliment was doubtful.

We reached Jenin late at night, and got into a house which had one room with a mud roof, and in the literal sense a ground floor, but we had looked forward to only having a cave to pass the night in, so this was only too charming.

We were far in advance of the mules with all the tents and baggage; they had been passed long ago while floundering in the mud, so we just made ourselves busy resuscitating a lady who fainted on arrival, and quietly, very quietly, waited the upshot of events.

Presently, the tinkling bell of the first mule, who had struggled through, greeted our ears. We rushed to the door and gave him a cheer. Even his bray was musical. One by one they all appeared with their faces and bodies covered with the mud, picked up in their many falls by the way, which gave them a most woe-begone appearance.

Then the luggage was unstrapped and carried in, but "Linden (or linen) showed another sight, when the drum beat at dead of night," because most of the mules had fallen in some river, and our portmanteaux were soaked through and through. A pulpy-looking mass was pointed out to me as mine, and by certain marks I found that it was indeed the immaculate Venetian structure that had always looked so nice and cost so little money. I got a friend to help me to carry it in. That trunk made the party jolly—a wild good-humour of desperation pervaded us. I ruefully unlocked it, when it was "flopped" on the floor. But why "renew the unutterable grief?" Handkerchiefs and boots, collars and tobacco, flowers from Gethsemane and relics from Bethlehem, shirts and water colours, pipe tubes and prayer-books, were all amalgamated in a hideous variegated "mush." I found myself murmuring "take it up tenderly, fashioned so slenderly," &c., but could only pour the water out of the boots and despondently lock it up, while the sides fell out in moving it. The tables were put up in no time, and at midnight we sat down to our regular table d'hôte. Towards morning our beds, which we won't call dry, were laid side by side on the floor, while the ladies were taken to another house where like comforts awaited them.

The door had to be left open to admit air to the snoring pilgrims, who each seemed to try to take more than their share of oxygen, and made a tremendous row over the gasping for it; but the open door had one defect: it admitted melancholy dogs and stealthy cats, who walked over us all night. This was very nice for variety, but it got "played out" before daylight, so I astonished one of these nocturnal intruders by **chasing her round the** room over the sleeping forms, helping **her** along with a brass-buckled belt, and I have an idea that that cat made for a sanctuary at Jerusalem when she got out.

Jenin is not a place **of** note. There were **no** biblical or historical events associated with the place that **we** could ponder over, which would have been very acceptable all the next day, for **we had** got into such a ponderous **way** of thinking that we felt the want of our desolate **cities** and magnificent **ruins**. For the latter, however, **I** pondered over my baggage, **and tried** to realize what it had been, and endeavoured **to** find sites for different objects, and to connect them in some way **with** the legends of their once being proud edifices reared in all the majesty of starch. Our most pleasant resort **was** on the house-top, which, according to the Eastern custom, had stone steps ascending to it; it was covered **with** grass, with a **few** vegetables growing on it, but I rather think it was originally intended for a cow pasture.

Jenin is the old Engannim, which means, "fountain-gardens," and if the appellation was as applicable in Joshua's time as it is now, it was well named. The strolls which my chum and I took in the suburbs during the temporary sunlight were very enchanting; crooked by-paths led past cactus hedges with prickly fruit hanging to the uppermost off-shoots in more security from invasion, than a palisaded garrison; through beautiful gardens watered by running streams, where vegetation, hurrying on before the advent of the summer solstice, put forth its almost visible growth, and where, around the majestic old palms, now so scarce in Palestine, the blossoming fruit trees held glistening diamonds pendant to each fragant flower; nor was our enjoyment marred by some hungry-looking rascals who we perceived were skulking behind us all the way, for we did not know till afterwards that Jenin is notorious for its robbers.

Two nights spent in the Arab house were quite sufficient to satisfy us of the internal delights of old Engannim, and we streamed out of the village the next morning, in the bright sunlight, descending into the plains of Esdraelon, called in the scriptures, Valley of Jezreel and Plain of Megiddo. A curious coincidence happened to us here while crossing the vast plain, which served more to bring home all the surroundings of the locality to our minds than perhaps anything else would. When Elijah was praying for rain he prayed upon Mount Carmel, which lay but a few miles to our left, and told his servant to go to the summit and look towards the sea. Each time he went, he returned saying there was nothing to be seen, but at the seventh time he said, "Behold there ariseth a little cloud out of the sea like a man's hand." And he said go up, say unto Ahab, prepare thy chariot, and get thee down that the rain stop thee not. And it came to pass in the meanwhile that the heaven was black with clouds and wind, and there was a great rain, and Ahab rode and went to Jezreel."

Just such another storm swept suddenly from the sea upon us while on this very spot; and, like Ahab, we went to Jezreel, and took refuge behind some of its ancient walls. It was short and sweet; sweeter than anything I can describe; the beating of the hail on any exposed part of the body was absolutely unbearable, and the story in the Bible of so many thousands killed by hail seemed then only too true. Those whose horses were under command rode on for shelter at the ruins, while others were helplessly moored out on the plain with their horses turned tail-wards to the storm. One old gentleman's horse plunged backwards as a clap of thunder went off in his ears, and being unable to extricate his hind feet from the soil, rolled over his rider, endangering his life for some moments.*

And here was the vineyard which Ahab, the King of Samaria, coveted of Naboth, and hard by was Ahab's palace; here the plan concocted by Jezebel for the death of Naboth was put into execution, and here Elijah told

---

* *I was continually afraid of Mr. M—— being hurt, and I was shocked to hear since that, on his return home, he was rolled from his berth in the steamboat and killed.*

Ahab that the dogs should lick **up** his blood in the place where they lapped up the murdered Naboth's, and that they should eat Jezebel by the wall of Jezreel. When Jehu was made king, he slew Ahab in Naboth's vineyard with **an** arrow, and had the body thrown where Naboth sank under the shower of stones.

We know well how Jehu came to the wall of Jezreel, and seeing Jezebel **at a window,** ordered some men **to** throw her down, then **trod** her under his horse's hoofs; and how, becoming compassionate after refreshing himself at dinner, he thought that the cursed woman should be buried, as she was a king's daughter: " but they found no more of her than the skull, and the feet, and the palms of her hands."

While cowering under the massive **wall,** we wonder if this might be the spot where the woman, who was no **better** than **a** Borgia or a Medici, could have been thrown, **and** we admit to feeling a lively interest in the large yellowish dogs belonging to nobody, which lay about the precincts smacking their chops, as if there was a tradition among them that they would again get fed on Jezebels, and leave nothing but the blood-soiled hands, which, like Lady Macbeth's, all the perfumes of Arabia would **not** sweeten.

Close at hand **is the** Fountain of Jezreel, where the camp of the Israelites was pitched, and the brook **where** Gideon chose **his three** hundred warriors from **the ten** thousand that were ready **to fight,** by the way they **lap**-ped the water from the stream; only this few drinking with their hands, while all the others lapped like dogs.

We are now on a battle-field more renowned than Waterloo, we gaze upon the scene **of** more battles than any other **spot** on earth. Alternately, through every age of reckoning, the broad expanse around us has seen the golden corn trodden down and glittering armies worse destroyed. More in number than its yellow sheaves have been the gory bodies piled upon its surface, and many a time have both been clotted together by blood shed for some insane idea. From **the** time when Pharaoh-nechoh came up from Egypt, and pursued Josiah the King of the Assyrians from the Euphrates and killed him here, and doubtless from long before that event, it has ever been justly chosen for the grand trials between foe and foe.

As we look upon the Pyramids after reading of Napoleon's battles, so we look at Gilboa rising to the eastward, where Saul had gathered all Israel together. As we stand in the carriage to catch the first glimpse of Quatrebras, so we rise in the stirrups to descry Shunem where the Philistines were pitched, and with the same interest as in viewing the Campagna and its Tiber, do we dwell upon the similar Esdraelon and its Kishon. The Israelites against the Amalekites and the hosts of Midian, the struggles between different quarrelling tribes, Godfrey against Saladin, when the Cross clashed against the Crescent; gendarme against janissary, when French cannon boomed across the plain, the Egyptian, Persian, and Assyrian—all have filled this plain with nameless graves, and perhaps the only good result of it all is the richness of the crops springing from a land so well fertilized. To my ungeneraled eye I cannot conceive a better battle-ground for fair contests of nations than this plain of Jezreel. What a sight it must have been, when the hosts of the ancients were drawn up in scintillating array, the bucklers reflecting dazzling rays, the shields sparkling, and the restless swords glinting as if blood alone would quench their fire. When the forces of Saul and Jonathan swept down from yonder mountain, what a mêlée must have ensued.

Now, not a tree, no obstacles of any kind interrupt the vision, and the many-coloured valley would, perhaps, be a more advantageous field of battle at the present day, than it was formerly. To be sure, there are mountains over which a general like Bonaparte could secretly bring new forces to swoop down upon his enemy, as the Mamelukes treated him, but there are no habitations to be desolated except Shunem.

Poor old Shunem! I looked in your precincts for one of

the fellow-town's-women of the old Shunamite woman to offer me rest and bread in vain. Nothing tempted me to tarry where Elisha was wont to sojourn awhile in passing. It was indeed a good gift to the **woman** who had often housed and refreshed the prophet when he told her that in her voiceless abode childish **prattles would be** heard, and that little feet would patter **about her aged** husband's knee; nor, **when** this child died, this **precious** boon from God, who, after sitting for hours one **morning** on his fond mother's knee, complaining of his head **and** suffering evidently **from** sunstroke after **exposure with** the reapers, did Elisha neglect **him.** The agony **of the** afflicted **mother** is evident from the haste in which she started to ride to the house of Elisha **on** Mount Carmel. As at the present day, she took a servant **to urge** the beast she sat upon, and having come to Elisha, he sent Gehazi forward with his staff to lay upon the child. **But of** what effect was the prophet's staff **in** the hands of the mercenary Gehazi? The lad slept **on in** death. The soul once severed from its earthly habitation has never **been** called back at once from the Unknown, except God's deputy approached perfection, **or** was divine himself. What passed while Elisha **was** closeted with the dead, none can tell; he **was not** perfection as **a man, but had to** pray long and fervently. We are told he lay **eye** to eye, and hand to hand with the **cold** body, **and as** he stretched himself upon it, God breathed the breath of life through the lips of the prophet till the flesh of the child waxed warm.

Abishag, the fair young Shunamite, who was selected **of** all the land to comfort the aged David, left **no** trace of **her** beauty among these women of her native town; through all the luscious orange-groves which rival Jaffa's excellency, we see no such face as cherished the ebbing life of the old Psalm-singer, and fatally inspired Adonijah with a tender passion. And as we pass on we come nigh unto a place where the gate of a city once stood where there was a dead man carried out followed by his widowed mother. We are at Nain, the same place where the Deity Incarnate, compassionate as perfect man, and potent as to

His origin, was arrested by the sorrow of a woman. In His boundless sympathy He said soothingly to the afflicted mother, "Weep not," and the Father on high, doubtless smiling on His Son, gave him power omnipotent. No long supplication was then necessary as when the prophets raised the dead. "Young man, I say unto thee, ARISE," was the divinely imperious command, and the soul that had fluttered off tremblingly for judgment came fleeing back to earth—to the dust it nearly left for ever. Well might a fear have come upon all, well might they glorify God, saying, "there is a great prophet among us," and well might all who even hear of the miracle glorify the majesty of Christ.

Before leaving this plain of Esdrælon, a retrospect must be taken to gladden the eye and mark well the scene of such varied warfare. Different enough were Gideon's tactics and implements of war to the cannon that lately rumbled over the plain; and yet they were more effective. Strange stratagem was it when the three hundred picked men surrounded the Midian camp by night, and stranger were the arms they carried; each man with a lighted lantern in a pitcher, and a trumpet, and at the signal they broke the pitchers and disclosed the light while blowing a blast and shouting the battle-cry. It was enough! The host below sprang to arms, but, in this uncertain light, imagined the enemy and legions of devils were in their midst, and in their flight stabbed their comrades instead of foes, and thirty-two thousand were routed.

To our left lies Endor, whither Saul resorted in the covert of the night to consult the witch, who, by clairvoyance, so common now-a-days, convinced him of the dead Samuel's presence. Samuel told him (most likely by the witch), that the morrow would see his death. This evidently unstrung the nerve of the giant warrior king, for when wounded on Gilboa in an encounter the next day, he ordered his armour-bearer to slay him, and in a frenzy died on his own sword, when his servant refused to obey him.

And now we are on the banks of the Kishon, "that ancient river, the River Kishon," where Sisera had gathered his multitude of Gentiles and his nine hundred chariots of iron against the children of Israel who, under Barak, were striving to throw off the Gentile yoke. And when the Lord discomfitted Sisera, and all his host, which was put to the edge of the sword before Barak, Sisera escaped to the tent of **Jael, the** wife of Heber who **was a** a Kenite; for there **had** been peace between Sisera's king and the family of the **Kenite. And** Jael induced him to **go** to sleep in her tent, and then approaching him softly **with** a tent pin and the huge **mallet,** which always lies about **a** camp, she drove the nail, as it is called, through his temples. Great is the praise **of** Jael for this action in the song of Deborah and Barak, **and** great **it always has** been, yet it seems to me to be as unwomanly a deed of **dastardly** treachery as ever was recorded. There **was no need for** this premeditated assassination, for Sisera's **army** had been slaughtered to a man, and, as the song says, the River Kishon swept them away; meaning perhaps the dead bodies were floated off, as it is improbable **that** the Kishon **at this** point was ever much greater in volume than when we crossed it. As it was, the rushing water tried hard to carry down our horses, and reached about half-way **up to** the saddle; so that to cross unwet, the feet had to be put up **by** the horses' ears, while those who could not conveniently **do this** were considerably *humid* when they reached the opposite **bank.**

Before us now rises from **the** plain the isolated **Mount** Tabor, with the village of Deborah nestling at the base. Beautiful for situation is this mountain which elevates its lofty cone in truncated form to the height of three thousand feet, from the ruined garrison, said to be built by Josephus, commanding one of the most extensive views of Palestine. " As surely as Tabor is among the mountains, and as Carmel by the sea," is a sort of by-word of Jeremiah, " Tabor and Hermon shall rejoice in thy name " says the Psalmist, **and** from each one's summit can be seen the other's crest. Gilboa and Little Hermon lie away in dreamy transparency to the south, while towards the north the Great Mount Hermon is seen far beyond the Sea of

Galilee. Many have been disappointed to find an old fortress on the flat top of the Mount of Transfiguration, which they imagined as depicted by Raphael, but it is probable that there were ruins here if not a perfect garrison at the time the great event took place. For when Samuel told Saul to go to Mount Tabor, he said, " thou shalt come to the hill of God, where is *the garrison* of the Philistines." *

And it is only reasonable to suppose they built it as a citadel on the summit. All the Christians of Nazareth wend their way up here, once a year, to a ruined grotto with three altars, one for Christ, one for Moses, and one for Elias, built as Peter had proposed, and here praise the Saviour whose face did shine as the sun, and whose raiment was as white as the light. Then, to this spot came that soft voice of the Father, who has ever been heard to speak in a voice neither frightful nor dreadful, but in soft accents of divine love, a voice that would betray fathomless depths of compassion, mercy and love, even if we knew not that such dwelt in His heart. A gush of melody shaping itself into words must have floated over the mountain sides when from behind the cloud came the voice, "This is my beloved Son, hear Him." We imagine it as the soft deep tones of the organ. It is that idea that stays our foot, enchains our interest, and absorbs all thought when from over head rich strains permeate the lonely aisles ; we wonder what possesses us, but it is the voice of God we hear ; notes that speak to us more deeply than any human eloquence.

---

* I Samuel, x. 5.

CHAPTER XIII.

NO more now will I sing of storms and lightning, and tempests raging. The last storm that tried our endurance had been passed through, the elements had got tired of waylaying us and saw that the Hadjis, the pilgrims from the West, could brave and survive the worst humours of Jupiter Pluvius.

Fine weather had now settled in, every day seemed more beautiful than the last, every sun that set seemed more gorgeous than ever seen before, every day's enjoyment seemed more thorough, and every tranquil pipe in the balmy night seemed sweeter than the last. It mattered not whether emerging from the tent by day to pursue the ordinary journey, or whether treading alone the holy ground at the small hours past midnight; all was serene, and contentment reigned supreme within me.

Henceforth I cared not where I was, the daily ride was only a transition from one spot of interest to another of deeper significance. It was enough to be free, to live under the bright sky, and to slumber through the starlit nights under the canopy that gathered the dews of Hermon overhead.

The mackintosh from this time mouldered in the knapsack, and waterproof leggings were ignominiously stowed away in the dilapidated portmanteau, gay white canvas leggings made their appearance, overcoats were forgotten in the daytime, and the red tarbouch shone out resplendent from its folds of gaudily-striped muslin. The riding dress became compact and as it should be; a flannel shirt and collar, and a loose cravat for appearance sake, riding trousers and leggings were all that the ladies exacted to sustain the laws of decency. We had no tents to pitch when we got to Nazareth, for the mules had given out far back on the plain, near Shunem, and the luggage was also lying in the mud where the animals and muleteers had completely lost heart together.

We took quarters in the comfortable Latin Convent, which astonished us dwellers in tents, with airy passages, stone floors, clean bed-rooms and large dining-room. There was a certain novelty in sitting on a wooden chair with a back to it, and at a window with glass in it, although we remembered having done so before, and there was a peculiar charm in getting into a real bed with muslin curtains; one of those Christian arrangements that never sink into the ground by the head, or give way at the foot and leave one half standing up all night. And though it blew hard one night we were surprised to find that no yelling Arabs were about, staying up the house, and driving in the pins to support it. Our own cooking was done in the house, as our French cook was too well skilled in all the witcheries of his profession to be discarded for monastic messes. The same cook, by-the-way, was a "regular brick." He and Floyd rode all the way back on the night of our arrival to where the despairing muleteers were sitting on the still more lugubrious-looking beasts which had succumbed on the other side of the Kishon. Now, when these Syrian chaps say they can't go any further, a dint of storming about and rawhiding will often instil new energy into their drooping frames; but when they lie down and say they won't move on, and call upon Allah and his prophet and all the powers that be, to strike them dead if they " budge an inch," the matter has to be treated in a different way. They will obey the man who gets in the most violent rage and strikes the hardest blow, and they must have got both from Floyd that night. The cook told me afterwards that they thrashed and pummelled and even kneaded the men in their gentle persuasion, but the muleteers swore they would die on the spot rather than get up. The case was now desperate, so Floyd, putting on a worse pitch of fury than ever, took the revolver he had borrowed from us and swore he would shoot them all, discharging a couple of shots just near enough to miss them. The muleteers wanted to die, evidently, but not in this way, so they got up and put the other mules on their feet, and during the rest of the night they were in the Kishon, supporting the animals as they forded the stream to prevent them from being carried away and drowned. It was well for us we had a convent to live in, for every thing was utterly soaked, and the few days we spent at Nazareth were absolutely necessary to dry our clothes and tents.

I forget a good many of the "spots of interest" about Nazareth, for I have scarcely thought of them from that time to this. The monks thrive well in the grotto business. I should like to have some stock in such certain and lasting institutions, but I'm afraid we can't make a "corner" on grottoes in Canada.

It was a favourite ramble for the boys, down to see the maidens of Nazareth at the rushing spring, called the Virgin's Fountain. The maidens generally looked about fifty years old, and, while washing clothes in an old sarcophagus, which the water ran through, they looked anything but the picture of our fancy's painted flight. A sort of jacket open in front, and a pair of blue cotton trousers reaching to the knee completed their picturesque attire ; but there were often to be seen exceedingly graceful girls coming laughingly to the fountain, who betrayed admirable native beauty in their skipping about among themselves, or in stooping to dip up the water, and returning with the shapely jar poised upon their heads. They wore, like all the Arab girls in the country, strings of large old coins of gold or silver, laid over the head above the brow, and stretching down below the ear. These ornaments among the poorest people are generally made of the common silver coin of the country, and from the large pieces of the size of a silver dollar in the middle of the string they dwindle down in shape to the smallest half-piastre at the ends, which are bound behind the ear. These are very rarely stolen from them, and I suppose, seldom, if ever, taken off; they are the hoardings of the parents given to the child as soon as she is able to wear them, constituting her marriage settlement, not being liable to be seized for the husband's debts. We often, out of curiosity, counted over this vast dowry that was to enrich the married couple and set them up in life, but we never found more than eight or nine shillings worth in the whole ponderous collection. It is an admirable custom, for the young men here know exactly how much their ladies will bring them in, so there is none of that delicate and awkward hinting about paternal settlements to be gone through.

The Church of the Annunciation is richly decorated; its trappings and gew-gaws placing it high on the list of Palestine churches; it is built over Mary's kitchen and parlour and sitting-room, and there is another church built over Joseph's Workshop. They are all *grottoes*. Some other equally credible spots are shown too, and, among others, the synagogue where Jesus preached to the people, till they became enraged at his doctrines and took him out to cast him down one of the neighbouring hills, "but he passed from their midst."

A pretty little English Church sits demurely on the hill, looking down over the narrow, ill-paved streets, and comparatively well-built houses of Nazareth.

It is a goodly sight to see a Church of England planted here, and to hear the organ accompany the people to a familiar psalm. It reminds us of a little girl who, losing her way, has found herself among a band of gypsies, and although they harm her not, she sits in their midst trembling at the unaccustomed scenes around her. But on emerging from the precincts where we hear of the Jesus who, as it was prophesied, should be called a Nazarene, and passed his youth among these hills, there is a revulsion caused in our minds, when we hear the well-known cry of the muezzin from the minaret calling the turbaned craftsman of the town to prayer. "To prayer, to prayer, ye faithful! God is great and Mahomet is his prophet!" is perhaps the burden of the song of this herald of a misplaced faith. He calls upon them to wash and pray that their Islam, their salvation, may be near and sure. But it is not through such reminiscences as these that Nazareth remains ever enchained in my memory. It is the wandering about the locality and the quiet meditations begotten by the memories of the place.

I have climbed the high cliff on whose sides Nazareth is built. I have wandered up from the familiar streets far from the sound of the busy workshops, where many a carpenter still plies his industry to support his Christian family, where far up the grassy slope the sound of Joseph's hammer had day after day ascended, and have strayed through the little graveyard where a few waifs from England should rest quiet if holy ground does aught to stay a wandering spirit such as led them here while quick with life. Up and up I climbed the steep hill side which, divided into gardens by rows of young cactus, presented the clinging harvest to the sun, and where, amid the rocks, the richly coloured vegetables thrived abundantly to supply the town below; and here at the summit I have sat when my shadow rested not on earth, but was cast through empty space by the western sun setting below me. All was deserted on the rocky pinnacle, yet it was not lonely here: the space was not so void as to be oppressive, for there breathed a companionship in the evening zephyrs; and as the glowing orb sank into the far off sea, it cast a halo around the land and warmly gilded the summit where I sat, as if to linger on the spot where He so often wandered.

How often had He watched from this point the sunbeams leave the town below and creep up the hillside to his feet, and observed the bluish brightness of the day mellow into evening hues and deepen into the purple shades of night. How often from here had His prayerful meditations winged their brief flight to an approving ear above; what temptations had He conquered here that had assailed Him in the town below, but in this purifying place troubled Him no more. Perhaps He came here with His sainted mother sometimes, or with Joseph after the occupation of the day was over; but we imagine the young man, on occasions like this, alone, rather than in the company of His family or His townsmen, for who could share in this communion between God and God. We reflect upon such an occurrence as one of the most private nature, for we feel convinced that in such moments the clay-mould in which the Deity was then enformed was forgotten and cast aside, and heavenly intercourse took place. Amid such scenery as this the young Saviour of mankind grew from a babe into boyhood; among these breezy hills His stature increased with His mind, and for a time both progressed together, as ordinary boys do, until the mind soared into omniscience while His human form, reaching maturity, increased no more. So little is known of His infancy, and the way He grew in the Lord, that it is ever to be lamented that the thirty years of His life spent here should not be generally known amongst all, especially the young. What a good thing it would be for us if we knew how He resisted temptation when a boy and how He conquered wrongful impulses which, as a human being He must have experienced. If we knew how He spent His time and what His occupation was, whether He studied from books or received all His knowledge by divine right. All we can learn is that He spent all that most dangerous part of a man's life in perfect innocence, in peace with God and man; and it is comforting to think that there really was once a perfect man on earth, even if He had the Holy Spirit within him from His mother's conception. It is humiliating and disheartening to think that we cannot, like Him, be perfect, that we have no connection with the Father that would give us power to be more than we are, save that infinite mercy and compassion which He will extend to us if prayed for. We can but see a man above and before us who was unique in all things good: He looks down from a pinnacle where there is standing-room for more than one, but our feet slip in climbing the difficult ascent, so that we cannot approach Him unless **He** stretches out His arm from above to aid us.

On such thoughts as these the mind dwells, on leaving the white-built Nazareth, with its hospitable convent and refreshingly clean-looking people, and we pass for the last time the spring where Mary doubtless came daily with her jar for the precious liquid, accompanied probably by her son, who could not have thought, as these people do, that woman should undergo all the drudgery of housekeeping, and who would not be too proud to bear His mother's burden as He now bears our sins. Oppressed as we might have felt on thinking over our imperfections, while about leaving beautiful **Nazareth** and its hallowed environs, we are yet far from being gloomy, for gloom is impossible amid such scenery and luxuriance; and Mount Tabor with its parklike groves appearing in the distance as the bluish plumage of the dove, will surely change the flood of thoughts from idea into reality.

Our pocket-bibles have to come into requisition again, for we are coming to where there was once a marriage; "And the **mother** of Jesus was there. And both Jesus was called and His disciples to the marriage, and when they wanted **wine** the mother of Jesus saith unto Him they have no wine." Christ's reply shows that His mind was not upon the festal scene around Him, but was piercing the dark future and dwelling upon the scene of His last great agony, when the woman's services would be required to take His maimed, bleeding and lifeless body from the accursed tree. He seems to start, half frightened, from His reverie at hearing His mother's voice, as if He had heard the same voice as it would sound in the future, and He gives **this** reply—"Woman, what have I to do with thee? mine hour is not yet come." But His mother, though she could not understand Him, had unbounded faith in her son, "and she saith unto the servant, whatsoever He saith unto you do it."

Jesus was an example from which the long-faced, joy killing professors of religion could not, as it were, take their cue. He had His own heavy thoughts which found partial utterance to His mother, but far was it from Him to cast a dampening influence over the scene of enjoyment. On the contrary, He changed the water into wine that they might be merry, and exhibited the power of God in an appropriate way, and, shaking off the future for the present, He most likely sat down in the house of the nobleman in Cana of Galilee and made merry also. The priests show the "six water-pots of stone, containing two or three firkins apiece," which had held the metamorphosed liquids, but I did not dismount to see them. I was only too glad to hear they had never been broken. Married men may look upon Cana of Galilee, where the bliss of wedded love was sanctioned and promoted by divinity, with considerable interest, for its name has become almost as symbolical of marriage as the bridal torch of the ancient, and is almost synonymous with their Hymen. There is now no more wretched place in Palestine than Cana at the present day, and henpecked husbands, with whom the torch has flickered and gone out, may take a malignant delight in saying that even the symbol of marriage has become wretched.

On entering the village, Floyd gave me a playful cut in passing, and poising his whip darted off through the rough alleys and around the mud huts with me after him at full speed; there was no catching him, for he rode like a madman, but on stopping I found that a large meerschaum had dropped and been snapped up by the thieving vagabonds about us. We searched and offered backscheesh for its recovery, but I fancy rank weeds are being smoked instead of tobacco at this day by some Barrabas in the companion that had seen me through many a night on fresh water and on salt. Soon after a pleasant lunch by a shady stream we came to the Mount where, on seeing the multitude, Jesus ascended to preach that discourse which is the embodiment of ten million sermons written since. It is called the Mount of

THE SERMON ON THE MOUNT.

Beatitudes on account of those declarations of blessedness on different kinds of virtue which He then dispensed, and it has two little humps like a camel's saddle, forming an excellent elevation to address a vast assemblage from. I should suppose that the meaning of the word "blessed" as appears in the beatitudes should be understood as "happy" or "fortunately placed," for in each verse is given the reason why they are blessed, and that it does not include, as in ordinary acceptation of the term, the idea of being also *saved* through all eternity. Here He could look towards the town of Safed, on a far off mountain, and say, "a city that is set on a hill cannot be hid," and among the many utterances of condensed wisdom that fell from His lips that day we notice that hard exhortation to follow, namely to return good for evil, in controversion of the old Jewish law of an eye for an eye, and a tooth for a tooth.

Here he lets people, that are openly generous, and inward niggardly, know that the prestige gained by laying five dollar bills **on** the collection plate while they privately **curse** the beggar on the street, **must** be looked for upon earth **only**; and, cautioning us against loud worship in public places and repetitions **such** as the heathen use, he gives us that beautiful prayer which seems more significant, more full **of** God's praise, and more inclusive of all our wants in life every time we search into its true meaning. Truly on a spot like this, He could consider the lilies of the field, without doing more than stooping to pluck them, and each one of **the** multitude could cull one also, and see that "Solomon in all his glory was not arrayed like as one of these."

Poetry reached its zenith in that speech!

Purity! Purity! how rare a thing thou art, how we adore thy image in all its forms, how often do we look in **vain** among earth's fairest faces for our ideal, and return **to** the lily which seems alone **to** bear no spot or blemish.

We are shewn another place, hit upon most likely because there **is** "much grass in the place," where the five thousand were miraculously fed; and cantering along over the undulating fields, where no fences or walls mar or limit the boundless view over the breezy, thymy hills, we suddenly halt.

The Sea of Galilee!!

There is that sea we always think of as in a dream, there are the shores, mountains, and peacefully rippling lake so well known to Him; the sea that lost its fury at His command, and supported him as the dry land.

As we wind down the cliffs a little way, Tiberias is descried with its old fortifications rent and scattered by earthquake. We are still a long way up and off; the sea looks like an azure patch of sky, and the mountains encompassing, hung in other shades of blue, look small in comparison with Mount Hermon lying to the north, grand and majestic, with its eternal snows glistening in the sun.

CHAPTER XIV.

I LEFT you abruptly in the last chapter, when approaching the holy waters of Galilee, for I felt the want of breathing time before copying out and adding to my letter, which appears endless before me in microscopic writing. Moreover, I feel a bewilderment in sitting down to add descriptions of these hallowed spots, where the great interest caused by sacred recollections was so strangely intermingled with the enjoyments which the nature of the localities themselves afforded. Rather than let you miss anything of Galilee, I will resume the thread of my winding path of travel where I left you, standing in mute admiration of the landscape, and as I lead you carefully down the break-neck cliff into the plain below, does it not strike you how small the Lake looks in comparison with our ideas of the "stormy sea?" Gordon, who swims well, is declaring that he will swim across, as his namesake Byron did the Hellespont, and others say they think he might swim that mile and a half easily; but we have no guide books with us, and do not know till Floyd informs us that the lake is *eight miles wide* at this point. So close appears the opposite bank, that we look into its nooks and crannies, and up its clefts and wadies most distinctly, but for all that, the intensely rarified atmosphere does not take away the perspective, and we are told that those mountainous banks, looking so small, are hundreds of feet high, so there must be a discrepancy somewhere.

The fact is, when a traveller comes to Palestine, he is totally at sea in regard to judging distances as viewed by the eye. It is so different from any atmosphere in America or Europe, that he is like a man blind from his birth, being suddenly cured and questioned as to distances. If he sees an object that appears to him only two miles away, he must persuade himself that in truth it is nearer ten; and if he climbs an exceeding high mountain, and views all the country that it has taken him days to travel through, he naturally ejaculates "how slowly we must have come here!" Soon we skirt the ruined walls of old Tiberias, and galloping over the grassy plain, come to where the mules, relieved of their burdens, are enjoying a roll on the sward, and the Arabs are busily pitching the tents.

I will not say that we stood upon the shore feeling sweetly sad, saying to each other "and this is Galilee," partly because we didn't say so, and partly because I know the nauseating effect experienced when reading books written apparently with one aim, which is to give the writer's own conceptions of the associations of the place conjured up in some tremendous and impossible reverie. That kind of rubbish has been served up for generations by people who went home and condensed all they knew into their "feelings on approach." In such a scene as this, where one by one we dash into the camp warm and excited, and hastily dismounting, select our luggage from the heaps lying on the ground, the idea of meditation is, of course, absurd; perhaps before the night is over, though, while boating over Galilee, I, too, may get touched with some comprehension of my position. To be truthful then, we took our towels and had a bathe in the clear and cold waters, where we had no extraordinary experience as in the Dead Sea, nor mud as in the Jordan, but simply had to swim hard to keep ourselves at the surface as in Canada's fresh-water lakes.

The water which had so lately melted from the snowy

mountains in the north was too cold for much luxury to be derived from bathing in it, and, after dressing, we strolled down the shore to Emmaus, where the ancient hot springs still bubbled and flowed from the bowels of the earth. On entering the range of domed buildings built by Ibrahim Pasha, one is almost overpowered by the sulphureous smell and intense heat of the steam that fills the building, the sense of which however, wears away after the lungs get accustomed to inhaling it. In the middle of the edifice was a large round cistern so entirely filled with water from the springs below that the splashing of the bathers sent it all over the floor where we stood; the ante-rooms connecting with the bath were lined with very dirty cushions, in imitation of the real Turkish Baths, where all the diseased and filthy inhabitants of Tiberias had lain.

The water has always been considered a **cure for** every ill, the temperature ranging about 144° Fahrenheit: how the people bore the heat was incomprehensible, for it would cook an egg readily: and there were two healthy persons bathing in company with a leper, enjoying themselves hugely, sliding off the smooth stone floor into the water.

We did not care to bathe just then.

All along the shore on the way from here to Tiberias we notice granite columns scattered over the ground, and standing in slanting positions out of the grass and water.

These are supposed to be the remains of the ancient Chinneroth, whose name during the earliest records, the sea before us bore: their appearance seems to indicate a higher antiquity than the time of Herod, who built a city probably on the site of present Tiberias. Josephus remarks that Herod's city was some distance from the hot baths; and, as these ruins appear all down the shore to the baths, it is reasonable to suppose that they do not, as many think, mark Herod's city, but one more ancient and thus, probably, Chinneroth.

As we had arrived quite early in the afternoon at the

lake, there was abundant time to read the stories connected with these parts from the Bible, when lolling on the shell-covered beach waiting for dinner, and it seemed strange that Raphael should hit upon the exact shape of the boats which now float on the Lake. One of these peculiarly-shaped crafts passed in front of us from Tiberias, filled with fishermen, the incident bringing up vividly the old cartoon of the miraculous draught of fishes.

Here we sit together and listen to the biblical narratives, while we select shells to take home as curiosities, and so thoroughly do the different accounts tally with the appearance of the place that we seem perfectly at home on the shingly beach; and we seem to look upon the shores and sea as if we had known them all our lives. Scepticism is forgotten here, we never seem to question the sites of the cities that were here in His day; there is but one feeling which intuitively impresses itself upon us, and into which all lesser feelings merge, that we are actually living on Galilee; and if Simon, Andrew, James and John were in that boat before us, we would not get excited, for we are so localized in idea that it would be only natural to see them cast their nets for fish, as they did before they became "fishers of men."

Our horses are being brought down to the beach to drink and be washed, the mules are stepping timidly into the water, the tents are set up as taut as drums, and from the glowing charcoal fire an appetizing odour, "as of goodly meats," is wafted to us on the evening air. As the day declines every shade of colour comes into play upon the landscape; from the glowing sunlight, the pink and orange, then the purple and darker hues take possession of it by turns. The shadows from the mountains behind us cover the camp and extend over the sea; Hermon still has a glow upon it; then, after a little twilight, the fair Selene, matured in her month's experience of earth, and alone in her glory in the sky, silvers every object with her beams, and the ancient hallowed waters now sparkle with a new sheen.

In the evening we floated off in one of those seemingly

well-known boats on the rippling bosom of the lake. We all know how strangely romantic it often seems when afloat drifting over some sheet of water on such a night as this; but how much more soul-inspiring was it thus to pass our Sunday evening gliding over Galilee? We had no aisles in the church where our evening hymns echoed softly; the roof was high; no walls shut us in but the mountains around, only one man could walk **upon our** floor. The rowers paused and rested on their idle oars **a** while to hear the melodious sacred strains swell out from the leader of our floating **choir,** and the lowly-sung refrain passed over the waters like the notes of the Æolian harp. We durst not even breathe too loud. There **was a** peace pervading, such as when He said "Be still," and the first harsh sound we heard was the grating of the boat's keel in front of the camp fire, announcing the termination of **our** evening service. That service will never be equalled again: no sermon, no prayers, no responses were heard, only the musical voice of praise and thanksgiving broke the stillness of the region, but, I think many an unspoken word arose from that boat, thanking God for this experience, and saying, "It is well for us to be here."

Next morning we had an early plunge and a ramble about **the** ruins before breakfast, and, taking the opportunity, we washed the mud off many of our things which had suffered in the previous bad weather. The day before we had come to several extraordinary places of bottomless sand which shewed nothing to betoken their presence till we found ourselves, whilst in the middle of a dry grassy field, suddenly clinging tenaciously to the saddle while the horses plunged heavily and in terror at sinking to the saddle-girths at each struggle. Many of the pilgrims suddenly found the terra *in* firma in a laughable way; some went over their horse's head and some fell over the tail, and, when the horses could not extricate themselves, the riders had to get off and help them up. Before breakfast was over the camp had been struck and sent off ahead of us, and soon we strung along the shore, passing through the streets of Tiberias. It would have been more pleasing, if not so correct, to have taken our remembrances of the old town as we saw it when floating past its sea-washed foundations the night before, for it is the most filthy place in Palestine.

It is almost wholly populated by Jews, and, like all the inhabitants of the four holy cities of their religion, they have a more squalid appearance than elsewhere. The Pharisees, with their long clothes, tall black hats, and long lightish curls hanging effeminately over their sickly, dirty faces were always particularly odious to me; and it was not on account of any biblical prejudice that made these men disgusting, for I had revolted from them before knowing they were the old sect of Pharisees. It seemed to be one of the great epochs in their lives to see us pass through the town, from the way they turned out to stare at us, and on passing the houses which were literally crawling with vermin, we were glad to emerge from the streets where the filth reached the horses fetlocks, and pass from **its** ruined walls forever.

The reason the Jews live here always, is that they expect the Messiah to land at Tiberias, and establish his throne at Safed, and most of the Jews at Jerusalem, here, and in other parts of Palestine are the descendants of Polish or Spanish refugees, driven from their native countries during the persecution of their race in the sixteenth century; and since maintaining a precarious existence, they are a degraded and oppressed people, living almost universally in poverty and squalor. They are interesting as a race, but not as individuals. There is but one better class seen at Jerusalem, having come independently from Asia, America, and Europe, with the hope of resting at last in the sepulchres of their forefathers.

Tiberias has a long history since its foundations were laid by Herod Antipas, in A.D. 16. It was captured by Persians in 614; by Arabs, under Omar, in 637, and by Crusaders under Tancred. In later days it fell into the hands of an Arab Sheikh, who built the present walls and towers. Earthquakes, especially the one in 1837, have desolated the greater part of the town, and in many places the walls **are** split open and fallen.

Once clear of inhabitants, the **most** enjoyable ride I ever had in my life commenced; the **shore** and the lake were teeming with life, and on the shingly beach, while passing through plantations of oleander, every beauty **of** the floral album conspired to give forth a most seductive perfume. Out upon the mirror-like surface **of the sea** of many names, the **huge** white pelicans sat **magnified** by their reflection and proudly indifferent to our presence, and the flocks of gaily feathered wild ducks treated the bullets whistling through their midst with perfect apathy. Above our heads, the kingly eagles soared about the beetling cliffs, and circling in the air for **a** long time **on** motionless wings, they would **swoop** suddenly down to the rocks or water, where their piercing **eye** discovered unwary prey. The path **at** times led far up the cliffs which seemed **to** tower above us sometimes with almost Alpine grandeur, and in looking down **at** the transparent depth of the sea rippling against the abrupt **and** rocky shore, the memory returned at once to those lovely spots **on** the Cornici Road, where I had wandered many a mile on foot, between Nice and Genoa.

Let those who come to this region in the glare and broil of summer denounce the beauty of Galilee, and tell of barren, shapeless hills, and neutral tinted water, and finding these banks parched and withered, describe it as a wilderness. **To** me it was simply paradise. How could we loiter through the groves below, and about the limpid pools and ponds where the tropical plants luxuriated, and **chase** the numberless turtles that basked so wisely in the **sun,** without the boyish love of **fun** coming out in **the** oldest of the party? How was **it** possible not to feel thus when gazing upon the heavenly-tinted small birds whose brilliant colours sparkled like gems amongst the branches, **as** they sang unto the Lord a new song that was as novel to **us as** their tropical appearance; how could we refrain from offering here an adoration to Nature as we found her in her stronghold, guarded by cliff and sea, and defended by floral barriers?

Some of us that did not bathe in the morning thought

it would be pleasant after a few hours on the move, so I stayed with them to wander on the shore, while the ladies rode on. It seemed a pity that the green oleanders were not in blossom yet, but we were well content with the fragrant seringa and glossy-leaved myrtle, the rich marigolds and a host of others. I could sit here on the shore and watch the lazy fish gazing fearlessly and interestedly at me from the water. They were of good size and well worth catching, but they had not been much disturbed by man since the disciples were wont to toil all night and sometimes return empty-handed in the morning. We had been feasting on the different kinds of fish that had once so laden the boat when they cast their nets on the other side of it; and along the shore the men may yet be seen casting the large net which was likened to the kingdom of heaven, that gathered of every kind.

The modern Arabs have a more lazy way to supply food for themselves, which reduces the gentle art of Isaak Walton to depths of degeneracy—they feed the fish with crumbs poisoned with bi-chloride of mercury or corrosive sublimate, then gather in their dead bodies with a stick. The more energetic stalk the game in the shallow places, and cast over them a hand-net weighted with lead. On coming out of the water, my friends did not follow the usual custom of pilgrims when bathing in the waters of the Jordan.

With them a piece of white linen is fastened about the loins before entering the water, and this is ever after kept sacred, to serve as the winding-sheet when they die; for they actually suppose that bathing in the holy river washes away every remaining sin, and they are said to come out of the water with the most radiant and joyful countenances.

Starting off now at a rattling gallop along the paths through the underbrush, we come upon our party gathered together around the village of Magdala, the Mejdel of the Arabs, where lived Mary Magdalene and where Jesus once landed after he had miraculously filled the multitude. The language of the Bible, where it says "he took ship and came into the coast of Magdala," loses much of its former significance when we look upon the small sheet of water beside us. I had got it into my head that Gennesereth was about as large as the Black Sea or the Caspian, and that to come unto the coasts of Magdala would require a very superior knowledge of navigation; whereas most likely he only could have rowed or sailed a few miles down what we should regard as a good-sized harbour. As to the storms that almost shamed the Atlantic in my puerile ideas, I have no doubt that a very choppy sea can get up here when the squalls strike down from the cliffs, or when the tempestuous winds from the cold mountains in the north are channelled down by the gorges so as to have a full sweep of the lake. After some experience of Palestine winds I can easily imagine the fishing boats of the disciples being "covered with waves," for the waves would be too close together to be ridden separately, but would splash over the bows in large quantities. It must have been one of these squalls that troubled them when the "waves beat into the ship so that it was now full," and it will be readily understood how a great calm should immediately succeed the shutting off of the wind, there being no expanse of water to keep up even a ground-swell. It must have been very sudden, because there is no place about the lake where they could not in a very short time beach their boat in safety, and with "rude Boreas," behind them they could run the whole length of the lake in an hour, and anchor in the harbour of Kerak, where Josephus collected his *two hundred and thirty ships* of war before attacking Tiberias.

At Kerak there was a *sea-battle* fought on this pond between the Jews and the Romans, and in proportion to Josephus' usual exaggeration, I should cut down that two hundred and thirty ships of war to a few dozen Feejee "dug-outs." Fancy two different navies on this expansion of a creek that measures thirteen miles by eight; what endless strategem there must have been, when neither could get out of sight of the other; how thrilling to see the Roman fleet becalmed, and the Jews throwing stones at them from the dug-outs of Josephus rowing about.

Magdala is like Nain and Cana of Galilee; it is not so nice as Howarah, while Bethany is a Paris to it. It's the worst place I ever saw. There are certain slums in every city we know well, when we rather pity the people that dwell there, but if the inhabitants of Magdala were put in the same places they would die of good fortune—they could not stand such prosperity. An Irish hunter could clear any house in Magdala, and if he did not, he could go through it. Around most of these villages they have fortifications of cactus, growing sometimes to the height of fifteen feet, forming a perfect defence against the barefooted Bedawin robbers, but I don't think Magdala has even that advantage which would serve to hide its frightfulness. About here we have to ford a stream rushing through a steep-banked gulley, escaping the quicksands said to lie at its mouth, and pass on through a rich tract of tangled underbrush, where no great amount of shade is received from the walnut and fig-trees described by Josephus, nor do we see the olives and grape-vines which once enriched the land. Then we come to Ain et Tiny (the fountain of the fig), where we might "Judge the summer to be nigh," according to the parable, "for the branch is yet tender and putteth forth leaves," if we regard the wild fig-bushes growing in the neighbourhood.

This spot is said to mark the old Capernaum, and it is interesting to wander about through the undergrowth in search of ruins, though I don't say we find very many ancient ones, it being very doubtful where Capernaum really was; but the remains of a ruined Khan are seen, perhaps of medieval construction. Topographers pile one supposition upon another concerning all the places about this shore, and it is useless here to follow their hypotheses, which all differ; and even if we continue on to the spot identified with Bethsaida, where some fishermen are casting their nets, we feel that there is nothing to create a conviction that it was here where those apostles who had a partnership in the piscatory profession were told to become fishers of men. We see here **a** curious old stone mill being turned by **a** crystal stream rushing past into the lake. We ride into the dark building to see a couple of men carefully dropping handful after handful of the precious grain between the revolving stones.

It is rather an odd thing to do, to ride into a man's mill, horse and all; especially when the door is his only window; but we **have a** new set of feelings and scruples to learn or overcome **when** travelling in the East, and most likely the Arabs would not understand our dismounting and asking permission **to enter.** They would then actually think they had some authority about their own premises and tell us to clear out **at** once, but as it is, they are very thankful if we do not take their grain **as** the Bedawin do, and gladly exchange the gracious "Marhabah" —the ordinary salutation of the country. Further on, lie the more extensive ruins of Tell Hûm which is thought by capital authorities to be Capernaum, and further still **are** the supposed ruins of the Chorazin which shared in the woe pronounced also on Bethsaida; that it should be more tolerable for Tyre and Sidon than for these towns. And certainly, if desolation means woe, the malediction is verified; for at Tyre and Sidon we see the fallen pillars yet remaining, the ancient names continue, and the sites are certain, but here there are no *sure* signs of either Bethsaida or Chorazin: so utter has been their destruction that **even** their locations are conjectural. It can be confidently said, that none of the scriptural names, which are as familiar to **us** as to the apostles themselves, can be located about here with any degree of certainty, except Tiberias, and poor old Magdala, whose name is perhaps perpetuated in memory of the good Mary. And why should we trouble ourselves about the circumstance? Is it likely that the curse of God and the denunciation of the Saviour will beautify a land and sustain the excellence or even the names of its cities? Does **it** then seem so very odd, when we know that God is true, that these scenes of Christ's teachings, miracles, and prayers should remain in doubt while every other important fact of Gospel history should obtain somewhere in

Palestine "a local habitation and a name?" No other spot witnessed so many of His great works, not even Jesusalem, —not even Olivet listened to so many of his discourses and parables; and in wandering about these shores the fearful doom of the Lord is ever present to our minds, " and thou Capernaum, which art exalted into heaven shall be brought down to hell."

But we can stop by the streams where the large oddly shaped fish elude our grasp, and lead us a lively chase along the grassy banks, and linger about the pure fountains whose grateful cooling waters flow in many channels to the sea. We can pause to think, that from here the soothing laving fountains of Gospel truths first welled up, and took their many courses to irrigate our parched and dried up human nature; that from here, as when Moses struck the rock, the apostles were called up out of the wilderness of sin, and from here began that grand organization of God's servants, the clergy, who, like the rivulets from the rock, have watered many a barren spot into fertility, and many a desert heart into an oasis of verdure and gladness.

No winter is ever known by these shores, six hundred feet below the Mediterranean. Thomson tells us that the flocks and their shepherds can therefore pass from winter to summer in an hour, and for several months can graduate their range so as to enjoy the temperature that is most agreeable to their tastes by ascending towards Safed, where the hills are often buried in deep snow. Up this ascent then let us go towards our destination, at Safed, which has been lying before us for days perched upon a mountain thousands of feet above our heads. We need not say good-bye to Galilee, for we will see it for a long time yet, but I must bid a long farewell to those delightful shores where I spent the happiest period of my whole journeyings from home back to home. I bid a long adieu to those hallowed places where the son of God Almighty in heaven had condescended to place his foot; and with a moistened eye, I now, while writing, again take my leave of the old fish, the gay birds, and dear old mud-turtles, for if ever I go back again it will not be with the boyish enthusiasm that then pervaded me and made me regardless of the sites of old Bethsaida and Capernuam.

We wended our way through fields of Grain, on each flowery summit, ever stopping, like Lot's wife, to take a retrospect of the cities of the plain we were loath to leave, but we could not put them much in the distance. The "litora relicta" seemed always the same distance below us, and the motions of a few fishermen in a sail boat were distinctly visible. Sometimes we descended deep ravines like the crevasses in the Alps, where the precipitous paths led to the bottom over rolling stones. One descent I remember in particular, when my head was almost touching the horses' tail while leaning back, when a single false step in the narrow path would have had a very dejecting effect on both horse and rider. Forming part of this terrific cliff, a little further south, there was a gigantic rock hanging over a precipice, rising fully five hundred feet in bold grandeur. It was all honeycombed with passages, having windows looking out over the abyss, and was, in by-gone ages, a famous den of robbers.

At length Safed was reached, "the city that could not be hid," and we found our tents pitched on the very brow of the mountain overlooking all the ancient world; and as usual, our abode was among the tombs. These graveyards were so suggestive of rest, that we felt in duty bound to sleep hard at night among the dead, and "bottle of" large quantities of "nature's sweet restorer," which the skeletons tried to monopolize. The modern Arabs' tombs are yet merely "a pile of stones to mark the place," and very rarely is a name ever seen to tell who the deceased was; which will prove a great loss to the world when the Arabs I have seen shuffle off their mortal coils of dirty rags and sneak into Hades.

There was ample time to see the newly-built Safed and its old ruined fortifications before dinner was ready, and mark the strangely diversified appearance of its Jewish population, gleaned from all the countries of the earth. It is another of the four holy cities of the Jews, and presents rather a cleaner appearance than their towns generally do, from the evident fact that the water must be drained off by the slope of the streets, and not suffered to accumulate and stagnate as the people would doubtless let it.

The present town, of course, lays no claim to antiquity, having been rebuilt since 1837, when an earthquake demolished the whole town, destroying five thousand of its inhabitants, which is about the number living in it now. A greater mantrap during an earthquake could hardly be conceived. The houses are of square stones, piled rather than built one above the other, on the slope, and with another shock would come down again like a pagoda of a pack of cards. Among the Jews, this Safed, their Zephath, is reported to be very ancient, but as it is not mentioned in the Bible, the fabulous accounts of the rabbis are uninteresting to us; its crusading stories, however, especially one account of Saladin beseiging it for five weeks, are attractive, and in climbing up to the old castle on the peak, it can be seen at once how Safed should have always been one of the greatest strongholds in Palestine.

The cannon lying embedded a hundred feet up here, in the castle ruined by the calamity of '37, were perhaps left by the French, for I find no mention of them in any books touching on Safed; and after crosssing the old fosse, and wandering among the ruined garrison, we see some very large bevelled stones, which are possibly the remains of the Seph which Joseph fortified in Upper Galilee.

CHAPTER XV.

"AGAIN, the Devil taketh Him into an exceeding high mountain **and** sheweth Him all the kingdoms of the earth and the glory of them. And saith unto Him, all these things will I **give** thee, if thou wilt fall down and worship me."

If this is not meant, as many people suppose, to be merely an allegorical representation of the temptations of our Lord, I should verily believe that this Safed, **or** its neighbourhood, was the identical spot to which the Devil brought Jesus to induce him while yet sharing our nature, to accept the power and wealth of earthly kingdoms, and thus to sell his divine soul in a moment of worldly avarice which always emanates from Satan. For here, in the heart of Naphtali, He could look over **a great** many kingdoms, and actually **see most** of the cities **whose** names we are familiar with, **or else** descry the localities in which they lay. He could **look** all over **the** Hauran where, **to** the eastward, "the giant cities **of** Bashan," then flourishing, might have shone out **to his** vision. Galilee and all its cities were at his feet. He could look clear over Zebulon to Issachar, **and** into their cities, and perhaps into Manassah. Carmel, and all the Phœnician Plains by the Sea lay to the west beyond Asher, with their great sea-ports, Tyre and Sidon. Lebanon and Hermon **rose** in the north, Damascus **lay** hidden in the region to the north-east; and a very large number of those cities mentioned in the Bible, which are not localized or even heard of now, must have added considerably to the grandeur of the view.

Was ever man tempted thus?

Would any ordinary man on earth possessed of a common love of power and imbued with the usual tendency to sin—with his ambition and belief that he was fit for great things urging him on—ever refuse this offer? If he had within him the makings of a great man, and even if in his moments of christian prayer, Paradise seemed more invaluable than all else, would he not in this temptation waver as to his prospects in eternity, and clutch the worldly power within his grasp? And if he were a little man, a small man, "a miserable varlet," would he not look down, as the Saviour could do from here, upon the place of his boyhood, where his neighbours cast him out, and accept the devilish potency that he might lord it over them in malignant revenge. If we may judge by the number that visibly sell themselves for gain, who amongst us would survive this seduction: and with the Devil as his friend and the fears of Hell thus mollified, what man of human weakness, no matter how good he had been before, would not, like the Fallen Angel himself, assume a lower dominion when he could never reign above?

The lost Archangel would tell him:

> "Here we may reign secure, and in my choice
> To reign is worth ambition, though in Hell;
> Better to reign in Hell than serve in Heaven."

You and I would not succumb, of course, but all other human nature would.

But this is idle dreaming.

We are not tempted in such an open way now, nor on so grand a scale, and no greater proof than this of Christ being the Son of God has ever been revealed to us, for any merely human being would have yielded. Hear his answer, in language by which Milton is eclipsed, "Get thee hence, Satan, for it is written, thou shalt worship the Lord thy God, and Him only shalt thou serve."

To such a commanding spot as this I stroll as the last shades of night are fleeing from Phæton's jewelled chariot, and as it approaches with all its oriental splendour, old Hermon, who is always last to sleep and first to wake, beams forth a radiant smile,

The Land of Bashan is lighted up and the **heights of** Gilead **now** have daylight on their summits; **at length** the sapphire hues **of** ruby, blue and yellow are lost **in the** grand effulgence **which now** shines down into Galilee, **and** the slumbering **waters** scintillate as a pellucid gem.

Another day **is** spreading over the ancient world, **which** counts its **suns** as the sands **on** the shore, and its decades as the hours of the year; **a** glory **shines** upon the holy spot **as** if the Dove were descending from on high, and the land again found favour in His sight. The sea lies small and beautiful below, surrounded by its wickered sides of osier—a fit cradle for the nursing of our Faith—for who can come to Galilee without feeling that he sees again the Gospel in its infancy? Frail indeed must **be** his standing ground, if those shores and waters call forth no holier emotions than lakes of beauty only. Gergasa can be seen on the opposite shore, where the swine ran violently down the steep place into the sea. The exit of the lake, where Kerak lay, and even the hot baths at Emmaus, and nearer Tiberias and Magdala, all lie within the vision, and it seems as **if** a stone hurled strongly would light in old Bethsaida. Directlly south **lies** Tabor, which, though some thirty miles away, seems **to** rest insignificantly **at** my feet; the peak beyond may **be** Gilboa, and nearer, the "hump-backed" Huttin, or Mount of Beatitudes is as a mole-hill on the ground. Nazareth **is** hidden, but perhaps that summit to the south-east may be the one I had climbed behind the town; and that looks like the abrupt bluff of Carmel by the sea.

The day is brigt now and illuminates the dark ravines and gorges of bluish-looking Bashan, which, in the distance, appear as the furrows of a plough; and though I may be wrong, I think I see fully a hundred miles to the eastward. It seems a ponderous statement, but the opposite shores of the lake are so close, and the view beyond is so limitless and searching, that a hundred miles hardly satisfies me.

But there goes tintom. **Ting-ting**, bang-bang, sound the tin dishes, too-oo-oot go the horns, ding-dong goes the dinner bell in Mahomet's hands, while he seems to give in extra tintinabulation outside my tent, as if he thought I needed it more than any one else. Then this leader of the fiendish band stops in the middle of the tents, when he is sure everybody is awake, and thus delivers an oration: he says. "Gentlemans, and ladies! It is a very bootiful day. Dere is no rain, or what-you-call-it, snow. De sun hab risen in de heavens, and am shining on de polish of your boots, it is very warm and"—"oh shut up, and get me some water!" cries a petulant pilgrim, at which all the tents give a sleepy laugh. "Yes, sare, I'm coming," he answers. "Gentlemans I have been too good to you dis morning and de breakfast will be ready in five meenits." This generally "fetches us" all; the pilgrims usually wanting five hundred things on getting up, a howling for servants ensues, who, answering loudly in whatever tongue they know, the replies of "yes sare, oui mam'selle, subito signore, aiwah howadji"—all help to make a din about the quiet camp I left before the daylight.

And now I notice that I have been sitting on one of those Syrian whitewashed sepulchres of the Jews which was the simile admirably taken of the hypocrite, that without is like a whited sepulchre, but inwardly is full of dead men's bones.

After breakfast we all assemble at the brow of the hill to have a last look at Galilee, and all the country that now seemed so familiar to us; then descend the winding path from Safed.

Between **Safed and Tibnin there is** but little to interest the Biblical student, but much to excite his love for nature, if he has any such.

The path which lies through the very heart of wild **Naphtalim** is not much travelled by tourists, or even natives; it takes its way over hill and dale, through verdurous thickets, under cliff and over torrent, till nature seems familiar in all its forms. Shortly after leaving Safed we pass a peculiar volcanic lake formed in the great 'quake of '37, said by the Arabs to be bottomless.

On a ride like this where there are not so many celebrated places of interest, and where the scenery is so variable, there is more real enjoyment to be obtained. Sometimes far ahead on the mule-path in the gorge where the road cannot be mistaken, and sometimes far behind the rest, we are tugging away at some bulb or root to add to the collections already gathered. Loneliness is not felt in this wilderness; the tombs hewn in the rocks around have more interest in them than all the monuments of Europe: they may be the tombs of the house of Jabin, or of Heber the Kenite's ancestors, or they may have held the dust of the mourning friends of the assasinated Sisera, the captain of the host. And do not the two great detractions from the full enjoyment of travel lie in the unwonted sense of solitude which involuntarily intrudes itself at times upon the most accustomed wanderer, and the breaking away from scenes that have become endeared through association, or from friends whose congenial society has become almost necessary to one's felicity? The yearning for the familiar, the deep sense of isolation which the whirling multitude often begets may be attributable sometimes, I think, to a failure of that self-reliance which buoys up the solitary wanderer, through which the petty vexations and trivial disappointments are looked upon with all the *bonhommie* of a philosopher. In that drear moment when one feels himself an exile rather than a traveller, and a weak creature dependent upon others, when the heart lies cold within him for the want of a well-known smile from some home-face—then the pleasure of sight-seeing wanes —historical associations pall upon the mind; the busy throng which was his delight yesterday has no interest to-day; holy cities possess no recollections; monuments contain but common dust; the gondola has no rythm of motion, and the Palatine is a brickyard.

All through this land, which ever reminds one of death in all its forms, whose barren rocks speak of earth's decay and man's nothingness; whose tombs lie open and expose the horrible remains, and whose living inhabitants are often more ghastly than the dead themselves, one might be supposed to long with a great desire for scenes about his home, and the simple amusements of his native town. When storms abrade the skin, and snows chill him to the bone; when the lame, halt and crippled draw near to him, and the lepers hold up what is left of them for alms, he may excusably wish to transport himself to a quiet fireside many thousand miles away. He *may* feel this, but, happily for me, no such utter disgust wound as a parasite about the enjoyment it would slowly and surely kill. In the cities of Italy, with every European comfort within reach, I have felt that sense of solitude, but never in the East. Are not one's thoughts enough resource for contentment when they have such food as is here offered? Is not the Bible the only book one wants? Does it not suffice to tread the precincts of His birth, to become familiar with His boyish home, to view the scenes of all His miracles, to move softly near the hill of His great passion and distress; to rest on Olivet, where "He had not where to lay His head," and to try to view the suffering people as they appeared to His compassionate eyes.

And, speaking of the afflicted people that always flocked in multitudes around the Saviour, it is remarkable how, at the present day, as in ancient times, the people congregate about any English *hakim*, or doctor, in whom they invariably repose implicit faith. The lame, the halt, the withered, and those suffering from ophthalmia, which is a very prevalent affliction, all came to Dr. ——, who occupied part of my tent, and at every village or town this kind old gentleman dispensed his small stock of medicines for their benefit, and wrote out prescriptions to be made up at Jerusalem, which was often many days' journey off.

The Hakin generally received them one by one in his tent, and as I had the spirit of Æsculapius strong within me, there was here a vast field of experience opening out. But alas! their ills could not be healed by human power or modern skill. God alone can cure those worse diseases to which man is heir. A horrible ailment of a hereditary nature was generally the cure we were called upon to effect. As was written in the tablets of stone, He visits the sins of the fathers upon the children unto the third and fourth generation, and far beyond that time the seeds of sin are apparent in the descendants.

One day a young Jewess came with her sister into our apartment to see the doctor. She appeared in good health and was very beautiful, wearing the long spotless white garment enveloping all but her little red slippers. I was finishing a letter to post before leaving, but I could not help gazing at the lovely face and lustrous dark hair disclosed by the long veil being thrown back upon the shoulders. She sat there looking modest and retiring, with a sad expression on her face. Soon the doctor came in; she arose and explained by the dragoman what ailed her, and then she disclosed her arm for his inspection. Gracious powers! what a sight! Her arm from the elbow was—but I won't describe it, it was too frightful. This poor creature, with the blue light of innocence shining in her eyes, suffering all the torments of the vicious, took her prescriptions, which may have soothed her for a while, and wrapping herself again and covering her face with the veil she crept silently from our midst and we saw her no more.

I fancy that pills of bread would have been as efficacious as the prescriptions, and quite as comforting to the trusting Arabs. But it is a sore subject to contemplate; the people of Canada will never know how blest they are, even though living in the smallest shanties, in comparison with the people of this and other countries, where the pangs of unavoidable disease are augmented by the straits of veriest poverty.

But here, on the top of a hill like a sugar-loaf, which rises a few hundred feet from the surrounding level, sits Tibnin, the termination of our day's ride. A fine old ruin crowns the summit that has figured many a time in the wars of the Cross under the name of Toron. After struggling up the steep ascent, we all dismount, and here Floyd misses the tents, which he knows were in advance of us, and, on walking to the brink of the hill, he sees them being set up below, where the muleteers would rather pitch them, than drive the tired beasts up here. Floyd just springs into the saddle of the nearest horse and goes headlong down the mountain. No mailed champion of the Cross ever went down so fast I'll be bound; perhaps some of Saladin's men might have, but an Englishman has to live a long time here before he has that confidence in himself and his horse. His terrific approach has a great effect on the muleteers, and those that try to remonstrate against striking the tents, which they know they have no right to pitch in the valley, soon let go the tent ropes when the koorbash whistles through the air. Floyd never strikes them very much, but he has a way of looking like a meat-axe possessed, and in half an hour those tents are pitched on the hill-top.

In the mean time we survey the village and ruined fortifications which frown over our camp. The inhabitants are a quiet-looking lot of dirty people; they cut up some tobacco and bore out long pipe-stems for the tchibook, they make slippers, and now and then mend a gun. They evidently don't eat anything, unless it is that white looking mess on the counter in front of their bazaars. Maybe those balls of boiled vegetables are for sale. I see a man taking a handful of boiled weeds out of an iron pot which has been on the fire, and patting it up like a snowball in a very questionable pair of hands, he slaps it down on the board in front of him—you can buy this now, for I think it was meant to be eaten, but I never tried it myself. An old coin-seller sits jingling the same ancient coins in his hand as he has been doing, year in and year out, for ages. He is a moneyed man, and will not even ask for backsheesh, but only rattles his "anticos" to attract attention, as a muffin man rings his bell. I doubt if he ever eats. How he buys his tobacco is a mystery.

On the whole they are a pretty respectable lot of people, for I always judge an Eastern town by the number of women seen in the streets. If they are not seen it is a sign they are kept in secluded and proper harems, and few were to be seen in Tibnin.

These old Crusaders' castles are always interesting because we have a better idea what took place in them than many ruins of much finer structure. The cypresses grow in clusters about the place, and among the debris are found tottering arches resting on columns of different coloured marble, where many a stalwart knight has fallen, and a pile of modern buildings forms an excellent elevation to view from the roofs the Mediterranean stretching blue into the west.

We are pretty well out of the Holy Land now, and as we are not to reverence Tibnin much, I might venture to say we had a shooting match among the ruins with our revolvers.

The fact is, I have been afraid to speak about such harmless amusements on going through the Terra Santa, because many of the people who read a little about those Holy places would set me down as a thorough reprobate if they knew I shot a crow or two about Nazareth; and if I described the steeple-chase on the "Galilee flats" my character would be gone forever. We had Olympic games here with the Arab young men who were well-built and handsome. They could not run very well and Gordon outdid the champion jumper easily before all his village. So fairly did he eclipse him that the Arabs didn't like it and one of the dragomans told my friend in a whisper, that he would probably get a knife in him if he beat them much more: so Gordon and I withdrew on our laurels, receiving the hisses and execrations of the people that were so smiling at the commencement.

It was an enchanting place to encamp on the hill at Tibnin. The prospect stretched for many miles over undulating hills, bushy ravines, and woody cones, clothed in the most charming verdure of spring, and after spending a long time in the dining tent, dallying over the dates and figs, nuts, raisins, and oranges, we were forcibly struck when we emerged with the landscape as it appeared under the brilliant moon. The hills were all frosted in the spectral light, and we were but a day's ride from Hermon itself, so it towered above us more grandly than anything I had ever seen. I must ever prate of Hermon. It is a real mountain. The little Tabors and Carmels and Zions would never be seen in one of its niches. Look at it from where you will, it always forms a striking tableau. From here it is positively awe-inspiring. Like a hoary sentinel of the "Old Guard," it has been watching over the land till the bottomless clefts, which appear to us as wrinkles in its visage, have been worn deep in its snowy brow. It looked down patronizingly on little Damascus, the oldest city in the world, when Uz, Noah's grandson, laid its corner stone, and ever since has sent a streamlet to lave its verdant gardens. The mystery of those mighty stones of Baalbec it could unravel, telling how they were set on end. It knew by sight the Jewish forefathers and could reveal the secrets of Machpelah. The Israelitish sway rose and declined before its eyes. It saw religions changing among the wretches at its base from God to Moloch and from Baal back to God, while its aged brow ever spoke of immortality, and preached the doctrine of eternity. It has seen the Dogs of War let slip, and its rivulets on the plains running red with every nation's blood. Rumours of the mighty power of Greece were wafted for two thousand years by occasional zephyrs to its summit. Rome received a well approving glance before she died, and in later years it sent down a chilling blast to careen the bold ships of Genoa and Venice. Ever has this mighty spotless crest acted silent umpire between the nations of the earth. Ever will man forget himself when gazing at this type of the Everlasting, this symbol of Eternity, this emblem of the Almighty.

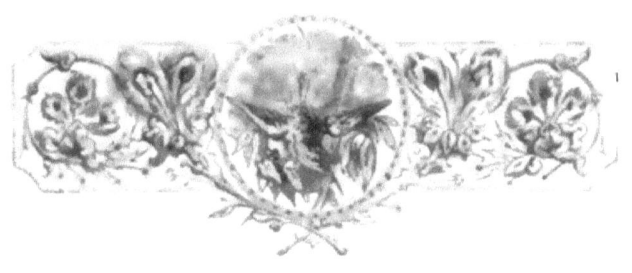

CHAPTER XVI.

WE passed from Tibnin towards Tyre, and soon entered a glen renowned through the East as being the winner among the many competitors for the apple of beauty which is so hard to give away here with an impartial hand. It is called the Wady Ashur. The precipitous sides are not far apart, and a path leads over the dry bed of a stream at the bottom. About halfway up to the patch of blue sky cut out by rugged cliffs, the sides are covered with trees, shrubbery and flowers. We notice the prickly oak, the arbutus, the hawthorn, and the sumach, with their roots and interstices filled in with ferns of the most delicate kinds. The hyacinths fill the air with a sensuous perfume, **and** we can here enjoy the far-famed " odours of **Araby**," which are always searched for in vain among the cities of the East. Continual scrambles for **new** flowers beguile **our** wandering journey. Away up, hundreds **of** feet, near that strip of blue we see the huge square-faced tombs of the ancients cut in the rock looking down at us, which, resisting storm and heat till now, by the washing away of the surrounding earth, and by their own disintegration, have become inaccessible to **even** the nimble goats. Large birds soar and swoop about these peculiar cavities, and make their nests in the sepulchres long since rifled by the rascally Arabs. From time immemorial it has always been usual for the kings and men of wealth to have their sepulchres desecrated by ruthless seekers for hid treasure, their sarcophagi exhumed and made destitute of all the rich adornments with which the ancients thought fit to inter the honoured corpses. Every day we read of new discoveries being made, and of engravings on sarcophagi bearing witness to the dead man's greatness, showering all the curses in and out of heathendom upon the greedy despoilers who should open the tomb. In a valley such as this, one loses his ideas about the general character of the land he has passed through, and forgets the miles of barren rock and bare piles of stones which form the backbone and ribs of Palestine.

It is a question quite settled among the Jews of course, but very open among others interested in these holy places, whether or not this country will ever flourish again in its old magnificence, and whether its people will ever take their old position among the nations of the earth. Many people think it will, and that, as Bishop Berkeley says, "Westward the course of empire takes its sway," it must, of necessity, come round here again. The same ecclesiastic undertakes to prove, I think, that there is no matter in the world, and Byron amusingly comforts us by saying, "no matter what Bishop Berkeley says," and this remark I would adduce in doubting that empire will ever take its way here again. One look at a good map will show at once how the country is nothing but a mass of mountains. The valleys, which are fertile enough, present but small tracts for cultivation in comparison with the great area of barren mountainous region. The rocky mountains were covered, when I went through the land, with flowers which grew in crevices between the stones, yet it was plainly discernible how in summer the whole country must be a glowing, quivering mass of glaring fiery rock, without a blade of grass to be seen anywhere. The earth has been so crumbled and washed down by the incessant rains of winter from the mountains, where all the fruits of the earth used to thrive, that, while it fills up and makes the valleys fertile, it leaves an unsightly skeleton where Solomon has sung of beauty in its life. These mountains are simply massive quarries which gunpowder will hardly move, much less a plough—and who would endeavour to farm a quarry? In summer the water is hoarded by the drop, even sanguinary combats ensue as to who shall fill their pitchers first at the scarcely trickling fountains. The whole idea of power returning here is simply ridiculous, and as for a thieving, ignorant native ever being a king, *Istugfar Allah!* God forbid! After ascending out of this wady we pass through Kanah, an Arab village of about two thousand inhabitants. There is nothing to remark here but the rather better appearance of the people; the more comfortable style of their architecture, betokening, I suppose, our approach to the sea. In the interior of the country one might expect the country to be more wretched than on the coast, on account of the continual oppression which they suffer from Bedawin, and the absence of any sea breeze to cool their stifling, fever-breeding atmosphere. From here now we catch our first satisfactory glimpse of the great sea lying deliciously blue out to the horizon, and on a promontory jutting out into the waters lies Tyre, sparkling like a diamond set in lapis lazuli. Those merchants of Tyre, whose wealth must have been enormous in olden times, no doubt, had their villas on these heights, and from here could watch their ships sail in and out with complacent satisfaction.

We have our luncheon under a kharub-tree, close by the tomb of Hiram, King of Tyre. Any Freemason can tell you more of Hiram than I can, but it seems that Solomon, Hiram Abif, and Hiram, King of Tyre, were the three grandmaster Masons from whom the society is said to have sprung, and, as I before remarked, he supplied Solomon with the wood to build the temple. Here, apart from all habitations, is the venerable old monument of remote antiquity. It is a huge sarcophagus, hewn from one stone about fifteen feet long and ten deep, supported on a massive pedestal, ten feet high, of solid masonry. I climbed all over it, and entered the interior by a small hole, and though averse to vandalism as a rule, I knocked off a bit or two for some friends at home, who are enthusiastic Masons.

This kharub-tree that we are lunching under is growing the very husks that the prodigal son would have eaten with the swine; the pilgrims gather about three hundred bushels as soon as they know what the pod-like fruit is.

It's just enough to give anything a scriptural name, and this howling band of despoilers light upon it like a flight of locusts, and carry off three or four pounds of it apiece, or if it's a small thing like a skull, they gather about like ghouls to get a morsel. There is, perhaps, half a ton of pyramids among them, and five or six pecks of sham Egyptian idols, and possibly five hundred-weight might balance in the scales their ancient coins. Necklaces from Bethlehem, olive-wood knick-nacks from Jerusalem, candles from all the grottoes, salt from the Dead Sea, mud and water from the Jordan, holy relics from Nazareth, shells from Galilee, and ferns, flowers, bulbs and roots innumerable, form their little souvenirs.

Diverging from the direct route to Tyre, we visited Ras el Ain (the fountain head) to see one of the most remarkable springs in the land, supposed to have been built by Hiram, and consequently as old as Solomon's pools. Four fountains gush up close together from the ground into a large reservoir, which overflows in great volume on different sides at the top into channels, leading the water to strong cylinders of masonry, where it again descends with considerable force. At the bottom of the cylinders the numerous ancient aqueducts take it up and convey it off. One of these acqueducts, of Roman architecture, once carried the water to a building about two miles distant; another, of Saracenic build, was probably for the irrigation of the surrounding soil. The Arabs want us to believe that the water is brought by a subterranean canal from Bagdad.

Changing horses here, as I did not want to ride mine too hard, a few of us galloped together around the surf-covered shore to Tyre.

Every one knows how a prostrate pillar strikes him with a sense of surrounding desolation, and how truly symbolical it is of ruin. We could look at a column standing upright for months at a time, and never feel struck with any feeling other than its symmetry, its quality, who put it there? and how did he do it? But when we find it prone upon the ground, or stretched supinely in the waters, when we can climb all over it, and stand on the defiled leaves of its graceful capital which was once exalted unto heaven; a deeper sensation pervades us, which has some connection with the thought that man's work can never be immortal.

On coming along the shores of Tyre for the first time, we are very ignorant of the prophecies concerning the overthrow of the city, and we know next to nothing about its history, but we feel that there is something extremely odd in seeing those pillars lying in the sea, and we have a sort of recollection of hearing the prophecy of its downfall. It's useless to pretend to have a full knowledge about a place before entering it, as many do, but after reading the 26th and 27th chapters of Ezekiel, those ruins grow more interesting every moment. As we sit at the tent-door looking at the fishermen returning in their crazy boats, we can't help seeing at once that the old Tyre has become a "place for the spreading of nets in the midst of the sea," and as from the cliff we see the scores of pillars standing in every position from the water, and only a fragment of the gigantic sea-wall now remaining, we have no more lack of faith in the old prophet that said, "and they shall break down thy walls, and destroy thy pleasant houses; and they shall lay thy stones and thy timber, and thy dust in the midst of thy water." When bathing in the briny surf we place our foot on something round and slippery, we know that that is a pillar of ancient Tyre, and on seeing a number of columns drawn up and laid side by side upon the shore for exportation, we know that in a few years, or perhaps months, the prophecy will be entirely fulfilled, and not a vestige will remain. "Thou shalt be no more; though thou be sought for, yet shall thou never be found again, saith the Lord God." Originally Tyre was built on a long island, nearly half a mile from shore, and the isthmus now joining it to the mainland was first created by the famous causeway of Alexander the Great. It has been destroyed and built many times. There was the Phœnician Tyre, a Roman Tyre, a mediæval Tyre, and now, but not upon the old site, a modern Tyre, and ruins upon the top of ruins cover the whole peninsula.

There is now only one gate to the town, but the rents in the wall give entrance everywhere, and it far exceeds many other places I have seen in point of cleanliness. Some very large red granite columns lie imbedded about the suburbs of the town, and an immense double column of the same stone joined together throughout its length, is found with a wall built over it. This is said to be a hundred feet long, though I cannot corroborate the statement, for one end is imbedded in the ground, both its pattern and its material, however, would suggest its familiarity with the Nile rather than old Hiram. Amid these ruins lay an old church built by Paulinus, Bishop of Tyre, described by Eusebius, who wrote the consecration sermon, as the most splendid of all the temples of Phœnicia. The bones of the great Emperor, Frederick Barbarossa, were brought here, after a long funeral procession from Tarsus, to be laid beside the remains of a greater man than he—Origen.

Recent excavations by the people of Beyrout, for quarrying purposes, have brought to light many interesting remains, such as fragments of fine houses, statues, and numberless other things. And now I am at it, I might as well add, that the inhabitants eke out a subsistence by selling their bad tobacco in Egypt. While here, Floyd gave me a stick of the same acacia wood as the horns of the masonic altar were originally made of, and although I did not value it as a mason would, it nevertheless formed an appropriate memento of old Tyre.

Who could have thought that the blooming mistress of the Seas would at this time boast of only a few old leaky boats in place of the bold galleys sailed by the navigators of Sidon, whose planks were Senir's fir trees, whose masts came down from Lebanon, whose oars of Bashan oak, with sails of broidered work from Egypt, propelled the ships of precious cargoes?

Damascus and Syria, Tarshish, Sheba and Ramaah were proud to be her merchants; Judah, and the land of Israel and all Arabia **were** glad to send the honey, oil and balm to her merchant princes who were clothed with Tyrian purple; and who could now wander out on the rocks among these ruins in the midst of the sea, which, sweeping over the fallen columns raises the long green mossy sea weed that floats like dead men's hair upon the surface and drops again as the wavelet ebbs, without exclaiming, "Where is this Tyre, this Queen arrayed in purple and fine embroidered linen?" No answer would he receive but the moaning of the ceaseless wave as it undermined another pillar, and as it took up **the** wailing lamentation for the fallen, would he not in **the** old prophet's words cry out, "What city is like Tyrus, like the destroyed in the midst of the sea!"

We left Tyre rather sorrowfully, for it **is** a fine place for rambling and swimming, and few ruins ever enchained my interest as did those in the waters of Tyrian blue. Besides that, we were fast leaving all ground sanctified by the footsteps of our Saviour, and we know that he came only once to the coasts of Tyre and **Sidon.**

We rode through the town and emerged on the sands of the shore, which we followed to Sidon. The surf was rushing in grandly after a high wind in the night, and as Tyre grew small, it shone out again in its old way, which I can only compare again to a diamond. Indeed, people ought not to spend all their enthusiasm on the Bay of Naples, and other European places, but reserve them till they come to ride along the coast of Syria, and then not drain their fertile minds before seeing some parts inland. The scenery in many places here was exquisitely lovely, where soft summer tints hung over the bold green headlands; while at our feet the grand waves came tumbling in from the restless sea with deafening roar. Toppling crested caverns of hollow, heaving billows rose from depths of deeper hue than the mild blue sky above. The ocean, like the peaceful eye of blue, which merely charms, in its serenity, like eyes of other shades, appals us while in anger, half with beauty, half with rage.

No mountains impeded our progress to-day on the level plain of Phœnicia and we soon crossed the river Leontes, which rises by the giant ruins of Baalbec. Some among us even after this experience in the saddle could not move off a walk, and it much retarded our progress. Some of the pilgrims actually never quickened their horses' pace from Dan to Beersheba, or rather from Jaffa to Beyrout. Most of the time they had a man leading their horses, and if the animals ever commenced a little trot they hung to the saddle and screamed till the horses thought they'd rather stop than go on with such a row. All the boys had great confidence in their horses' speed, and as long as the ground was good, my little fellow could get away from them, but in the sand he lost, for his legs were too short to take the stride. There was a grand race to come off after lunch between Mr. T——'s horse which had been the subject of much admiration, and the other fleetest of the cavalcade. This animal was a very fine grey, evidently with a good deal of blood in him, but as he had not had any racing all the trip we were all in doubt about his speed, so Mr. T—— asked me to see if his horse could not settle which was to wear the ribbons of victory. At luncheon, I changed the saddles and we left encumbrances in the way of clothing with the Arab grooms, and on mounting, the big horse seemed to appreciate the preliminary canter amazingly. I took him on in front for a mile or so to warm him up, and, on coming to a water course he hesitated for a moment, but felt persuaded to go over. He was stiff yet, but with a few more trials did it nicely, and now his blood was up, with the run and feel of the spurs. At the signal, all the horses got off well together. It's a grand feeling when, at the dropping of the flag, the spurs touch lightly, and the first bounds of a splendid horse, try the firmness of the seat to the utmost.

There is a mad exhilaration in feeling the animal working like greased machinery between the knees, when the second horse's nose comes near one's leg and we have the race in hand, and keep the sharp heels as a *dernier resort;* and as we land past the belle of the party, who is acting winning-post, we would fain let our horses go on forever rather than stop that delightful motion; even though it is to ride back for the prize bouquet. We race past Sarafend, the old Sarepta or Zarepath where Elijah raised the widow's dead son, after living on the miraculous cruse of oil and barrel of meal, but it would hardly do to get pathetic after horse-racing, nor will I say we were moved in any way on being told the name of the place. We said we were happy to hear it and proceeded to get up another race. Elijah's tomb is shewn, so he must have returned from heaven to get buried here.

Sidon was reached, where we encamped in one of those cheerful graveyards, and soon the boys of our party were strolling through the town; and, by-the-way, these boys were all (except myself) well out of their "teens," and one was married, but I must always call them *boys* now, even if they don't like it. We poked about the bazaars of Sidon "the mother of the Phœnicians," buying rich dates at one stand and goody-goodies at another, till we came to the remains of the old bay.

A most perfect **picture** of **a** quaint old seaport town **is** Sidon. Its old lighthouse and rocks, at a distance **from** the shore, under whose shelter the sailing craft were anchored, the beach shelving in, where the stealthy fisher casts his net over the lethargic fish, the weather-beaten strand and rusty piles of cable, shapeless anchors, and broken gear of them that go down to the sea in ships—all bespoke the old maritime port—the home of the sailor when ashore from the deep. The rambling old castle running out into the sea with turrets and battlements and oddly formed cannon scowling from the port-holes, where, from its Gothic-looking tower, the Star and Crescent replace the standard of the Cross planted by King Baldwin long ago—this brought a mediæval era to our minds. The granite columns like those of Tyre imbedded and forming part of the structure of the castle and its bridge, and the heaps thrown out from the ancient manufactories of purple dye which was for the luxury of Kings—this all carried us further back, beyond the time when the haughty Pharoahs from Egypt, the ruthless Assyrian from Nineveh, the Chaldean and Persian from Babylon, and the cohorts from Rome helped to bow the crest of mighty Sidon. And yet we see, while on this shore, that it has been "more tolerable" for Tyre and Sidon than the cities in the wilderness of Galilee.

How replete with memories is the curious old town built up from the sea! Shall I tell of the pleasure of straying about here, of searching every cranny and recess of the vast old castle's ruins, where, on the tower, we dream of ancient days and watch the sea leap up the foundations far below; while we view, with a different interest, the timid vessels running in and bringing up under the lee of the rocks for shelter? Old Sidon's history is not so interesting as that of Tyre or Akka; she has been more an observer of their troubles than a partaker in them; but she has been the school of sailors, the builder of navies, and better than all she discovered the tight little island we look up to. What a tale her mossy rocks could tell! As she was an umpire rather than a combatant, a spectator rather than a gladiator, they could tell a more clearheaded and a more interesting narrative than any rocks we know of.

The present town extends up the hill from the water, and is rather well-built and clean; of course everything is of stone, but it is of that same soft rock which throughout the whole country is used for building purposes, and which soon dissolves by the action of the weather, and again, as dust, mingles with the marl of the mountains. This will explain how nothing but the marble or granite columns are seen about a ruin, because all the foundations and walls built of this stone have long since returned, like all that was mortal of their builders, to the dust from whence they sprang, and the houses before a very great length of time become as the scripture says "laid on heaps." One would hardly think that some seven thousand souls are cooped up in little Sidon, but these eastern people pack like herrings, and although the orange groves are extremely fine, they scarcely equal the orchards at Jaffa.

On leaving Sidon we pass the village of Djoun, where Lady Hester Stanhope led her peculiar life, and died her solitary death. Her story is too well known to need repetition. Every one knows of the eccentric lady who once graced the courts of England, who forsook her friends and noble home in Somersetshire, and after the death of her lover, Sir John Moore, at Corunna, here, among the Lebanons, for years maintained despotic sway among the Arabs, both by the power of her wealth and her reputation as a prophetess and astrologer. All know how, when her star began to wane, her health to ebb, and her purse to dwindle, she was plundered right and left by her faithless servants, and left to die alone in poverty, and how, at her sad burial out on these hills, the only English spectator, besides the clergyman, was, strangely enough, a man by the name of Moore.

About here, on the shore, we come to the place where that prophet, who was averse to the briny deep, came ashore in a whale. Well, now, I said, we were very ignorant and did not know much about this coast, but this announcement startles us. It is almost too much, but sure enough there's his tomb, and they have boxed him in well, too, so the whale can't get at him again. But didn't Jonah go off to Nineveh or somewhere? I always thought he did. But then he must have come back to the scene of his great event to accept the offer of this nice sepulchre. Josephus says he was cast up on the shores of the Black Sea, but he is wrong, for I see his tomb here and I know that whenever any person in ancient days hankered after a nice tomb he was sure to appoint his death in some place quite handy; perhaps Jonah died in the Khan close by. So many pictures have I seen of the whale getting uncomfortable and retching Jonah to the shore, that it is a rare and pleasant incident of travel to stand upon the very spot.

All along this Phœnician plain, we trample on the most beautiful kind of lilies I ever saw. The flower itself is, perhaps, seven inches long, and the leaves, turning black at the top, are of richest purplish maroon colour, with exquisite black petals. They are, I believe, never seen anywhere but here. We were now able to cull them in a peculiar way, having practised during the journey the Mexican trick of picking anything from the ground while riding past, and the Arabs had taught us their equestrian manœuvres, which often afforded great amusement; especially to-day, when, in turning sharply, Timoleon got his forelegs twisted in the sand and suddenly stood on his head, which I did likewise out of pure courtesy.

In our journeying we used to get camels and have a cruise on the "ships of the desert." I don't care much for it. It's risky. Of course they lie down and you sit on a wooden saddle, like a hen coop, though not so soft. The beast roars all the time you get aboard, like Van Amburgh's lions on being poked up. All at once he raises up behind, and throws you forward to gaze at his head in the most helpless way. Then he surges up in front, when you feel an intense desire to roll over his tail. Once fairly up he starts off, but I am unequal to a description of the motion. It is like riding an earthquake. You don't want much of it. The novelty and one's trousers soon wear off. Perhaps you get off all right, and perhaps you don't. Perhaps your hen-coop turns and pitches you to leeward. Ten to one you dismount over his head when he drops in front to let you off, and if you don't fall off he'll turn his head around and roar in your face.

The commissariat department had been well looked after by the dragoman before starting on this journey, and in addition to the many canned articles of diet, we always had the mutton, chickens and eggs of the country, and these we had in every conceivable form and variation. Beef was never seen, and pork was equally scarce. I think I only saw one pig in the East, and that was kept by an "unbelieving Gentile." For luncheon we always had hard eggs and heavy native bread of a dark colour, sliced cold mutton, and, of course, the inevitable cold fowl. Somebody said, "Well might the witches of Macbeth say 'fowl is fair.'" These breaks in the day's ride for refreshment were very enjoyable, and on going to Beyroot we had a fine bath in the Mediterranean, and it was with reluctant rein that we guided our horses towards our final destination that day.

Jimmy had never entered his horse in any of our races. He had a beautiful little cream-white steed with flowing mane and tail of purest white. Jimmy said he thought it could run, though he had never tried it much, so I mounted on his father's champion horse again, and we started on a long race across a sandy tract. Jimmy had a lot of mackintoshes strapped behind him, and he didn't profess to sit his horse better than a bag of wool, but he started off, all legs, and wings, and bags, and ran clear away from the big horse. Whip and spurs availed nothing. The cream-white steed floated away from me like thistledown on the wind, and here, at the end of the long journey through the country, it turned out that Jimmy and his horse were the champions of the party, and the rest of us all had to "take a back seat."

It takes a long time to get into Beyroot, for the path winds through miles of plantations, fenced with high prickly cactus, but at last we rode into the town, and stopped before the hotel. I would rather have parted with all my luggage than with my little horse. He had carried me without a stumble over arduous mountain paths, through miry valleys, down break-neck precipices, along shelving slopes of rock while other horses were going down like nine-pins, and he landed me at Beyroot sound and hearty as he was himself. The only subject of admiration in the thieving, marauding, lying life of a rascally Bedawin is his affection for his horse, and even then he does not treat him as he should. There is no animal alive more affectionate, sagacious, long-suffering and fleet than an Arab horse, and nothing so clearly expresses poetry of motion as his pace; I took leave of mine, feeling sorrowful indeed at his going back to experience the same hardships again, with most likely a harder master.

There were quite a number of Europeans at the hotel, so it was more than filled by our addition; several of us boys had the good fortune to secure apartments in the proprietor's house adjoining, where we had all the comforts of home, combined with the luxurious divans, airy sitting rooms, and fragrant nahrghillis of the east.

We found out, and in fact, knew long ago, that the road to Damascus and Baalbec was quite impassable with the snows on the Lebanons, and there were in Beyroot, people of Damascus, who had been waiting for months to get home. It was a sore disappointment not to be able to visit the oldest city in the world and the great ruins of Baalbec; but for such contretemps the traveller must be prepared, and keep a boundless stock of patience with him always.

Though living in semi-oriental style here, everything seemed strange and almost unnatural after our long camp life. The mere fact of standing on wooden floors and sitting on chairs at decorated tables with English faces about us sufficed to make our lives a novelty, but of all the blessings of civilization, the return to the postal system seemed the best. I found a stack of letters waiting for me, and although there was much pleasing news conveyed in them, I heard of several deaths of old friends, that had the effect of saddening my rest at beautiful Beyroot. There was ample time now to write these long letters home which I had generally kept posted up at intervals during the camping, since we left our last post office at Jerusalem; and looking back at it all, while I grieve at not being able to describe the profit, advantage, and joys experienced while living in the saddle, I feel also inclined to say nothing of our hardships.

Like the words around a sundial,

"*HORAS NON NUMERO NISI SERENAS.*"

"So let us note those hours alone,
On which the sun of joy has shone,
And leave unmarked the sunless past,
O'er which the shade of sorrows cast.

CHAPTER XVII.

THE Hotel Bellevue, where we stayed in Beyroot, was very appropriately named, for it commanded a prospect unsurpassed, I suppose, by any hotel in the world. The waves dashed up almost to its doorsteps, and the view extended over all the harbour, and the ships tossing and tugging away at their anchors; it included all the front of the town, and the mighty Lebanons rising out of the sea some nine or ten thousand feet. In the appearance of the town, which is built in a semi-European style, the peaked and slanting reddish roofs of the houses, that contrasted forcibly with the flat or domed roofs we had of late been accustomed to, seemed its oddest features, and the life and variation of colour about the general appearance of the place was refreshing to our eyes. The town ascends the slope from the sea for several miles, broken up into gardens, vineyards and orchards; no spot in Syria being productive of so great a variety of fruits and vegetables. Inside the cactus-guarded plantations, the creeping plants flourish luxuriantly around the mulberry, orange, and lemon trees, and even the more numerous olive trees seem to have a brighter and greener tint than the dull-coloured, dusty and scraggy ones seen further south. As in most eastern cities, now-a-days, there is a more modern portion of the town as well as an older part, and the ancient districts being smaller and dirtier, are rather the more interesting of the two, because the people there maintain more of their old customs and peculiar kinds of garb. We knew its ins and outs pretty well in the few days we spent there, and enjoyed the numerous attractive walks through the orchards beyond the town. A favourite stroll was to follow the coast a few miles to the south-west, there, upon the shapeless rocks, to sit and doze in the sun, while one of us read a book aloud. But it was a melancholy fact that a couple of engagements had sprung up between some young spinsters and bachelors of our party, and we could not go in any direction to rest in perfect solitude, without seeing these unfortunate people sitting very close together out on the crags; where the waves breaking on the rugged wall of rock in front of them, dashed skyward in sparkling spray, sending the foaming water rushing to their feet, adding much to the romance of the situation.

On Easter Sunday, we all repaired for service to a large room in another hotel; each having his best tarbouch and clothes on, with all the mud and horse-hair well brushed out; and I believe, in fact boldly assert, that our boots were blacked. I spent a long time in the selection of my clothes for the occasion. I had but two suits with me, but to select the least worst was the great difficulty. However, after considerable mending done in my own way with the thimble on the thumb (which I maintain is the correct way), I thought at last that my appearance was intensely respectable. It is generally thought more proper not to work on Sunday, but the wear and tear of riding and climbing, had created such devastation among the buttons so necessary to one's happiness and comfort, that we were constrained to sit on the divans and provide the necessaries for reuniting our garments. There is nothing more conducive to peace of mind than knowing that one's buttons are all right. I had been tied up in different parts with sundry pieces of cord, which were called my "body and soul lashers;" and there were among my goods and chattels, divers sailcloth needles, which now proved vastly useful, and when the string was doubled, with a reef knot on the end, I never knew my clothes to "carry away" in the same spot again.

In a day or two we sighted the steamer rounding the Cape and coming to anchor in the roadstead "on time" to a minute, so we packed our things once more, the poor portmanteau again being stuffed with all the old relics, besides **some** cones of cedars of Lebanon, and some more long leather tubes for the nahrghilli.

The sides of this mouldy old receptacle had to be strapped up to prevent the things falling out; it was such **a** disgrace to the party that I **al**ways used to pretend, on coming into a hotel, that I didn't own it, but was **looking** after it for a friend.

About five o'clock that day I raised my foot from **Holy** Ground, and was soon tossing over the bay to mount the steamer's black walls, where, after setting the luggage in the state-room, I came on deck to view Beyroot from the sea. Of course the town looked its best from this advantageous position. Built, as it was, up a slope, we could see into all the rich gardens and orchards extending far back among the habitations of the Druses. But the mountains formed the charm of the place. The snows of the mighty Lebanons towards the east towered cool and refreshing from the blue sea. What a roseate tint they bore as the setting sun shone on them once more for our benefit, before darkness enveloped the scene, and left it forever in our memory. How like the alchemist's magic bowl did the colours change on that glorious landscape!

> "Now upon Syria's land of roses,
> Softly the light of eve reposes,
> And, like a glory, the broad sun
> Hangs over sainted Lebanon;
> Whose head in wintry grandeur towers,
> And whitens with eternal sleet,
> While summer, in a vale of flowers,
> Is sleeping rosy at his feet."

I stood alone at the taffrail in the evening breeze as the steamer swung round and bore me away from the Holy Land, the land of miracle and wonder—from Jerusalem, from Galilee, from Nazareth, from the pleasant valleys and flowery mountains where I remembered,

—" the mingling sounds that come,
Of shepherd's ancient reed, with hum
Of the wild bees of Palestine,
Banqueting through the flowery vales ;—
And, Jordan, those sweet banks of thine,
And woods, so full of nightingales!"

My eyes were looking far over the maze of lights on the shore, and rested, in imagination, on the top of Zion. Had it been good for me to have been there? Had any change been wrought upon my life by visiting the Holy city? Those were the questions I put to myself. The Italians have a favourite expression, which may mean a great deal or a very little, according to the shrug that accompanies it; and their accustomed *Chi lo sa*, (who knows) was all that recurred to me as an answer to the difficult questions.

Next morning we were running along the coasts of Cyprus, the ancient Chittim, where the purplish peaks of old Olympus were dreamy in the distance, and dropped anchor off Larneca where we flew ashore in one of the fleet lateen-rigged barks sailed by Cyprian sailors. Here the goddess rose from the milky froth of these lovely waters, and here reigned supreme the native beauties, who even rivalled the model loveliness of their deity.* Here, in a splendid temple, Venus was adored, where incense from a hundred altars swept over the thymy hills; and though exposed to the air in the roofless temple, no chilling rain be-damped the shrines of tender worship.† And from this atmosphere of love, and love alone, a Zeno might be looked for, as a contrast to the daily scenes surrounding, who, with his Stoic followers, hardened like clay in this warm sunshine, and drew the clammy air of joyless life around them.

We quaffed of the Cyprian vintage, and the noble-looking Greeks were most welcome to our sight after our long intercourse with the son of Ishmael, of whom we generally lacked appreciation. We liked to look

---

* The beauty of the Cyprian women seems to have been almost worshipped by the ancients.
† Rain is said never to have fallen into the Temple of Venus.

at these dark and handsome faces about us, even though in the eyes there lurked a shade of treachery. A native dignity shed itself around the manly forms, whose symmetry their strange and rugged garb failed to hide; fit devotees they seemed to worship at the shrine of Venus.

And here we found the old remains of Aphrodite's grandeur, in mutilated forms which once graced her splendid temples with all her wondrous symmetry, which the woman fashioners of marble had only need to copy from themselves. But it was with no hope of beneficial change in our unfortunate physiognomies that we gambolled in those azure waves, whose loveliness, once condensed, gave birth to beauty deified, who, with her zone-bound archer boy driving errant course with sparrow, dove, and swan and swallow, hovered round this shore.

Another day passed over the tranquil Mediterranean which was like a millpond in its calmness. The awnings were put up to keep the soot from dropping on us and to form a cool retreat on the deck, the only place where any motion of the air was perceptible. There was not wind enough astir to drive its currents into our submarine cyclopean furnaces for cool breath, and ventilation, and draught for fires. The storm-king could not have more kindly hushed his infant tempests if we had even been his pets.

All along the horizon on the right rose the saw-like peaks of the Taurus range where, in the City of Tarsus, lying at their bases, the apostle Paul first saw the light of day. (Jimmy said "that Taurus range makes a *bully* view," but we let it pass, for once.) After night-fall we crept carefully in towards the lights of Rhodes, and rattled out the cable when we stopped. We did not see much of this island where tradition said, no day ever passed without sunshine, which the ancients explained by saying, Phœbus was in love with Rhodes. Pindar, in his finest ode, took, perhaps, the most poetical view of volcanic eruptions when he describes this island as raised from the waves like Delos, by Apollo, and even staid old Virgil tells us that it is "too good for mortals." Here we live among the ancient poets and philosophers. **Now we** pass the small but fruitful Cos, with **its** groves of cypress casting mournful shadows, as **widow's** weeds over a beautiful face.

The **cypresses may** mourn for the victims immolated **on the altar of science, for Cos** was consecrated to Esculapius, **and here Hi**ppocrates, the great physician, **like many of his followers, was** bound to kill or cure.

Every **half hour seems to** raise the isles of old renown **like magic from the sea.** They appear at first as a pin's head on **the sight and grow** to masses of bluish steel, then approach **with every rock, and** tree, and blossom, showing plainly on their slopes. Their precipitous sides **drop down from among the gods** above to the very bowels of **the earth, and we plough and tear** our way in perfect **safety through the depths that** leap and **lick** their rocky walls. **Then they pass again into** the distance, as when **the** nymphs **had kissed and wept** over Perseus, " he **leapt** down **the** mountain, **and went** on, lessening and lessening like a seagull, away **and out to sea.**"

There, **to** starboard, lies old **Samos where** the wise Pythagoras investigated **the labyrinths** of the mind, where he and his followers **assigned** peculiar sounds to the motions of the celestial spheres. So much did he appreciate **the power of music,** that he thought the world was formed by **a kind of harmony, and** the Pythagoreans had the pleasant custom **of** being awakened **by** the sound of the lyre, **and** lulled **to** sleep at evenings **by its** strains. It may be **of interest to** ladies to know that **he** discovered that **the square on the** hypothenuse **of a right-angled triangle is equal to the sum** of the squares on the **other sides.**

Here is Patmos towering from the cerulean depths, with a village perched half-way up its terraced sides, where the **Apostle John wrote the apocalypse.**

At sunset, we run into the harbour of the ancient Chios, which **the modern** Greeks **call** Khio, and the Italians Scio. Now **we revel in what was called** the Paradise **of Greece,** and, **though the name is lost, it yet** bears all the beauty. One might gaze for weeks at Scio and not be sated. It is a bliss for an artist or a poet: blind old Homer must have *felt* its beauty inspiring his wondrous verses. How he must have longed for sight when they told him of the scenery around him, how he could, whilst sitting on the rocky shore, conjure up those words to suit the sounds his ears perceived. Here amidst the loud roaring of the sea he could rumble out his πολυφλοίσβοιο θαλάσσης, and among the groves of olive and myrtle, mulberry and pomegranate, could tune his lyre to softer song to emulate the nightingale.

We speed ashore as the four stalwart rowers move in perfect time over their bending blades, the light boat skimming swiftly past the threatening hulls above us whose tapering spars seem to knock at heaven's gate, and we spend the evening wandering about old Scio. The melodious strains of vespers often draw us to some fantastic church, where the Greek priests, among the gorgeous trappings of the interior, by costly dimly-lighted lamps are performing solemn service. Or, while sipping of the "best Chian" that Horace speaks of with so great a relish, we feel a pleasure in the manly bearing of the native men, and mark the modest noble carriage of the fair Greek women, who together take their evening stroll past the café where we sit.

A marked change is perceptible on coming here from among the Arab women, where all is slavery, squalor and peculiar kinds of modesty, and seeing these tall handsome women, whose uncovered faces speak better for the moral atmosphere in which they live, than all the doubtful modesty of their Eastern sisters. The weaker sex here begin again to assume more of their true position in society, and the very neglect of covering their faces speaks better for the men, who can trust themselves to look on fairest woman, which the Mahommetan confesses he cannot do.

On such a voyage as this the panorama of ancient views and memories is always on the move, and changing as the winds that bear us on; one is loth to leave the deck at all, and we often desert the dining-table *en masse* to witness some new passing scene of interest; while going to one's berth seems mere sacrifice of opportunity.

But the sun has hardly risen when we again assemble on the decks where half the previous moonlit night had echoed with our songs; even before appearing at the hatchways we have our heads out of the ports—wondering where we are. These brazen port-holes often frame the rarest pictures upon earth. For instance, when we wake and peer out upon the sea all motionless around us, and discover ourselves anchored off Smyrna, amid the flying squadron of English men of war, and in one glance take in those floating forts of England, and Smyrna, "the ornament of Asia" crowned with citadel and cypress—this is one of those surprising views a port hole sometimes frames. Smyrna looks exceedingly well from the harbour. It is packed together on a slope in front of a mountain, like a dish of peas, presenting nothing extraordinary in the way of architecture, yet relieved of any tendency to monotony by minarets and occasional domes. The hills extend from the back of the city around the bay—the part crowned with dense groves of cypress trees and the ruined citadel being the Mount Pagus of the Scripture; the site of that one of the seven apocalyptic churches of Asia* which was located here in the first century of our era. And among the multitude of graves on its summit, we find the tomb of Polycarp, who was bishop of Smyrna about eighteen hundred years ago, and was one of the venerable apostolic fathers as well as a disciple of Saint John. Here the fine old man, whose writings have been nearly all destroyed, suffered martyrdom for his faith, and, as he was led to death, the pro-consul offered him his life if he would revile Christ. "Eighty and six years have I served him," was the grand reply of the gray-haired old man, "and he never did me wrong; how then can I revile my King and my Saviour!"

After selections were made from the many gondola-shaped boats that swarmed around our ship like flies, and after bargains had been struck with the rowers, a course always necessary to pursue, we all went down the vessel's

---

* Dr. Cumming's seven churches of Asia Minor.

sides, and embarking in the cockle shells threaded our way through ships of war to the embankment. I don't know how it is, but the boatmen and people living in a similar way about harbours are always the greatest rascals in the world. It would seem as if there was something in the air that made them mean and underhand, or perhaps their profession educating them **to** bargain over the smallest things, makes them think **that** every advantage taken is fair gain; but if I can't **explain** the phenomenon, I **can** vouch for its existence, for **both at** home and in the East, and particularly in Italy, **they** are the most plausible, cheating rapscallions on the face of the earth.

But what a surprise awaited us at Smyrna! **We** were going to Ephesus by rail, and forsooth! real carriages awaited us in a station. We bought our tickets for Ephesus. We were booked through for Ephesus. We were going **to** have a *little run* down to Ephesus. Oh Diana, where **are** you now? Great goddess, whose praise once rang throughout this land, do not return to be rattled up to your city by **a** whizzing, puffing, snorting invention, and be bundled out into a miserable station by a barbarian conductor!

Everything about the road was of English manufacture. Under the words "First class for Ephesus," would be seen a collection of whirligigs and spider's legs, that meant the same thing in the native lingo. It was some time since we had been in a railway carriage, but we got in quite naturally, and were whirled off through forty miles of fine scenery, till we slackened up at our destination. The few horses that were to be had for extortionate prices were snapped up by the first comers, and the rest of us started off on foot for the four-mile ramble: the first things that struck us being the numerous high columns of masonry, where storks that had lived unharmed for ages now looked down from their huge nests at the band of intruders, who would dare to throw occasional sacrilegious stones at them. Then we crossed the deserted marshy plain, where, in the dry spots, we could see the serpents that infest the locality gliding into their holes, and many large ones were found dead about our path, where they had been killed by other travellers.

If anything can add to the desolation betokened by a fallen pillar, it is to see the glittering forms of snakes occupying the ruin, and the idea is connected remotely, I have no doubt, with the wily form of Satan when he viewed the ruin of our race and occupied the garden deserted by mankind.

In an unsightly hole, where excavations rendered all the scene an eyesore, lay the foundations of one of the seven wonders of the world—its great architectural ornament—the temple of Diana: an edifice which of itself exhausted all the quarries in the neighbourhood, and whose erection occupied more than two hundred years.

"It was four hundred and twenty-five feet long, and surrounded by a colonnade of one hundred and twenty-seven marble pillars, seventy feet high, twenty-seven of which were carved in the most exquisite manner, while the remainder were polished." Scopas executed the bas reliefs, and the altar was the work of Praxiteles, the first sculptor of all antiquity. We could climb over the immense fragments of the deserted shrine standing in pools of water, and could gaze in wonder on the gigantic masses of purest symmetry which had been but atoms in its composition, when, from its splendid pinnacles, it smiled haughtily upon all the buildings of the earth.

And when Paul was come here by the upper coasts from Corinth, Demetrius the silversmith, who made the silver shrines for Diana, called together his fellow workmen, and told them that Paul had "persuaded and turned away much people saying that they be no gods, which are made with hands." The smiths were full of wrath, and, making a very common use of religion for the purposes of business, cried out "Great is Diana of the Ephesians"; the whole city was filled with confusion and they caught Paul's travelling companions, and rushed with one accord into the theatre. Now after encircling a small mountain we come and stand in this vast theatre. The mountain at the back forms a natural part of the immense place, and is shaped like the tiers of seats of any large theatre of the present day. If the building was round it must have extended a great distance over the plain to form the circle of which now we only see a segment. Among this wilderness of fragmentary marbles the seats were placed tier upon tier, and, imagining the whole construction, as it most likely was, of circular shape, partly natural and partly artificial, it is difficult to say how many more people it would hold than the Coliseum. Perhaps three times as many. The Coliseum held 87,000. For this circus we should say then at least two hundred and fifty thousand, and they certainly would not build a larger place than was required for the theatre-going population. Imagine now the scene and **crush** when the "*whole city*" rushed with one accord into this **vast** ampitheatre. "Some therefore cried one thing and some another: for the assemblage was confused, and the more part knew not wherefore they were come together." Alexander was put forth to address the multitude, and beckoning with his hand he would have made Paul's defence, but for the space of two hours before the people were appeased there arose that fierce, unquellable, idolatrous cry, "Great is Diana of the Ephesians." It makes one almost quail to think of that stupendous uproar.

We climb in and out and over the beautiful masses that strew the plain and hills for miles. Frieze and cornice, column and capital, headless Dianas and bucklered warriors, temples and theatres, all lie glistening in the sun in the same position and on the very spot where they fell in the long centuries past, when the tree of our Gospel which now offers rest and grateful umbrage to the weary was first spreading its roots into all the cities of the world. The whole place looks as if God had swept away the city in his wrath with the besom of destruction. In the British Museum we may see some trifling ornaments of which Ephesus was pillaged, and at St. Sophia in Constantinople we may recognise the great columns of green granite which Justinian took from among their fallen brother-pillars lying here in heaps. We have but to use the spade to exhume, in half an hour, more graceful statues, more fragments of precious floors, more chaste capitals of purest marble, whose carved leaves drooping over seem almost as natural as the foliage of the old acanthus. Scores of richly carved sarcophagi are laid open to the view by a few feet of earth having been thrown aside by the excavators. Each massive mausoleum with its wreaths of stony flowers, worth a small fortune in England, lies among dozens of others in this wilderness, with nobody to take care of or to value them; and on one sarcophagus I noticed an inscription in characters of the purest Greek, but I forget now the words themselves.

A small theatre, probably a place of amusement built by some Ephesian Crœsus, has the very windows remaining in the walls, and even the rows of seats which have long waited to be repeopled, and to hear the festive mirth of jovial Comus ringing from the stage. We are struck, nay, startled by the maimed figures and staring faces that look up to us as if beseeching us to remove the tons of ponderous stone that have for ages crushed their life out, and near by, standing on the plain, made of porphyry and fully complete, is the baptismal font of St. John, about as large as a medium-sized circular dining table; the ruined church of the same apostle is also shewn. The great charm about Ephesus, as it stands now deserted and uncared for, is the fact that there are no people about —no officious loiterers or priests to disturb one's pleasure in viewing the wrecks of early grandeur—no noisome grottoes horribly connected with stories that are cherished by us all—but simply the marble masses themselves, telling their story better than any man or book could do it for them. But it is impossible to keep out the biblical topographers who are bound to find a site for everything, for in a hole filled with refuse splendour is shown the tomb of St. Luke. Out of all the thousands of tombs about, which are unidentified, St. Luke's alone is pointed out. It does make me so wild. Why can't they let the apostles, who died obscurely, rest in obscurity, and let their memories form their only graves and epitaphs, instead of having one set of dead apostles and graves in Italy and another set in the East. Surely they were ubiquitous enough in doing good in every country, whilst in life, to merit a quiet resting place in death.

We were not alone among the ruins, however. The middies, lieutenants and other officers from the fleet at Smyrna, were also lunching in the great theatre, and refreshments were being again handed around among the old *amphitheatre stalls*, just as in Covent Garden, where those knowing individuals who tread on everybody's toes go about, chopping out the word, "Shill'ngices, sir, sh'll'ngices?

The middies who were handsome young duffers and fine specimens of English boys were all dressed in their shore-clothes, and their great ambition being to get to the top of everything, when they came to some huge piers supporting arches whose stones were as large as a piano, they appreciated them much more if they could scale their topmost pinnacles. They looked with no great emotion upon the massive arches, said to have been the gates of the city, and they entered the cave of the Seven Sleepers with what might be almost called indifference, not knowing any more than we did who the Seven Sleepers were; and the way they chucked crackers at the sacred heathen statues propped against the wall was refreshing, after the sanctified looks and deportment that some of our pilgrims had always maintained in going through the Holy Land.

Is it not strange that, whilst passing through countries which are noted for certain exports or manufactures, one either sees none of the speciality, or at least does not see the best. Better figs can be seen in Canada any day than one sees in the bazaars of Smyrna. The soap we prize so much I never saw in Marseilles. Instead of streets flowing with perfume, as I always thought it did, Cologne has but few manufactories for its celebrated water. Beggars of Genoa are not clothed in velvet, and if we only stay at home, we get the best of everything without the worry of foreign bargaining and the annoyance of custom houses. Some people think they actually save money by buying abroad, whereas, the tips to the custom-house officers alone will generally make up the difference between the prices.

Above all things remarkable in Smyrna are the *hamals*, and the camels. The hamals, or porters, of Smyrna come nearer to that epithet of an "ox" than any people in the world. On large pads slung over their backs, they carry burdens generally weighing about five or six hundred pounds. They are not very tall, but are immensely built and wear a small jacket, heavy boots and knee breeches, which expose their huge calves, and after the burden is placed on their pads which alone would be enough for some people to carry, they march off like Atlas with the world on his back. A story is told of one of them, who, upon a wager, took fifteen hundred pounds on his back, walked across the street, slipped and fell under his load, and was crushed to death.

When the camels are carrying cotton or anything bulky they fill the whole street, often delaying the pedestrian in a bazaar for some time while passing by, and in Smyrna they have the finest specimens of the genus ever seen. Instead of having that very lean and emaciated look that most camels have, they are stoutly built, immensely strong, and on different parts of their bodies are covered with dense patches of long hair, valuable for many purposes.

"Smyrna the lovely," as they used to call it, has been rebuilt six times, and it is one of the few ancient cities of Asia that has retained in modern times any approach to its former prosperity. Situated on a secure and capacious harbour, with a good anchorage, and being, as it were, the door of the store-house of Asia, this result is only natural. In the course of its many revolutions, it has, in a manner, slid down the hill to the sea, and the sole vestiges of the ancient city, not obliterated, are the vaulted foundations of the Stadium, a few relics of the theatre, and the immense walls of the castle crowning the hill. The name of the great philosopher Anaxagoras is inseparably connected with Smyrna, also Anacreon, the famous lyric poet, and many of those mythological or historical characters, whose names are now every day expressions of the different attributes for which they were famous, are reputed to have been visitors or dwellers in Smyrna. It was one of Homer's birth-places. Apollo and Diana, Bacchus and Hercules, and **the Amazons** with whom they combated, were its **visitors**. Antony and Cleopatra, Augustus, Pompey, and a **host of** others knew Smyrna well; also Parrhasius, who **first** gave symmetry to painting, and made hair flow in natural elegance upon his canvas, and who, while painting the dying Prometheus from a captive slave bound to naked rocks, might have **said**:—

> " Ha ! bind him on his back
> Look ! as Prometheus in my picture here—
> Quick, or he faints ! Stand with the cordial near !
> Now—bind him to the rock !
> Press down the poisoned links into his flesh,
> And tear agape that healing wound afresh.
>
> So, let him writhe ! how long
> Will he live thus ? Quick, my good pencil, now !
> What a fine agony works upon his brow !
> Ha ! gray haired and so strong !
> How fearfully he stifles that short moan !
> Gods ! if I could but paint a dying groan ! "

We spent a day or two wandering through the bewildering maze of Smyrna's bazaars, in which we **were** never sure of finding **our** way, **and** through whole streets where they sold nothing but ancient and modern Turkish weapons, rarely-worked old pistols, yataghans, guns, daggers and Damascus blades, all richly mounted, chased with gold or silver, and ridiculously shaped as compared to our arms of the present day. We explored all the cafés and tried the beverages that looked most tempting behind the bar, generally seeming to be composed of sugar and colouring matter, mixed up with strongly scented hair oil. We didn't drink much in Smyrna.

The farewells of pretty foreigners are always interesting, because they take leave so warmly at parting, and get over it so quickly afterwards. Nothing could be more satisfactory than the good-byes which some eastern ladies, who were going off in the "Urano" with us, gave the gentlemen who came down to see them off; of course they were *all brothers*, and considerable display of delicate handkerchiefs was indispensably necessary to obliterate the streams of imperceptible tears which the owners of those melting eyes and rosy lips evidently supposed were flowing; but the chiefest charm lay in their getting over their affliction so quickly, and pacing the deck in great spirits with their husbands or cousins. I don't know who the ugly fellows were, I'm sure.

The Pacha had been invited to review the English squadron which was anchored all about us, and at this moment he was going aboard one of the ships. A gun boomed out from the Admiral's ship, all the rest taking up the salute, and before the smoke hid their hulls, the strings of flags that covered the ships from the trucks to the decks, floated gracefully down several times in courtly salutation. Then the sailors were put through their drill; at one movement the yards of all the men of war and gunboats were manned with myriads of tars; at another, they disappeared like magic from the rigging. The way they ran up and down the slack rigging was marvellous. Now the air was shaken continuously by thundering concussions. Nothing could be finer or more majestic than the rolling clouds bursting from the sides of the stately ships, curling far over the water before the report was heard. A regular engagement could hardly look more imposing, when, as the strong breeze carried off the smoke they blazed into each other's sides; nor would they be as beautiful when drawn up in line of battle, for then, I think, it is customary to house the tapering topmasts, and partly dismantle the ships. While the firing continued our anchor rattled up, and we swept through all the fleet like a reviewing monarch, and as I looked down on it all from our dirty rigging, waving farewell to some blue-coated fellows we met at Ephesus, I could not help feeling proud of old England and her navy. Soon Smyrna, "the crown of Ionia," and the ships striking awe into its inhabitants, dwindled in the distance as we ploughed

down the matchless harbour that would give anchorage
to the fleets of all the world, and before we got tired gazing
at the passing landscapes, darkness set in, and at night we
dropped a claw off Mitylene.

There is a certain feeling of quiet amazement and surprise, engendered often by the familiarity of the name and
the many ideas associated **with** it, that calls forth on certain occasions from profane people, when being shown a
place like Tenedos, the exclamation of "the deuce it is!"
When we tumble up **from** our berths, half asleep, rubbing
our eyes, and looking stupidly **at an** island covered with
old fortifications, which seems at early dawn to be a floating artificial delusion anchored in front of us, it takes some
time to realize that we are beholding one of those localities
we had wished never created, while plodding for the first
time through Virgil's Æneid. And after stamping around
a while on the motionless deck, we begin to wonder where-
abouts the wily Greeks hid their ships and themselves,
and, by the way, those "cognita litora" of Troy must be
on the other side of the smoke stack, and lo! it is even
so—about four miles off are the identical "well known
shores" that were left behind with the old "hoss" waiting
to be pulled into the Trojan walls. We have it all in our
minds now, but the Greeks must have gone to the other
side of this little island to escape being seen by the Trojans
rejoicing then at the apparent termination of the siege.

All the morning was spent in running up the Darda-
nelles, with a fresh breeze from the south, in company
with some large sailing ships, and two small piratical-
looking Greek "fruiterers." It was an exciting race. The
four ships were having it out among themselves and with
the Lilliputian mites that sailed like witches under a large
mainsail, two jibs and huge square top-sail; and even our
good ship, with all her rags hung out, and all her steam,
could afford to be no idle spectator of the scene. We followed them a long time before catching up, and ran in the
cluster along the narrow straits for miles. It was a grand
sight to see those fine vessels coming safely into Constantinople from the ends of the earth, with every boom, yard

and bowsprit bending with the swelling clouds of canvas that covered the masts from the large sails below up to where the knitting needles, piercing the heavens above, each spread its own little handkerchief to the breeze. They ploughed on with their bluff bows carrying huge " bones in their mouths," while once or twice a few skyscrapers were clewed up on the ships, and the topsails came fluttering down on the little boats as the squalls off the shore became more lively ; but as soon as the wind decreased a little, up went everything again, in the determination to carry on every stitch, and " the divil take the hindmost." Each would jockey the foremost out of her wind, so they had turn-about at the lead ; the small boats entering and leaving the water as cleanly as a knife hugged the shore for smooth sea, and laying down to the gunwale distanced the burly John Bulls ; while they all hung in our wake till night-fall.

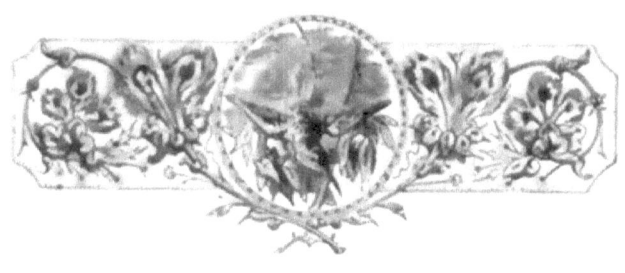

CHAPTER XVIII.

CONSTANTINOPLE was the one city left in the world that I hoped would fully reach the excellency of the encomiums bestowed upon it, and verify the accounts of its many panegyrists.

It matters not in what country we travel, or what cities we visit, there is always more or less disappointment felt when coming face to face with the objects of our inexperienced dreams. Their very reduction from realms of fancy to certain materiality is enough to have this effect. Where only fine streets, and parks and houses are looked for, there is more satisfaction experienced than when we have interwoven the imagery of poetry with the meshes of its streets, and made ideality the piles on which we built the city. Paris is, at first, more satisfying than Venice, because we only look for a fine city. Give Venice but the pale orb she worships, and in the silvery light of evening she again becomes a poem.

Her streets are then lines of perfect cadency, her mossy-based palaces are words containing each a new idea; the sparkling lights and skimming craft give life to every line, and in the song of the gondolier we hear the poem read. We may rattle into Rome, and the huge modern railway station breaks at once the first link of the chain of fancy, and before the hotel is reached whole fathoms of that cable have gone overboard. Naples' beauty is somewhat marred when we view it among odours not wafted from the Gardens of Cashmere, and even Edinburgh's fairness will not stand her drizzling rain.

Now we have laid in our thoughts of Constantinople, all such scenes as are described in every oriental tale, and we look for the footsteps of Aladdin rather than the Cæsars,' and the works of his Genii rather than those of Raphael or Angelo. The name of the city seems a synonyme for "domes and minarets," for who ever wrote of the one without speaking of the other? We think of it as a collection of cupolas floating in the air, of golden kiosks and marble fountains, of a confusion of flag-bearing masts and towering minarets, of marble palaces washed by flowing waters, where great ships could anchor at the very portals. For years we approach Constantinople in imagination when Mount Olympus is resplendent in the rising sun and the swelling globes and gilt-tipped minarets, glittering palaces and lofty towers are dreamy in the first blush of morn. For years we plough through blue waters past the Seraglio Palace rising on a point half-hidden by its foliage, and into the mouth of the Golden Horn, where we see Scutari across the Bosphorus, whose waters are filled with craft of every kind, and ships of every clime. Often have we gazed on St. Sophia, the mosque of Sulieman and all the others, where, in old Stamboul and Pera, domes were piled on domes, and have had visions of whole cities bristling with arrowy towers, whence the muezzin, like our Christian bell, proclaimed the hour of faithful prayer.

We dreamt of all this fondly, and cherished it in our bosom as the image of one long loved.

And it was so.

None will have to reduce their expectations very much when, on waking up, they find the ship anchored in the Bosphorus, and view for the first time the several divisions of the one great city, and the waters dividing them clasped by bridges or strung together by the ceaseless ferries. As long as a nearer approach than the deck of the steamer is not made, no one can say that too much eulogy has been passed upon it. If this position is held, where the myriads of caiques cleaving the waters, and where every craft, from yawls to ships with royals, can be seen sailing almost into the very houses before they come about, then it must be said that this is the most peculiar, as well as the most beautiful view that any known city can present.

Of course there are some things wanting in the surroundings, without which the city seems unreal, but which are fully supplied when one goes ashore; for instance we see, from the deck, no mangy dogs that have been scalded and worried till their dearest friends would not know them, thus we lose one of the great features of the town. We see no people with their legs in the middle of their back, or having two sets of arms, neither have the natives rowing near us anything particularly interesting about them. We see no men with horses following us by the half hour thinking we want to ride, and are too modest to ask. These are draw-backs, but they may be lived through.

A rigid custom-house examination is to be passed here, both on coming in and going out of the City; passports also must be shewn. I never had a passport, but I was always the son of the most respectable-looking old gentleman in the party, and a few piastres so obscured the official vision, that they were blind to all dutiable goods. My wrecked portmanteau was never touched. They didn't think it was a portmanteau, but only a fender for a boat's side. A lot of hungry looking porters were waiting to carry our luggage to the Hotel, and one of them seeing I valued in some way this *fender* took it up too, and charged double for the loss of character sustained in carrying it through the street!!!

After we had had "a scrub" and a light *repast* in which the hotel must have lost about two days' profit, we strolled out towards the post office, forming, in our best clothes, an eminently respectable group. The old spurs and leggings had long since been discarded, but we still carried our whips with us, because they saved us from being annoyed too much by pedlars and beggars, who knew then what they would get if they detained us by holding on to our clothes.

Very marvellous were the improvements that a few hours in the hotel made among our ladies. They had somewhat lacked in style whilst in the Holy Land, and had had a general appearance of "Sweetness long drawn out." Anything that was likely to be damaged by their sticking their heads into the mud had been then stowed away in the trunks, and their deportment while walking among tents was much too natural for Constantinople, so it was changed here.

I am not versed in the mysteries of the toilette, so I can only say, that when they came out to-day their appearance was very charming. Their cheeks were no more wan with much travelling, and their eyes sparkled with renewed glow; coils, plaits, curls, tails and fringes, and all those heavenly ideas as to the shaping of " woman's glory" made their appearance. All the edifices in the science of capillary architecture were now well exhibited, their carriage was most exquisite, and there was an indefinable *something* about them that imparted queenlike grace to their movements. Jimmy suggested " newspapers," but what had newspapers to do with such inimitable style ?

We entered an immense tower, and after climbing clear out of the world to the top, the guide said it was not the post office, but the tower of Galata, where we could have a fine view; but we implored him to take us to the post office, telling him that then we could see all the way home. He seemed so puzzled that we took pity on him, and looked out from the windows with impatience. He evidently thought us insane to refuse such a view, and so we would have been.

The wilderness of roofs stretched below us covered hill and dale for miles. On every side lay splendid mosques whose domes seemed to multiply out of calculation. We counted on one mosque between fifty and sixty domes, including all, both small and large. The arm of the sea called the Golden Horn extended far away from its bridges and ships through sylvan groves and glades to the " Sweet Water " pleasure gardens; Stamboul appeared on its opposite side, with its countless houses and bazaars forming a mass of varied colour; the Seraglio rose from the Bosphorus like a fairy palace and we looked across that beautiful sheet of water to Scutari, where so many of England's heroes found an honoured resting place. We followed the Argonauts' course, as they sped on towards the Euxine that no Hellen had ever crossed, and we now knew their course as they had come past Olympus, the seat of the immortals, and past the wooded bays of Athos and Samothrace, the sacred isle; past Lemnos to the Hellespont and by the narrow strait of Abydos, into the Propontis or the Marmora, that now stretched beyond our almost boundless range of vision.

Then we got our letters which supplied the mind's eye with a new lens to peer into our far-off homes, and reading them as we followed the guides along the ill-paved streets, we descended steep declivities and climbed wearisome hills, stumbling over the dozens of dogs that never move for mortal man, and going into places of interest, perfectly unconscious of our position on the face of the globe. I speak more for myself when I say this, for I received nearly a dozen welcome letters, and wandered on reading them, continually getting separated from the party, and heartily *blessed* by the Turks I collided with, till at last, I looked up, and found myself in a room with extraordinary figures in all postures around me. Some were threatening me with swords, and others had frightful daggers with waving blades in their hands; fierce Tartars glared over their terrible moustaches and clutched their spears beside them; ferocious Janissaries were advancing towards me, but had apparently stopped to make sure that I was the right victim, while the door closed behind me with an an ominous sound. I took it all in at a glance, and for an instant recoiled, then realized that I had unwittingly followed a treacherous Turk into a *museum of ancient soldiery*.

The first effect was peculiar. I wasn't afraid, I only wanted to see Constantinople at once.

Some of the figures were of wax and some of wood, constructed life size. They represented all the different costumes of Turkish janissaries and priests from the earliest ages, and not only were the weapons interesting, but the immense turbans and other head gear, which had always been varying in style and shape, had for us an almost greater attraction. Folds upon folds of muslin were wound together into all possible shapes, such as patent pails, Canadian cheeses, sugar loaves, pyramids, garden flower-stands, and from mosques and minarets down to paper collar boxes. I had never realized while reading of the thousands of Turks slain in ancient wars that they were really like these fellows, and it seemed rather a good thing that none did live on to the present day.

There was another place where, on descending a hole leading under the ground, they showed us the one thousand and one columns of Constantinople. About fourteen feet of each pillar was seen, and as much more might have been buried under the ground. A bewildering maze of columns stretched far away into the vast subterranean vault, and, for all I know, there may have been more or fewer pillars than the number named. We had no guide-books with us, and I have never since seen the locality mentioned in any Eastern works, so I need only add that if some holy-grotto makers would only affix some well-known biblical event to it, they might make these the most interesting ruins in the world.

Constantinople is a place where a good deal of fun can be devised by four or five fellows who are inclined to hunt it up, but the street scenes and city sights are too well known to bear new descriptions, now that one can rattle across from England in a few short days. It was a sort of week's do-nothing. We delighted in decent hotels and revelled in Turkish baths, we rejoiced in the street saddle-horses which replace the donkeys of Egypt, and we gloried in beating down the prices of articles in the bazaars, often buying things just to see how cheap we could get them.

The Dancing Dervishes are seen performing in their octangular place of worship, where the spectators are seated in the gallery surrounding the room, and also inside a barricade on the lower floor. We pay the fee and take our slippers from the boy who carries them from place to place, and thus entering with undefiling feet we watch the scene from within the barricade among a crowd of unperfumed natives. About fifteen men, dressed in pale green cloth dresses, girded about the waist and extending to their bare feet, are spinning about in the central space. They wear a peculiar white hat, of conical shape, about eighteen inches high; the eyes are half closed, as if in an ecstacy, and their heads are either thrown back or else placed on one side, so as to follow around the revolving shoulders. The arms are either placed about their sides or are held half in the air, which position imparts more grace to the movements and conveys a better idea of the transport they are supposed to be in. The dress floats out to its full extent with the whirling motion, exposing the feet and cotton trousers, and it is difficult to say how they manage their feet. The motion is perfectly free from any unevenness, they seem to make a half turn on the toe and heel alternately, propelling themselves with the other foot. There is just room enough for them to spin without touching one another (which they never do), while they imperceptibly follow each other around the room; this continuing for about twenty minutes, the chief dervish sitting at the head of the room calls them to prayer, when they kneel in couples before him while he reads aloud a sermon, and after a prayer, they commence the spinning again. There is no *dancing* motion about it, but simply a spinning as of a top, which becomes very monotonous after viewing it for a little while.

In such hot weather, the idea of one's religion being judged, like the governor of a steam engine, by the number of revolutions per minute, is revolting; and, strangely enough, a similar odour pervades both machinery and dervishes.

Our watches were left at home when we went for a

bath: they might, it is true, have been left with the savage who took care of our clothes, but we were not trusting enough. On a raised platform, in the first room we entered, were divans and bathers reclining, but we ascended to a smaller and more private apartment, where the attendants assisted us to undress. With a large shawl girt about us we descended the stairs and received on our feet some high wooden clogs to raise us from the heated and wet marble floors. I thought at first these were only for the wet, so I kicked mine up to the ceiling in disdain, however, when I got into the room where the steam was suffocating, the floors were so hot that I had to get the clogs again. In the centre of this room, where we waited, there was a circular marble platform, while all about the sides were niches, each one having a fountain from which hot and cold water could be turned on.

When we had begun to visibly disappear in this soft and enervating atmosphere, Turkish boys, as scantily clothed as ourselves, set us each down by a fountain and rubbed our arms and bodies, softly at first and then more briskly with hot water, till the epidermis rolled off in such a way that we thought we could have never been clean before. With closed eyes we let them continue in this way till they brought large dishes, and whipped up huge lathers of soap with mops of palm fibres, and then, with these wisps laid heaps of light suds upon our heads and bodies.

This felt nice any where but in the eyes. They doused copious bowls of hot water over our heads and washed us a little more, then led us into a cooler apartment, where they laid towels about the wet forms of four skeletonized young men, and wrapping our heads in turbans of soft towels, brought us through cooler chambers, to where the broad divans invited repose. Here we lay in great enervation, swathed in many towels, till we got dry, and while chatting among ourselves and making our narhghillis bubble lazily on the floor, another servant brought some strong coffee in little china cups without handles, and set in lower cups or sockets of silver filagree work. This seemed to be just the stimulant the exhausted frame required. The coffee is most pleasant to the smell, and is taken without milk; although generally condemned by Englishmen on account of the fine grounds that half fill the cup, it was, to me, delicious. We could sleep or doze here by the hour, and return to the air as new men; but several found that their first trial pulled them down **so** much that they refrained from trying it a second time.

On visiting the mosques, we went in a body with guides, who arranged about the entrance fees and told us what little they knew concerning the place. The great Sophia, the St. Peter's of the Turks, does not appear as well either inside or out as several others; the guides say it was built by Constantine after his conversion, and was turned into a mosque by conquering Turks. My letter never reached home from Constantinople, so I give somebody else's account of it.

" It was built by the Emperor Justinian, and completed **in** A.D. 538. The world was made to pay tribute to this temple, dedicated to the Divine Wisdom, and so named Santa Sophia. We come to the door and take off our shoes; for no foot that has trod the unhallowed earth may stand in these sacred precincts. By a winding path, in total darkness, we feel our way up by the tower, **and** come into the gallery for the women, from which we look down upon the interior of the temple. The **vast area** startles us at once; but we soon begin to admire its proportions, and then to contemplate the wonderful variety and beauty of its pillars and walls. Four huge columns support a glorious dome, and four hold semicircular cupolas on each side. These columns are of porphyry, and once stood in the Roman Temple of the Sun. Those green granite pillars, supporting the gallery, once adorned the temple of the great goddess Diana of the Ephesians. There are forty columns, some of serpentine marble, some of Egyptian granite, and others of white marble with rose-coloured stripes, and all of them plundered from temples of paganism; so that this temple is sustained by pillars of Isis and Osiris, of the Sun and Moon at Heliopolis and Ephesus, of

Pallas at Athens, of Phœbus at Delos, and of Cybele of Cyzicus.

"The walls are of polished marble, and the paved floor is covered with Turkish carpet and mats. Overhead and around on the walls are inscriptions from the Koran, instead of paintings, and the place is shown where the gold letters and stars are made to conceal a picture of the Virgin Mary, which was an ornament of the temple before Mahomet wrested it from the Christians, and defiled its courts with his Moslem troops."

This all sounds very well, but the interior is dingy and dusty, and does not equal the other cleaner and brighter mosques, such as that of Sultan Achmet or of Suleiman; while none, in my estimation, attain the excellence of the Grand Mosque at Cairo. The domed roofs are generally supported by four immense piers of costly stone, and at the heads of these, texts from the Koran are frequently seen flaringly painted on huge gilded disks; while the whole appearance of the vast interiors is that of void barrack-like vaults, poorly decorated with a few ornaments quite out of keeping with the architecture, set with hideous taste about the walls.

Whilst in this region of Stamboul there was an ancient and modern armoury to be seen, where a place like a church was filled with stacks of modern breech-loading rifles. About a hundred thousand arms were here, waiting patiently for the day when they would be called upon to belch forth their contents at Russian bears, English lions, American eagles, or at any other animals in the menagerie of nations. All around on the walls and ceilings were ancient arms fashioned into tasteful devices, and in other rooms were rare collections of breastplates, greaves, and helmets, guns used before locks were invented, and fanciful weapons of ancient days; while extraordinary little brass cannons and curiously-wrought arms bespoke the early uses of gunpowder. The famous swords of all the sultans, from the splendid Damascus blade of Mahomet the Second, were seen in the gallery, with the keys of all the cities of Turkey, mounted with gold and deposited in token of their fealty to the Porte.

One morning we went on board a **steamboat at the** long wooden bridge which crosses the Golden Horn, to take a trip up the Bosphorus. This bridge, that we start from, completely out-rivals London Bridge as **to interest** in passers-by. Every nation in the earth has **its** delegates representing them **here at** all hours of the day, and it must be the best spot on **earth** for observing "all the world and his wife," or his many wives, as the case is here. Even while waiting for **the** boat to start, we may see the Turkish gentlemen, who **now** dress **as** Englishmen with the exception of the red fez, riding past, and **the more** polite Frenchman who is careful of treading on other people's toes; the hadji or pilgrim who has been to Mecca, wearing the green turban as a sign of his holy journey, trudging along, clothed in dark garments reaching to his yellow boots; and the Yankee jostles him **as** well as the rest, although there is an adage among the Eastern people, who expect hypocrisy in religionists, that "if a man goes **to** Mecca once, be careful of him, if twice, have no business with him, if thrice, avoid him. The dark Arabs pass quietly by with their long tchibooks sticking out of the back of their striped abbas, which expose the lower part of their legs and the parched skin, "the vellum of the pedigree they claim," and the hugely-turbaned Persian swathed in white is returning to his bazaar in old Stamboul.

An officer of the Turkish Army caracoles **past** on a noble charger, which, prancing through the moving mass understands and finds his own way with slackened rein, and the surly, heavy-looking rider, clad in richly-coloured tunic, and girded with belt and sword of shining brass, sits in a fine saddle over a saddle-cloth of gold, paying no more attention to the people his horse knocks aside than if they were dogs. Then some of the Sultan's wives come slowly along with a guard in front, and a lot of eunuchs behind, who scowl death itself on anyone who gazes into the covered carriage. The way is blocked in front of where we are perched, and the four occupants, who fill the carriage with **a** cloud of rich silks, are amused at our position. They have a light gauze over their faces, which heightens the wondrous beauty it is supposed to hide, and, alas for the frail sex! those looks bestowed upon our young men would have cost them their heads had the Sultan seen them.

Our boys may have been an improvement on the Sultan as to good looks, and their eyes may have opened in undisguised admiration, which the others, as women, doubtless perceived, for they returned, while nobody else could see, long melting looks from their glorious eyes half covered by the silky eye lashes, and their pouting lips smiled in a way that would soften an iceberg.

A coal-black giant of Nubia soon rode his horse between us and the carriage, as he perceived a reflection of glowing lights in Gordon's eyes. We could have set fire to that fellow with pleasure.

Now the steam-boat starts, and we are whisked through a perfect Pall Mall of boats and steamers which get out of the way in a marvellous manner. The magnificent marble palaces, lining the north shore of the Bosphorus, that are almost endless in extent, are now passed. Some of them have just been finished, and stand as spotless as a statue fresh from the studio, with every pillar and corner stone shining in the sun—unused heaps of imperial splendour—matchless piles of rarest workmanship and design, some occupied by the wives, and some empty, because the superstitious magnate slipped at his first entry, or had some other unpropitious accident. We head towards the Black Sea, stopping at villages every few minutes, and darting across from Europe to Asia and back again, at each village finding people penned in on small wharves till the boat stops, when they are allowed to go aboard. Part of the little steamer is divisioned off by canvas curtains for the Turkish women, but none are seen that are worth such close concealment.

Every headland we pass opens up a new vista between the ever changing banks, that sometimes are undulating at the top, and at other places partake of a sterner and bolder nature.

Picturesque villages, looking like exotics from Switzerland, are dotted on the rising shores, and in every cleft a little hamlet nestles beneath the shade of cypress trees above. Italian villas are transplanted on the verdant slopes, where the **owners** of the kiosks or country seats that line the hillsides to the water's edge have borrowed all the graceful beauties of Italia's gardens, that moderate and temper the luxuriant **overgrowth** of **oriental** splendour.

As we pass **some** ruined castles hanging over green, precipitous banks far above **our** heads, we might think we were on the Rhine—that pales before these scenes—if it were not **for** the rich depths of transparent blue that could never remind us of the nondescript neutral tints of the German river of grape **and** goblet. When we **tear** along under some bold and purplish bluffs, we might imagine that the heights of Catskill towered above us, and that New York would ere long heave in sight along the flowing Hudson, but an airy-looking mosque or two, with crescent-tipped pinnacles, perched half way up the mountain side, or a garden full of sparkling fountains and eastern arbours, recalls to our minds that the vaunted river of the States is not **set with** jewels such as these. And where the vineyards, kiosks **and** villages cover not the intervening **spaces,** dark groves of mournful cypress crown the summits, or spread a pall over part of the scene, telling of the dead amid such light and life; and that even here, among these endless beauties, man must die and leave them all. Presently the Black Sea spreads wide and limitless before us, as it did before the heroes in the ship Argo, when they saw it stretching out in front of them without a shore, and "trembled for all their courage, when the ice-cold wind, from the wandering blue rocks that shone like spires and castles of grey glass, swept down and chilled their hearts."

Then we land and beguile the time in wandering through the native village, like many others, built so close to the water, that one could almost leap into the second story windows from the steamer that rushes past the shore in several fathoms of water. Another boat takes us down the Asiatic side repassing all the scenes, and threading our way through the large ships slowly tacking through the straits, landing us at Scutari, opposite the main city, where we mount our horses to visit the Howling Dervishes and English Cemetery. The horses clamber up the stony streets of Scutari, not like our trusty old Arabs, but clumsily slipping and striking fire from the stones, and we dismount at the top of the hill and enter a small building, with a gallery around the interior, where we rest in our stocking feet, with several of England's Lords, similarly shoeless, who have come here from their yacht to view the scene. The room was low and intensely hot. Below us was a semicircle of men, dressed in ordinary costume, commencing their religious performance, and several small children at the ends of the circle were following the motions of the men. They were swinging their bodies back and forth, and from side to side, bending their heads down till near the ground, then springing suddenly erect with all the activity of acrobats. The ceaseless chorus of Allah! Allah! Allah! accompanying each motion, became more guttural and indistinct every five minutes, till it grew into a sort of gasping howl, horrible to listen to. There was no cessation to the violent swaying and bending, which became more frantic as the minutes dragged by. The fanatics were pouring with perspiration, their eyes were starting from their sockets, their mouths were open and their tongues were lolling out; still they kept up the motion with redoubled energy as if possessed of devils, and the little children seemed nearly dying with the fatigue of the exercises they were forced to keep up. The more energetic frothed at the mouth as the gasps degenerated into moans, yet no one could bring himself to that pitch of religious frenzy or choking fit, which is supposed to be the visitation of holy spirits to the devout.

We could see upon the wall rude drums and cymbals for other rites; and knives, steel hooks and instruments of torture, with which to tear and mutilate their bodies in some of the more frenzied orgies. We left the house, that reeked like the Black-hole of Calcutta, before any of them actually went into the fit, and were glad to get out from such horrid scenes that almost equalled the old worship of Moloch. The high priests of the Dervishes sit in the middle of this circle and pronounce benedictions on the **devotees** afterwards, and then children are brought in to be miraculously cured of **their** diseases by his power. An American writer **says:** "The first was a babe not two years old, wound up **after their** fashion in many folds of cloth, so that it can **move** neither hands **nor** feet. It was placed upon the floor upon its face, and the sheikh, who would weigh certainly one hundred and seventy five pounds, placed one foot across its legs, and then carefully raising the other, placed it in **the** middle of the back, and stood with his whole weight upon the child. He stepped off cautiously and the servant took up the child, which seemed to be unharmed by the pressure."

A gallop of ten minutes brought us to the English Cemetery, walled in and kept by an Englishman, where those brave fellows were buried that fell wounded in the Crimea, and lingered in the hospital at Scutari till they died. It was a spot whose very beauty would reconcile many men to being soldiers if they were sure of having such a resting place in death. It was a spot where the poetry of a soldier's life and the fine essence of martial glory, that passes death into eternity, could **be** better sustained and perpetuated here, by the similitude of the beauty around their graves to the ideality of their lives. Here, side by side, were England's heroes laid, that had left their homes **and** friends never **to** return, ranged together, as soldiers, **in the rank** and file of Death, quietly awaiting the last clarion **that is** to marshal all into the field of Judgment; when, at the last roll of the drum, they will again meet their comrades, and together await the orders of the Most High. Flowers grow up about the tombstones where no dear hand had strewed them when the graves were freshly made, and from a giant monument of granite, angels of peace, spreading forth their wings, cast mournful shadows over the honoured tombs; and cut in stone as lasting as the memory of man, as eternal as the glory there engraved, in French, Italian, Turkish, and English, are seen the records of their fame.

The view is like the Bay of Naples, as we see it from Vesuvius. We have a Sorrento, a jagged Capri, and a rugged Ischia standing out of the horizon to seaward, called the Prince's Isles, and to the right we have a city— not Naples, but Constantinople, lit up in all the hues of the setting sun, with every crescent tipped with gold; and far below the quiet graves, at the bottom of a perpendicular cliff, the waves of the Sea of Marmora sing a ceaseless requiem. I had a distant kinsman once, who lived a while at my home in Canada, and one of my earliest recollections is being shewn his handsome portrait, and being told that he had been shot in the trenches before Sevastapol and had died at Scutari. I have stood by many graves, and have entered many sainted tombs, but I never rested by any of them with such feelings as now pervaded me when lingering by his monument above the blue and rippling sea. Though not lachrymose as a rule, I have to confess to brushing away the first and only tear that ever kinsman shed over this soldier's grave. I thought of all the fond mothers too, and loving widowed wives, that would give years of their lives to visit these graves of the sons or husbands that lie buried here among strangers in a foreign land; and I thought what a relief it would be for certain others to give vent to the silent sorrow that had saddened all their smiles since 1854, when manly forms had bent over them in a last caress, then rushed away—forever.

We passed out, and remounting, hurried over the commons to take a ferry back to Pera, and while crossing these waste spaces in the country, occupied only by hordes of wild dogs, we noticed the vast tracts of Mahometan cemeteries lying to our right. I made a hasty detour to view these, while a savage pack of wolfish beasts followed jumping at my feet. The tombs I found were generally of costly construction, gilded, carved or painted in peculiar ways. Each Turkish Mahometan tombstone had carved upon the top of it, the shape of the covering for the head which the deceased wore whilst in life, and thus his rank and importance are always known as long as the stone remains. The effect, as may be imagined, is very peculiar, on account of the stones, which are gaudily painted at first, being suffered to get mouldy and slope in all directions from the ground, giving the graveyard an appearance of a collection of Turks, wearing every kind of turban and fez, and suffering from the effects of too much "arrack." Over each grave the Mahometans also plant a cypress, which they think has the effect of absorbing all infection from the corpse, so that whenever a grove or forest of cypress is seen, we know that there is another of Death's orchards, from whose roots he gathers in his fruit.

The bazaars of Stamboul, always of such interest to the traveller, have become more Europeanized of late, and although the keepers of the little shops in the arcades dress in the old way, there are more goods sold that have been made in occidental countries; and the more wealthy merchants, many of whom have travelled a little, copy the English dress more than a stranger to Constantinople would suppose. But once in the interminable arcades one can wander for miles through many of the old scenes of purest orientalism, witnessing the bargaining between the shrugging vendors and deprecating customers, and see streets full of rich dresses, and slippers embroidered with gold and silver, and stacks of the patchwork tablecloths and cushions that have made Constantinople remarkable. We nearly all had to procure new receptacles to carry away the purchases of slippers, cushion-covers, bottles of attar-of-roses, and numberless other things which we had been spending our idle hours bargaining for.

While the remembrances of old Nablous, Jerusalem, and Cairo, are fresh in my memory, I will not describe the well-known Eastern peculiarities of Constantinople for fear of repeating myself or tiring the reader. I will not describe the pleasant little journeys in the caiques, that cleave the waters of the Bosphorus with their upturned pointed bows, nor the trip in one of these fleet skiffs pulled by brawny oarsmen up the Golden Horn, where we pass from the hospital for old ships of war and refuge of many a battered vessel, to where the stream, passing verdant shores and picturesque villages, grows as small and tranquil as the little Isis, where Oxford students pole their shallow punts. Nor will I speak of the pleasant groves and leafy glades that here begin to line the shores, where the rich resort in carriages or in graceful boats of many rowers, and all classes breathe the fragrant meadow air and dally by the river side; nor of the clusters of Eastern maidens from Pera and Galata, that move slowly about the sward, each dressed in flowing garments of some single colour of great richness, forming bright bevies of beauty to deck the landscape, and appearing in the distance, while sitting together, as garlands of dahlias scattered by the spring side.

One day a few of us took a stroll towards the marble palace on the Bosphorus, expecting to see the Sultan proceed to his mosque, which he does on every Wednesday. Vast crowds were waiting about the gates and thronging the streets through which he was expected to pass, and two or three regiments were drawn up with their bands to accompany him to the mosque.

But the Sultan is very capricious about his movements; often changing his mind at the last moment, and going in a different direction. Some say he is in constant fear of assassination, and takes a different course to frustrate any conspiracy to take his life that might be in project. To-day we heard, after waiting some time, that he would go by boat to his mosque on the Bosphorus, so we all followed the Turkish soldiers like so many *gamins* through the streets. The music was a wild barbaric march, that rings in my ears yet, and was unlike anything I had ever heard. The instruments were of peculiar shape; some men carrying large brass rattles, shaped like huge maces, and surmounted by large crescents. At the mosque we took a caique and rowed out towards the ships of the Turkish navy anchored opposite the palaces. It had been a source of considerable dissatisfaction at other times to view the excellence of these foreign men-of-war. If anything, they looked superior, and seemed better supplied with modern inventions than the English war ships we had seen at Smyrna, and they certainly made as much row.

Presently, a gun boomed from the furthest ship, as the Sultan was seen to start from his palace, and all the others took up the firing, discharging their guns on the port sides while he passed to starboard of them.

The flags, that almost enveloped the rows of men on the yards, dipped several times in salute, and the crews of each ship gave a single shout as he passed. Now we could see the regal galleys approaching like lightning over the blue water, with twenty-six rowers in white stepping upon the seat in front of them to take the stroke, then throwing themselves back upon the gilded oars till they sank flat upon their backs. They took these strokes with great quickness and unison, fairly lifting the craft from the water. A long gilded prow rose gracefully in front of the boat, running into a horn projecting about ten feet in front. The galley of pure white and gold, was, perhaps, over sixty feet long, and under its golden canopy sat the Sultan, dressed in blue clothes, with a sword girt about him, and the inevitable fez on his head ; while behind the throne was posted a helmsman. He took no notice of the guns firing, or of the band that struck up a wild tune, but gazed stolidly downward till the boat headed up by the steps leading to the mosque, and the man in the bow threw the silken line to the shore. As the Sultan passed up, each regiment gave a single shout—not the warm ebullition of loyalty—not the heartfelt hurrah that springs from a London mob, as one voice, when royalty makes its appearance, but the forced, soulless, discordant shout of slaves of a despotic ruler.

The Sultan walked slowly, with stooping frame, up the steps, and turned into the mosque without any recognition of his subjects, and perhaps a feeling of relief passes through him as he found that once more he had escaped the assassin's bullet.

Now let me finish this chapter. Borack, the old pen, who has for hours been tearing over foolscap, is completely used up, and will no longer sip of the little Stygian pool in front of me, which alone can sustain his powers and impart utility to his movements. In his fatigue, Borack finds that, like Achilles of old, the dips in the Styx leave him weak in some points yet.

CHAPTER XIX

THE fair Ægean is fast asleep: neither laughing ripples play upon its countenance, nor do troubled furrows mar the serenity of its brow. Its breast may, perhaps, be gently breathing, but the slumber is too peaceful, and the silence too profound, to mark the rise of inspiration and the ebbing fall that speaks of life within its depths. It has the tranquillity of stone, of pure and newly chiselled marble, resembling most the beauty of Pygmalion's maiden statue through which life has been infused. We have seen its glistening arms, as immaculate as ivory, stretched with bridal fondness around that neck of land where Leander met his love, as if the soul of Hero still possessed the waters, and lingered round the spot that saw her love and death. But now we have come down from among the few rare jewels that form a diadem for her brow to where the Cyclades lie as a necklace of amethysts around her; and, farther down, some sparkling pendants nestle in her gently undulating bosom. And strung upon this necklace the emerald Syros is admired above all others, and in its very heart is set a gem of gems, the lovely town of Syra, rising cone-shaped from the sea.

We cannot but gaze delightedly at Syra, as the vessel

stops as if she too were spell bound; the varied colours of the vine-covered houses, and the shape of each picturesque Greek cottage on the hillside make such a grateful change from the monotonous views of Turkish and Arab towns, that we feast the eye upon it gladly. No minarets or mosques claim old acquaintance with us here, for we are getting nearer home, and no more will be heard the *muezzin's* daily call to prayer that was always grating on our ears. And having parted now from these stately ornaments of every Moslem town, no great loss is felt. We could hardly have a surfeit of them; but when from Constantinople we rushed through the old Propontis towards the setting sun, leaving a glorious sight behind us, we felt that any dwarfish domes or stunted pinnacles that we should see henceforth would only disenchant our memories of the Osmanlis' places of worship.

The quarantine, that formerly proved such an annoyance to travellers, having been removed from Syra, we were enabled to leave the "Jupiter" and go on board the little paddle-wheel steamer "Schild," that was to take us to the Piræus. A few hours were spent in roaming over the town, or scudding about under the gracefully shaped lateen sails, and, after dark, the anchor left its weedy bed, and we paddled quickly away into the night, leaving rolling waves of phosphorescent sparks behind us, and only a pyramid of twinkling lights to mark the place where the lovely city of the day had been.

If the days had become so continually serene as to dispel all thought of cloud or storm, the nights were even more celestial, making slumber seem a useless waste of time, when, instead of breathing the confined air of the cabin, we could be watching the glories of the firmament. Several of us preferred to sleep the few hours between our last chorus and sunrise rolled up in rugs upon the deck, and the refreshing rest that came to us here left us in the morning as bright as bells, while others from the stuffy cabins looked feverish and stupid.

As the night was furling her starry banner before the approaching god of day, we descried, when first raising our heads from the trembling deck, the long low shore line of Greece; and as the hosts of the night were fleeing in myriads before the arrows of the powerful sun-god, he hurried on, taking mountain peaks at first, and before deigning to set foot into the valleys, the old garrison of Athens capitulates before his shafts. No need to tell us what that ruin is, planted like a speck upon a distant mound. It would be like pointing to the smoking mountain by the Bay of Naples, and saying, "Behold Vesuvius!" to tell us that it is the Parthenon, set in the Acropolis, that, even at this distance, presents each column to **our** view.

With the day came a rattling breeze, that made the stout Grecian fishing boats keep up gamely with our swift little steamer: an hour's run along the coast, and we glided into the ancient harbour of the Piræus. Here all thoughts of ancient Greece had to be forgotten. They were dispelled in spite of us. The small harbour, lined by a stone embankment, was alive with gaily-dressed Albanians and picturesque natives watching our approach; dozens of boats flocked about us when we anchored; others flying from the shore, like vultures to a carcass, rounded to, and dropped their wings to have each a peck at the prey.

At every port around the eastern part of the Mediterranean these flotillas of small craft congregate about the steamers, covering the sea for as much as sixty feet around the steps let down the vessel's side. Every anchoring is a scene of a perfect civil war between the inhabitants, half of whom seem to be boatmen: fighting like maniacs for the nearest place at the steps, they try to insert their strong boats by rushing them with full force between the others, while the expected prey look down amusedly from the decks above.

Then come the bargains for the passage to the shore, when the wily Charons ask double the tarif, the passengers trying to look as if they didn't want to go till they get the charge lowered. This had been arranged for us by the *commissionaires* of the hotel in Athens, so we came ashore and popped into carriages to be whirled for six miles through an avenue to the little metropolis.

Nothing we suffered in the desert equalled that drive to Athens. The dust enveloped everything, so that we could not even see the carriages following, and each driver, unwilling to be left in the clouds raised by our horses, tried his **very** best to pass us, making a regular chariot race, without any of the pleasure. So fine were the particles that they entered the tightly-closed eyes. It seemed **as** if the *souls* of the ancients were quiet enough, but **that it was** their *dust,* pulverized by centuries, that bothered us.

What a relief it was **to have** a rest on a shady balcony **outside** delightfully situated apartments, and after washing away the grit from our eyes, to watch the people passing in their native dresses, and the regimental bands marching gaily through the Grand Square below. Hearing these fine strains every day, which we had long been unaccustomed to, intensified the different moods in which we happened to be, as music always **does** ; **for does it** not drive the happy perfectly wild, and seem, to the superficial gazer, to increase sadness into sorrow whilst bringing tears to the parched eye of grief ? Does it not fill the listener with a sweet melancholy sometimes, a nondescript sensation, which shows itself according to the situation ; if we are near those we love, does it not **draw us** more tenderly close ; or if separated by thousands of miles, does it not waft us into scenes of home dearer than earth itself, and produce a weary longing to transport ourselves whither our minds can fly at once ? **In** other **words, does** it not change the lover into a devotee, and in **its very strains bear** the malady **of** homesickness **to the traveller ?**

Those were halcyon days spent in that cool room, and shady balcony. More poetry **was to** be extracted from the ruins of **Athens** while sitting there with the Acropolis frowning down in front of us, than in continual meditations among the debris of ancient temples. All day a mellow warmness pervaded the air, not a glaring heat, but yet enough to make us seek the shade, and while it disposed to laziness of body, rather seemed to stimulate **the brain.**

We sat here most of the days, thanking our lucky stars at having seen all the ruins in one day's drive; exempted from further worry about sight-seeing, but able to stroll out on moon-lit nights to form our own ideas of them then. The "Times" was literally devoured by the pilgrims hungering for news, and the few books, that were to be had, soon found their **way** to my comfortable retreat.

Ernest and I had shared tents, state rooms, and apartments everywhere, living as congenial spirits—never even squabbling the whole time **we were** together. We had with us part **of M.** Simeon's translation of Horace's Odes into French verse, Corinne, and a few Italian and French newspapers which we bungled through **to** our heart's content; and after a daily dig into the history of Athens, there ensued a dessert of some of Thackeray's works, thus the hours passed away as quietly as the smoke-curls that marked their course.

It was in my first stroll after arrival, when feeling the difference between the Italian-looking town and my visionary Athens, that I entered an open space and saw, apart from all habitation, the mighty remnants of the once unrivalled temple of Jupiter Olympus. Before me rose part of that fane whose splendour and magnificence were the glory of Athens, where the supreme pagan deity was propitiated, supplicated, and worshipped. Here was erected the colossal statue of the Olympian Thunderer, formed of brass and fashioned into the shape of **man**; also the shrine of Chronus and Rhea.

> "Here, son of Saturn! was thy fav'rite throne :
> Mightiest of many such ! Hence let me trace
> The latent grandeur of thy dwelling place.
> It may not be : nor e'en can Fancy's eye
> Restore what time hath laboured to deface.
> Yet those proud pillars claim no passing sigh ;
> Unmoved the Moslem sits, the light Greek carols by."

Who does not regard Athens as the very zenith of travel—the reward to be received after education among other countries' ruins—the perfection of a ruined world's remains.

No ordinary pleasure and privilege was it to walk

through this colonnade. It had been a long cherished anticipation to thus end my wanderings through many ruins among the remains of the "City of Sacred Streams." But I could only feel my utter inability to comprehend them when I trod like a pigmy upon the floor of the mighty Olympium. Inexpressible admiration was still left to me however, and with that I had to be content, while deploring the limited range of speech that would give my feelings utterance, and longing for those productions of pure intellect which even the heathen say man was once possessed of.

The structure itself could not fail to remind one of our imperfect state, when, Peisistratus having founded it, six hundred and fifty years elapsed before its completion by Hadrian. Plutarch compared the unfinished "Atlantis" of Plato to the Olympium in its imperfect state: and now it is "a sad simile for the awful wreck of the mind where only a few rays of reason occasionally beam, to show the chance observer that the once glorious habitant within hath not as yet totally abandoned its slowly-sinking tenement of clay."

One can climb upon the bases of the upright pillars, and where one of them has been cast down by storm or earthquake can walk between the portions of the column separated by the fall, and try to make his own height equal the diameter of the massive fragments, while between, the marks of the chisel are as fresh as on the day they were made.

About twenty-three hundred years ago these thirteen columns, with one hundred and seven others, came down, pure and spotless, from the neighbouring Pentelicus. Since then they have been the models from which every town, from St. Petersburg to San Francisco, has had its copy. The Corinthian column, most to be admired of all, is here seen in all its early perfection; modelled with all the skill and science of the ancient Greeks, and combining, in reality, the massiveness of the Assyrian and Egyptian works; though, at first sight, its immensity is not noticed through the extreme grace and symmetry of its outlines, and the perfect uniformity of its proportions. The enormous capital lay upon the floor of the old temple, with every leaf shining in the sun, as the helmet wreathed with laurel lies upon the battle-field apart from the warrior when motionless in death. And it recalled the old story of the Corinthian virgin, who, after death, had placed upon her grave, a basket containing those little trinkets and knick-knacks that maidens dearly love. The basket, covered with a tile, was accidently placed upon an acanthus root, which shot forth, towards spring, **its** large foliage, and, in the course of growth, reached the angles of the tile, thus forming the volutes at the extremities.

While continuing my walk through the suburbs **of the** town, I saw a handsome young man, sitting by the wayside, singing a low melody as he thrummed on a small guitar. He was dressed in the short, open, dark-blue jacket, half covering the rich shawl around his waist into which a pair of ornamented pistols were thrust. The high red felt hat was crushed down and hanging to one side, in the customary way, so that the long blue silk tassel drooped **and** spread gracefully over his embroidered shoulder; the many folds of his stiff white skirt fell over graceful limbs clad in leggings shaped as greaves, and his feet, encased in red slippers with large rosettes at the toes, were crossed carelessly in front of him. While regarding him, **at a** little distance, and wondering why he was singing **there** alone so sweetly, a rattling of hoofs called my attention to a horse, that had been startled in the town, rushing wildly towards us. I sprang into a recess to let it pass, but the young man, in endeavouring to do likewise, was hurled, stunned and bleeding, to the ground. I hastened to him, but I was not the first to aid him. A shriek rang out from **the** lattice above, and a beautiful young girl burst from **a** door to be the first to raise his head and place it in her lap; and, in a moment, I saw that fonder ears than mine had been listening to the serenade that seemed so innocent of design. The incident is hardly worth recording, but the look of unspeakable tenderness and love that came into the young man's eyes, as he returned to consciousness, was beautiful to behold. It recalled and confirmed the idea that love—the cream skimmed from the surface of passion—will heal our deepest wounds, and while it sometimes makes its own incisions on our hearts, supplies itself the soothing balm.

Eleusis lay near the Bay of Salamis, within a few hours' drive from **Athens,** and our carriages were guarded by a small body of cavalry, all the way back and forth. On **account** of the brigandage, hitherto rife in the country, every carriage travelling along the roads is thus guarded **by** armed horsemen, who follow a certain distance, then deliver their charge to others, who continue the protection without a word said to any one. We felt like governors-general on the occasion, and were glad to see that the young king had provided us with a body-guard suitable to our rank.

Some book says Eleusis possessed a magnificent temple of Ceres, and gave its name to the great festival mysteries of the Eleusinia, celebrated in honour of Ceres and Proserpina.

I don't know much about the place. Perhaps the heaps of huge broken pillars and statuary are the remains of Ceres' Temple. No "flood **of** thoughts came o'er us with a rush" as we scrambled over the fragments of cornices, capitals, and columns, and we walked over the old floors where the devotees of old had performed the rites of their poetic worship with no other feeling than the hope of finding a nice place to have our pic-nic. We found a table and a couple of benches outside an old **wine-house** by the wayside, and there we spread the contents of our hampers. The "vile offspring of the brave," that kept the tavern, had nothing to drink but sweetish syrups and fiery aqua-dente, so he offered us some very fair muddy coffee, which we ate as well as drank, and a horde of hungry children, with several dogs and various cats, watched us "tucking in." These were partial drawbacks, but after having had the Arabs watching our every mouthful, these children seemed like seraphs; we even gave the improved set of dogs a new lease of life with the **scraps.**

We bathed in the clear waters of the bay, down by the old stone mole, where Themistocles or Aristides may have embarked, and were shown the Straits of Salamis, into which the Armada-like fleet of the Persians was decoyed, losing five hundred of its large ships, while the valiant Greeks darting about in their nimble triremes achieved the victory with a loss of but forty; and we saw the hill on which Xerxes' throne was raised to view this great naval combat, that might be likened to the duel of David and Goliah for inequality and result.

The way home led through glens and glades, between forests and under frowning cliffs, and when we had rounded the shore of the bay and ascended into a gorge in the mountain, the view, on looking back, framed by the banks of rock near by, stretching over the waters and shores, renowned both in history and in poem, presented a picture of surpassing beauty and interest. Greece seemed more than ever like our visions of the land of glory and of song; a place fit for the wars of gods or the revels of poets. The craggy shores seemed the natural altars for the sacrifices to the Nereids, and spots of shingly beach still offered smooth surface for their pattering feet, when, decked with coral and pearls in their sea-green tresses, they danced along the shore, till Triton blew a blast from his silver-sounding shell, summoning them to the blue depths to attend the car of Amphitrite. In such leafy copse as we were passing through, the piping shepherds might have seen, in their imaginations wrought upon by a fabled faith, the phantom shadows of the Naiads retreating from the rivulets, their feet glancing white among the ferns; or, in the dusk of evening, they might have thought the distant sheep upon the mountain side, were Nymphs assembling for their dance with the Dryads from the woods, when the dreaded Satyrs would join the Bacchic orgies, to the flute of old Silenus always mellow with old vintage.

In the vales the baffled huntsmen may have seen the fleeting deer double back and pass him as if chased by pursuers more than mortal, and with his brain all reeling, and his horse drooping with fatigue, may have imagined Artemis, the huntress queen, her yelling pack and immortal train of Oreades passing close beside him in full cry.

There was a fascination, that lingers with us yet, about the faith of these simple folk who peopled their dark groves and sparkling fountains with light and fairy deities; who felt that, after their quiet pastoral life was ended, their shades would be in no danger of Cerberus, or of the punishment of Tartarus, like those of impious men; and that the burning lake and rolling stone of Sisyphus would have no terrors for them after death. The phenomena of nature seemed to them to have some immediate relation to the powers divine. And how much more attractive was this religion of the imagination, even with all its terrors, than the prosaic sceptical belief of many of the present day, who, crediting only what can be proved by demonstration, cavil at their church's creeds, looking for a miracle to persuade them, and, ever seeking for the tangible, thus have no belief at all: men who see no charm in the sunlight streaming through the oaks, throwing fanciful lights and shadows over the secluded dells, where fountains swell and bubble among the lilies and the moss; men who view the glorious rising sun merely as the lamp that lights them to their constant strain for gold; who perceive no beauties in religion or in nature—soulless creatures, who are dead to the true enjoyments of this world, and hardly, we should think, fitted for the next. Over Christianity, such as this, the mythology of the heathens takes exalted rank; for did not their old poetical beliefs, whilst in undiluted ignorance, seem better than a half knowledge and neglect of the Almighty.

And if their veriest ignorance was to be admired, how much more was the wisdom of the enlightened philosophers and statesmen of Greece, who illuminated the darkness in which they lived, and left their maxims to be folfowed by all good men, both Pagan and Christian. They seem to have travelled through most of the then known countries in quest of that knowledge, parts of which have come to us; and opened schools to give the Grecian youth the benefit of their lore, and an education which, except among the Stoics, always savoured of Arcadia; for the Ionian loved the lyre and song, and hymns of poets formed the staple of Athenian education. Yet the constitution of Solon demanded in the people a great knowledge of the law, with a large share of its daily administration. Thus the acuteness of the lawyer was grafted on the imagination of the poet, and these, with the calculation of the mathematician, and the practiced oratory of the bar, gave birth to the qualities which constitute earth's greatest statesmen and lawgivers.

In such an atmosphere as this was passed the youth of Plato, whose philosophy left so deep an impression on the Jewish and Christian schools of Alexandria. Its great effort was to unite the contemplative mysticism of Eastern sages with the accurate sciences of Greece; to combine, in short, the two qualities, intellectual and moral, argumentative and spiritual, into one harmonious whole. It is not wonderful that so magnificent an idea attracted the desires, and rivetted the attention of thoughtful and contemplative minds ever afterwards.

On walking through the modern Athens, we look in vain for some trace of the spirit of these great men among the present people and their works. The site of their old Academy is almost conjectural, and each remaining work now seen, gigantic in conception and execution, only serves to show the change between the past and the present. One stroll through those vast repositories of relics—the Vatican and the Capitoline museum at Rome, will show how, in the imitative arts, the powers of executing the fair ideal was manifested in the Grecian mind. The Dying Gladiator, the Venus, the Laocoon, of Grecian sculptors, are alone sufficient to show the superexcellence of the ancient art of Greece. Ten minutes, in the yet perfect Temple of Theseus, now used for a museum, or a glance through the treasures of the Acropolis, will convince one of the fact, that the great metropolis also carried off the palm for fine arts from all her sister cities. Of course it would be unreasonable, judging by histories of the rise and fall of other countries, to expect that Athens would maintain her sway any longer than she did; but her death, after **she had** lost her manly mind and virtue, was peculiar. **It was** like that of a warrior who had lived through **all** his battles and sank at last through internal disease. Her contests she survived with ease, **but it was the** inward splenetic disorders, and the never-ending **cabals, that brought** her slowly but surely to the grave.

On going to the Acropolis on a bright evening to view **it by** moonlight, we pass the Theatre of Dionysius or **Bacchus.** The marble seats of the small amphitheatre are nearly all there. Part of the stage, or more likely the proscenium, remains with its inlaid pavement, and the low barrier between the actors and spectators is yet standing: a semicircular row of marble **arm-chairs surrounds** the stage, much more comfortable than the cramped seats the opera houses give us nowadays. At the bottom of each **chair is** engraved the name of the person who seemed **from his** office to have had a life estate in it, and you will remember enough of the old Iliad to know that ἱερέως **means** *of a priest*. This, then, is the priest's row, and **there are** the old names whose pronunciation so troubled our spirits at college. In the centre of the semicircle is the large throne **of the** high priest of this order of Bacchus, well-shaped to accommodate the portly form of this dignitary, who lived among revels **in** his early life, and with few prayers and much wine, he could sit here in after life fulfilling his position as master **of** the orgies, with his fat **old sides** shaking at the comedy, and his guffaw still sounding among the loudest **of the loud.**

It was pleasant to wander here often where Œschylus, **Sophocles and** Euripides displayed their heroic dramas, **and where the** art **of acting** other men's emotions and **desires, of** depicting their eccentricities, virtues, failings, good resolutions and continual falls was first exhibited. This is the stage that would more particularly occur to me when Shakespeare says "all the world's a stage;" and what new transformation scenes, tragedies, comedies, and burlesques, has that stage seen since the time of Sophocles! What new inventions have been used to effect those transformations, and how repeatedly have new lights shone out of obscurity, illuming the whole stage for a while, and on going out left nothing behind them but their ashes in the pan and a remembrance of their effulgence, till a light from another quarter gave the stage perhaps a more crimson hue.

The path winds up the rocky mountain that rises out of the town towards the citadel, and at the only gate leading through the massive walls that crown its precipitous sides there is admittance given by the guardians of the almost deserted garrison. You enter and clamber up the slippery ascent, noticing that the way is worn into ruts by the chariot wheels and feet of the horses that for centuries gradually made the indentations in the rock, and then enter the vast Propylæa or "entrances" flanked by large columns, and stand within the stronghold of Greece. Now you are treading where every general and warrior, every statesman and citizen in togas of scarlet or purple, where Pericles and Demosthenes, and hosts of other Grecians of mighty name have trod. Yonder is the place where the colossal statue of Athene stood, whose spearhead, like the pillar of smoke in the wilderness, was by day a guide to the mariners at sea, and on going a little further, before you stands—at last—the Parthenon with its bold grandeur brought out in relief against the sky, and its capitals and architraves tipped with silver by the moon, the Selene of the Greeks, who thus kissed her sleeping Endymion.

> "On such a tranquil night as this
> She woke Endymion with a kiss.
> When sleeping in the grove
> He dreamed not of her love."

Battered by siege, blown up by bombs, "stormed at with shot and shell," the bull's-eye for every Venetian or Turkish missile of destruction, the Parthenon yet stands as a model of sublime architecture. Stern as is its purely

Doric style, which admits of nothing but the severest of straight lines, it has a dignity and character about it like the sculptured head of some Roman emperor. It suggests at once the emanation of such a people as the Greeks were at its founding, four centuries and a half before our era, a race of warriors, philosophers and mathemeticians, who, unspoiled by luxury, sought not the beauty of the curved line but tried and succeeded in imparting majesty and grace to a sternness of outline so typical of their lives.

Approach those fluted weather-stained pillars of Pentelic marble, so destitute of ornament, and step into the "Chamber of Virgin Athene," and view the deserted shrine and the destruction within. The moon makes it positively appalling. Not only does every scattered column add desolation to the scene, but in the mystic light the white forms of the ghastly statues propped against the walls people it with every victim murdered in the precincts. Mutilated heads, battered torsoes, maimed figures draped in white, loom up spectrally on every side. Hands and feet, broken arms and legs, lie about as if unclaimed by the ghosts at this resurrection. Frieze, cornice, and bas-relief of exquisite workmanship are merely thrown to one side, and yet these are the master-pieces of Praxiteles and Phidias. Each would be a treasure any where else, but here they are trodden under foot. Of the forty-six columns, forming the peristyle, a few at the sides have been overthrown by explosion; the rest remain as fast and massive as the Pyramids. The marble has partly assumed the colour of its native mountain, and the whole structure seems less like the fabric of man than an overgrowth of nature, so perfect are its various proportions. But I despair of describing the Parthenon. Let us go instead to the battlement hanging over the precipice, and view Athens lying far below—a mass of twinkling lights. Mount Pentelicus lies towards the north, and near by is Lycabettus; Hymettus in daytime still has "the sound of bees' industrious murmur" about its slopes, and provides us with delicious honey; and the dry bed of Ilyssus, besung as the "whispering stream," is seen beneath.

I should only weary both reader and myself, to describe the other ruins here. The Erectheum with the caryatides or female figures supporting the portico, the temple of Victory and others, shall go untarred by my brush. It seems like painting the lily, like trying to adorn rich cabinets with home workmanship; every touch is a daub or a gash.

On descending, however, we pass a place **that calls for** another thumbing of the pocket-bibles, that show evident marks of the usage they received in the Holy Land, and every name now seen therein seems **as** familiar as that of **a** travelling acquaintance. Every locality mentioned seems **to have** a deeper significance **when** we remember that only a short time ago we trod upon the very spot. The Bible, the Koran, and Josephus have been laid aside while writing about Greece, and it is a pleasure once more to search the pages of divine Writ, to say a word about that admirable character, St. Paul — the hero of the apostles who counselled with the Athenians, and endeavoured to change their attractive belief into a purer, beautiful, and true faith. It would seem as if no other of the apostles was capable, or at least so eminently fitted for the great task of preaching in the face of such a thoroughly established belief, and of counselling among the wisest of philosophers.

But St. Paul was a scholar, **a** traveller, **a** sailor, and a man. While he feared God above, he seemed to have no dread of the dangers of earth, nor of the rulers that governed its countries. He could act calmly in his perils, and speak of them without boast. When they had to gird the ship, whilst in imminent danger on the Mediterranean, he never seemed to quail like the fishermen on the Galilean pond, but acted **as** if feeling that if he died, **a** great work would go unfinished, and that his death was of minor import to himself. He said himself, to his little flock at Ephesus, " Neither count I my life dear unto myself, so that I might finish my course with joy, and the ministry which I have received of the Lord Jesus." A Pharisee, and **a** persecutor of the faithful himself, till that voice came to him, "Saul, Saul, why persecutest thou me!" he could now speak with boldness to the sages whose philosophy concerning the immortality of the soul, and whose maxims laid down for the regulation of society, only wanted the divine light he could shed upon them to fill up the deficiencies in their crude conjectures, to form it into a glorious and comprehensible Faith. He could enter Athens with the same resolution and confidence as he afterwards entered a prisoner into Rome; and here, on Mars' hill, he could confront the Epicurean and Stoic philosophers, and reveal to them, in language they could fully appreciate, the mystery of the true God.

We stand on the bare rock where he endeavoured to convince them, and we think the spot is as sanctified as any we have visited. We know, too, that it is the last time we shall stand on holy ground in this life, unless perchance our footsteps should at some future period be turned to the East again; and in spite of the longing to return to the West, there comes a feeling of depression on descending to the common earth.

CHAPTER XX.

A HURRIED WIND UP.

THERE were partings to be gone through and survived shortly after leaving Greece, when Jimmy and I, on our way up the Adriatic to Trieste, left our friends at Corfu, who were going into Italy by Brindisi. We went back to the island of Syra after leaving Athens and the Piræus, and spent a Sunday there, having service in a stifling little box of a church with an inaudible sermon from a toothless clergyman, and singing that set our teeth on edge.

It was a relief to leave the hot island for the cool sea, and pass another five days in doubling capes and dashing past bold headlands, rushing through straits and threading our way through "spicy Isles." On rounding Cape Malea, an old hermit who has lived on the face of the precipice for a great many years, came out of his rocky abode and waved a flag to us. I suppose the only excitement he ever looked forward to was seeing the gay vessel pass occasionally, and his only knowledge of the busy world, the sight of groups of travellers clustered on the decks. My friends disembarked at Corfu, and then I was almost alone for the rest of the voyage.

But it was the perfection of steamboat travelling. I lay in my berth at the open square window nearly all day, reading books from the ship's library and enjoying the delightful breezes, matchless scenery and gorgeous sunsets. It was a grand opportunity to review the trip. We think of such an experience as we take a running glance at a collection of photographs; but put any of them for a moment into the megalethescope of the memory, and they are at once peopled with natives in strange and peculiar garbs; the cities are lighted up with the myriad lights; the hurrying, loitering, jostling throng is seen again; all the surroundings appear in the natural way, and according as we arrange the instrument we see the views in white sunlight or silvery rays of moon.

After another survey of Trieste I went by rail to Venice, where "The City of the Sea" was looking more as it should at this visit, but as I was not suffering from oppressive opulence, it seemed more full of poetry around a certain Bank, where some shekels awaited me.

It was somewhere about this Grand Canal, I think, that I first met the reader, and here I intended to take my leave; but it does seem a pity not to speak of Italy as she appeared to me, when running to Milan, in all the beauty of spring, with the Alps towering on one side, and for miles in every direction the feathery vines, gracefully strung from one gnarled fruit tree to another, transforming the country into one vast arbour. It does seem a pity not to speak of Milan and its drives, shops, theatres, and cathedral; nor of the lovely Como where Nature with a partial hand has strewn her best beauties for art to render perfect; nor of the quiet little Menaggio where the tourist, as he sits in the garden at his hotel, is at a loss to know whether to be appalled by the grandeur of the mountains, to be enchanted by the fairy lake and its snowflake sails, or to be lulled to sleep by its rippling. It seems an actual shame not to mention the drive to Porlezza,* where the road, winding up over the mountains from Menaggio through woods and shrubs with foliage just changing from down to feathers, opens up at intervals a seemingly new

---

* It was a special pleasure, whilst in different parts of Europe, to tread the same paths as my parents did twenty years before.

vista at each turning, where we view the many-coloured water reflecting Italian villas on its shores, the hoary-crested mountains, the picturesque villages and rushing little steamboats that all lie before the eye as a vision of something not of earth.

The motionless lake and sleepy town of Lugano, where the old monastery bells on the distant hills break out occasionally into an audible snore, requiring but a doze through the sunset while floating on the mountain-bound water to be perfectly in keeping with all surroundings, and where, about the gardens of the villas or hotels, one may hear an occasional whack of a croquet ball, or prick up his ears at an English peal of laughter ringing through the air—this must all be left out. Nor would it be consistent with my intent to mention starting early with the old stage driver to help him worry along his five elderly martyrs who knew the road so well that they stumbled on every stone that happened to have been thrown there in the last month, as if they hadn't regulated their pace yet to escape it; and if our Jehu's whip *was* as heavy to wield as King Richard's sword, he certainly did it to perfection, for every thirty-two seconds he gave a grunt, and struck the same horse in exactly the same place as before; then he gave a tug at the reins to prevent the beasts from falling into reveries, and every half minute he delivered a savage poke at the nigh wheeler, though this sometimes varied through temporary abstraction. The whole performance brought us to Luino on Lake Maggiore, where the steamboat swept me down to Pallanza, to dally awhile about the Borromean Islands; but I didn't row out to see them; there was a little Italian girl at the stage hotel who spoke French, and while making my arrangements for the *coupé*, there seemed to be numberless other things requiring her advice. Perhaps she did only keep the books in a dead-and-alive hotel. I didn't care about that. She was sweet. Peace be with her; she seemed to like English, but I had to leave Pallanza, to reach Domo d'Ossola on my way over the Simplon.

Next day I crossed the Pass; ascending imperceptibly

from the sunny valleys, by the winding road that led slowly from the pleasant vineyards to the sterile regions of the upper air, **and** through the Ravine of Gondo, the wildest grandest scene of all the Alps, where the brawling Diveria, swollen by the thaws of spring, flowed clear as crystal in the deepest parts, and threw a fountain over every stone that broke its rush ; while slender bridges, cast across by fallen trees, were moistened by the spray of little cataracts beneath.

At every mile the walls of rock grow nearer ; at times we enter long galleries or tunnels, through rocks that completely block the way. On looking up, the mind cannot realize the thousands of feet of sheer precipice above ; light cascades descend from unknown heights in feathery spray ; huge misshapen boulders hang threatening above, and, far in the abyss below, gigantic masses splintered **in** their fall and vast avalanches of snow ominously warn the traveller of what his fate may be at any moment.

After toiling up thousands of feet to where the snows towered above the carriage top on each side, I alighted and rushed into an Inn to have a bite ; and here, on the top of the Alps, I found myself thawing out round the fire with a Swiss family I had once met before, on the blazing top of the Ghizeh Pyramid. In spite of the absence of the gaudy Eastern headdress, and in spite of being enveloped in two overcoats, they recognised me at once, so we hobnobbed over hot soup and mountainous loaves of bread.

A few miles more of ascent, and the St. Bernard Hospice is reached at the highest point of the road. Nothing is **seen but** the snow that walls the way and extends in menacing grandeur towards the heavens further than the eye can pierce the mist. The great glacier gallery, where the icicles make a fairy grotto of the tunnel, is passed ; then we begin to descend ; along precipices where from a dizzy height, we could see houses resting on verdant farms, thousands of feet below, like dice upon a gaming table. Presently we come among some stunted fir trees clothed with snow, and soon their coating disappears, and further down, others are **timidly** putting forth a suspicion **of a leaf. A change** of horses at Berisal ; **then on again,** round mountains, over bridges, through forests; and as we descend from the snow, vegetation commences again and grows under our very eyes.

An hour's rest at Brieg; **and,** as the shades **of** evening grow more sombre, we are dashing through avenues of dimly visible trees, with the bases of huge mountains **on** one side, **and** the rushing Rhone on the other. Dark night settles down upon the valley; the lamp throws its light over the five snorting jet black horses that are making short the journey to Sierre; anon, as in the days of yore, we pull up by the way side, and now five greys replace the panting blacks. Off again, and under the flickering light the gallant greys loudly clatter over the smooth road; the driver has my flask and I have his reins in hand; **the** greys are better than the blacks; the music **of** the whip rings out on the night **air**; the conveyance **sways** and swings from side to side; the cheery "yoick" **of the** driver makes the horses bound again; hi **on**! hoop-la! let them go! I am free! I am **alone**! I am wild!

And should I leave all this out of my sketch book? I **trow** not. Charles Dickens, the great photographer, went over the Simplon, but why should not I make my little sketches too. But this is the last of them, for I am getting into too much civilization, **and** running past Chillon and Vevay, I see painted on some large signs, "English boarding school for young ladies. What could I say of Lausanne or Geneva, or indeed any other part of Switzerland, that is not known to all. Berne, Basle, Strasbourg, and Mayence contained **no** mosques or minarets; the Rhine was not the Bosphorus; Cologne and Brussels had no dreamy narghillis; Antwerp possessed no turbaned merchants, but some sailors who swore in musical English. A few weeks in London at the height of the season, dispelled the last remnants of Eastern dozing; I made my salaams to the Czar; George Frederick was kind enough to win the Derby, and do it well; England smiled everywhere, and Scotland glistened in her dews; Glasgow was sooty, and Edinburgh was, &c., &c.; let us shut the sketch-book with a

BANG!

www.ingramcontent.com/pod-product-compliance
Lightning Source LLC
Chambersburg PA
CBHW031944230426
43672CB00010B/2047